REWRITTEN THEOLOGY
Aquinas After His Readers

Challenges in Contemporary Theology

Series Editors: Gareth Jones and Lewis Ayres
Canterbury Christ Church University College, UK, and Emory University, USA

Challenges in Contemporary Theology is a series aimed at producing clear orientations in, and research on, areas of "challenge" in contemporary theology. These carefully coordinated books engage traditional theological concerns with mainstreams in modern thought and culture that challenge those concerns. The "challenges" implied are to be understood in two senses: those presented by society to contemporary theology, and those posed by theology to society.

REWRITTEN THEOLOGY

Aquinas After His Readers

Mark D. Jordan

Blackwell
Publishing

© 2006 by Mark D. Jordan

BLACKWELL PUBLISHING
350 Main Street, Malden, MA 02148–5020, USA
9600 Garsington Road, Oxford OX4 2DQ, UK
550 Swanston Street, Carlton, Victoria 3053, Australia

The right of Mark D. Jordan to be identified as the Author of this Work has been asserted in accordance with the UK Copyright, Designs, and Patents Act 1988.

First published 2006 by Blackwell Publishing Ltd

1 2006

Library of Congress Cataloging-in-Publication Data

Jordan, Mark D.
    Rewritten theology : Aquinas after his readers / Mark D. Jordan.
        p.   cm.—(Challenges in contemporary theology)
    Includes bibliographical references and index.
    ISBN-13: 978-1-4051-1220-8 (alk. paper)
    ISBN-10: 1-4051-1220-4 (alk. paper)
    ISBN-13: 978-1-4051-1221-5 (pbk. : alk. paper)
    ISBN-10: 1-4051-1221-2 (pbk. : alk. paper) 1. Thomas, Aquinas, Saint, 1225?–1274.
    I. Title.   II. Series.

    BX4700.T6J67 2005
    230'.2'092—dc22

                                                    2005012330

A catalogue record for this title is available from the British Library.

Set in 10.5 pt Bembo
by The Running Head Limited, Cambridge
Printed and bound in India
by Replika Press Pvt. Ltd, Kundli

The publisher's policy is to use permanent paper from mills that operate a sustainable forestry policy, and which has been manufactured from pulp processed using acid-free and elementary chlorine-free practices. Furthermore, the publisher ensures that the text paper and cover board used have met acceptable environmental accreditation standards.

For further information on
Blackwell Publishing, visit our website:
www.blackwellpublishing.com

Contents

Contents

Preface

"A small error at the beginning is great in the end, according to the Philosopher in *On the Heavens and the Earth* 1." Thomas Aquinas begins his first treatise with that allusion. In a gesture typical of hasty reading, the opinion is now attributed to him. Such gestures are repeated at much larger scale. Many a fat book on Thomas is undone by hasty presuppositions about reading that occur in (or before) its opening lines.

Thomas could certainly have added a happier corollary from his own experience: a small inspiration in the beginning counts for much later on. When I was a junior in college, I finished reading Bernard Lonergan's *verbum* articles and promptly wrote to him for advice (as undergraduates are liable to do). Lonergan wrote back a remarkably patient letter in which he explained that I should always read Thomas actively and comparatively, putting my mental habits at stake. His single letter sparked what other teachers, nearer to hand, had been saying. From them, I heard that nothing happens in the action of Platonic dialogues by accident (Jacob Klein), that attempting to *write* philosophy or revelation must remain a dangerous risk (Leo Strauss), and that Aristotle's texts, in whatever form we inherit them, present consummate acts of teaching (Robert Neidorf). In graduate school, I heard from Louis Mackey that elaborate charts pretending to arrange all of writings's possibilities should be painted only in sand. These inspirations helped me to read Thomas again – and better. If my style of reading still strikes many Thomists as eccentric, I would plead my genealogy not as an excuse, but as an argument. We should continue to worry about how we read Thomas not only because he is grandly canonical, but also because his practice of writing theology challenges (or rebukes) many who would write theology today.

What follows is offered as a book and not merely a collection of chapters. Though first drafts of its oldest parts were written 20 years ago, and published in earlier versions over the years, the newest parts were written in the last months. No page of the whole has escaped rewriting. The order of consideration has been changed and changed again.

Any book on Thomas must be selective in its topics, but especially in its attention to scholarly publications. Two decades back, when Clemens Vansteenkiste sacrificed himself to publishing an annotated bibliography of books and articles on Thomas, the yearly total ran well over a thousand pieces. Today the total must be higher – and the sum of originality somewhat less. *Recentiores non deteriores*, the philologist's rule holds: more recent copies of a text are not necessarily worse. The rule applies to Thomistic reading as well, but only with the explicit caution also applicable to codices: more recent studies often add nothing to earlier ones. Sometimes they subtract. The latest scholarship can be astonishingly innocent of earlier discoveries. So I try to sample various strata in the last century's Thomistic scholarship, without pretending to be comprehensive. Those who want a bibliographic compilation, or even a recap of the last decade's publications, should consult the databases.

It remains only to thank my colleague, Lewis Ayres, for originally proposing this venture to me; David Mellott for his help in preparing the manuscript; Blackwell Publishers for bearing with my lengthy revisions; and the many colleagues who have spent the time, in print or in person, to challenge my readings and to correct my errors. I also thank the editors or publishers of the following publications who allowed me to revise earlier versions of some of the material that follows in order to present it here:

Chapter 2: "The Competition of Authoritative Languages and Aquinas's Theological Rhetoric." *Medieval Philosophy and Theology* 4 (1994): 71–90.

Chapter 3: "Medicine and Natural Philosophy in Aquinas." In *Thomas von Aquin*, ed. Albert Zimmermann, pp. 233–246. *Miscellanea Mediaevalia* 19. Berlin and New York: Walter de Gruyter, 1988. "*De regno* and the Place of Political Thinking in Thomas Aquinas." *Medioevo* 18 (1992): 151–168.

Chapter 4: *The Alleged Aristotelianism of Thomas Aquinas*. Etienne Gilson Series 15. Toronto: PIMS, 1992. 41 pp. (published and paginated separately). "Thomas Aquinas' Disclaimers in the Aristotelian Commentaries." In *Philosophy and the God of Abraham: Essays in Memory of James A. Weisheipl, O.P.*, ed. R. James Long, pp. 99–112. Toronto: PIMS, 1991. "Aquinas Reading Aristotle's *Ethics*." In *Ad litteram: Authoritative Texts and Their Medieval Readers*, eds. Kent Emery, Jr and Mark Jordan, pp. 229–249. Notre Dame: University of Notre Dame Press, 1992.

Chapter 5: "The Protreptic Structure of the *Contra Gentiles*." *The Thomist* 60 (1986): 173–209.

Chapter 6: "Aquinas's Middle Thoughts on Theology as Science." In *Studies in Thomistic Theology*, ed. Paul Lockey, 91–111. Houston: Center for Thomistic Studies, 1995 [1996]. "The Ideal of *Scientia moralis* and the Invention of the *Summa theologiae*." In *Aquinas's Moral Theory: Essays in Honor of Norman Kretzmann*, eds. Scott MacDonald and Eleonore Stump, pp. 79–97. Ithaca, NY: Cornell University Press, 1999. © Cornell University.

Chapter 7: "The *Pars moralis* of the *Summa theologiae* as *Scientia* and as *Ars*." In *Scientia und ars in Hoch- und Spätmittelalter*, ed. Ingrid Craemer-Ruegenberg and Andreas Speer, pp. 468–481. *Miscellanea Mediaevalia* 22. Berlin and New York: Walter de Gruyter, 1994.

Chapter 8: "Theology and Philosophy." In *The Cambridge Companion to Aquinas*, ed. N. Kretzmann and E. Stump, pp. 232–251. Cambridge and New York: Cambridge University Press, 1993. © Cambridge University Press.

Chapter 9: "Esotericism and *Accessus* in Thomas Aquinas." *Philosophical Topics* 20 (1992): 35–49.

Abbreviations and Editions

There is no single best edition for the works of Thomas Aquinas. When finished, the Leonine *Opera omnia* (so called because commissioned and funded by Pope Leo XIII) will be a superb edition of the complete works. The Leonine is likely to remain unfinished for a long time – and in two senses. First, not all of Thomas's works have been edited for the series. Second, those works published before 1950 need to be revised in varying degrees. The best *complete* edition now available is the one published by Roberto Busa as a supplement to his computer-generated lexical analysis and concordance, the *Index Thomisticus*. Busa's edition contains the best available texts as of December 1971, including then unpublished Leonine versions.

Many libraries lack both the Leonine and the Busa editions of the *Opera omnia*. Certainly many scholars do. They consult Thomas in a ragtag collection of different editions, especially those published by the Italian house of Marietti throughout the twentieth century. The Marietti editions often reproduce texts taken from earlier printed versions of Thomas, the so-called "vulgate Thomas." They add to these not only notes of varying quality, but also an immensely useful system of paragraph or section numbers. These "Marietti numbers" are widely used for quick citation, especially for Thomas's expositions of Aristotle.

Faced with the proliferation of printings, I cite Thomas's works by their medieval textual divisions. These do vary occasionally from edition to edition, but they are the closest thing to a uniform system of citation. The citations are condensed. I do not specify, for example, the kind of textual division. "1.2" will mean question 1 article 2 in a series of disputed questions, but Book 1 chapter 2 in an exposition of Aristotle. A reader familiar with Thomas will know what is meant. A reader not yet familiar with him will be able to sort things out by taking the text in hand. When I refer to these medieval textual divisions, I use the conventional English terms even when these are a bit misleading. For example, in the *Summa of Theology* the opening arguments are conventionally called "objections" in English – as though Thomas's position were already established. In fact, they are dialectical arguments on the way to a determination, and Thomas frequently incorporates parts of them into his own position. Since English-speakers stubbornly continue to call them "objections," that is the word I use in order to be clear.

I give below my abbreviations for the works of Thomas that I cite. Each abbreviation is followed by the standard title as in Torrell's catalogue.[1] I then mention the edition(s) in which I read the text. For the so-called *Contra gentiles*, where the medieval divisions units are long, I supplement them with the section numbers from the edition of Pera, Marc, and Caramello. Some might have wished that I did this as well for Thomas's expositions of Aristotle. My only plea is that the most efficient way to search for texts in Thomas is at the magnificent website directed by Enrique Alarcón from the Universidad de Nevarra. It may be found at *www.corpusthomisticum.org*.

Collected Works

Leonine *Opera omnia: Opera omnia iussu impensaque Leonis XIII. P. M. edita*, edited by members of Leonine Commission (Rome: various imprints, 1882–).
Busa *Opera omnia: Sancti Thomae Aquinatis Opera omnia*, ed. Robert Busa (Stuttgart – Bad Canstatt: Fromman-Holzboog, 1980).

Individual Works

Catena aurea	*Glossa continua super Evangelia (Catena aurea).* Busa.
Coll. Symb. Apost.	*Collationes in Symbolum Apostolorum.* Busa.
Compend. theol.	*Compendium theologiae seu brevis compilatio theologiae ad fratrem Raynaldum.* Busa.
Contra err. Graec.	*Contra errores Graecorum.* Leonine vol. 40 (1967–1968).

---

[1]   Jean-Pierre Torrell, "Bref catalogue des œuvres de saint Thomas," *Initiation à saint Thomas d'Aquin: Sa personne et son œuvre* (Fribourg: Éds. Universitaires de Fribourg, and Paris: Éds. du Cerf, 1993), pp. 483–525.

Contra gent.	*Summa contra gentiles. Liber de veritate catholicae fidei contra errores infidelium seu "Summa contra gentiles,"* eds. Ceslaus Pera, Petrus Marc, and Petrus Caramello (Turin: Marietti and Paris: Lethielleux, 1961–1967).
Contra impugn.	*Contra impugnantes Dei cultum et religionem.* Leonine vol. 41 (1970).
De art. fid. et eccles. sacr.	*De articulis fidei et ecclesiae sacramentis.* Leonine vol. 42 (1979).
De malo	*Quaestiones disputatae De malo.* Leonine vol. 23 (1982).
De potentia	*Quaestiones disputatae De potentia.* Busa.
De rat. fidei	*De rationibus fidei ad Cantorem Antiochenum.* Leonine vol. 40 (1967–1968).
De regno	*De regno ad regem Cypri.* Leonine vol. 42 (1979).
De spir. creat.	*Quaestiones disputatae De spiritualibus creaturis.* Leonine vol. 42/2 (2000).
De unitate int.	*De unitate intellectus contra Averroistas.* Leonine vol. 43 (1976).
De verit.	*Quaestiones disputatae De veritate.* Leonine vol. 22 (1970–1976).
De virt. comm.	*Quaestiones disputate De virtutibus in communi.* Busa.
Expos. Iob	*Expositio super Iob ad litteram.* Leonine vol. 26 (1965).
Expos. Isaiam	*Expositio super Isaiam ad litteram.* Leonine vol. 28 (1974).
Expos. Pauli	*Expositio et Lectura super Epistolas Pauli Apostoli.* Busa.
Expos. Pery	*Expositio libri Peryermenias.* Leonine vol. 1★/1 (1989).
Expos. Post.	*Expositio libri Posteriorum.* Leonine vol. 1★/2 (1989).
Lect. Ioan.	*Lectura super Ioannem.* Busa.
Lect. Matt.	*Lectura super Matthaeum.* Busa.
Lect. Sent.	*Lectura super libros Sententiarum.* Oxford, Lincoln College MS 95.
Post. Psalmos	*Postilla super Psalmos.* Busa.
Princ.	*Principium "Rigans montes de superioribus" et "Hic est liber mandatorum Dei."* Busa.
Qq. de quolibet	*Quaestiones de quolibet.* Leonine vol. 25/1–2 (1996).

Scriptum Sent.	*Scriptum super libros Sententiarum* . . ., eds. Pierre Mandonnet and Maria Fabianus Moos (Paris: P. Lethielleux, 1929–1933).
Sent. De anima	*Sententia libri De anima.* Leonine vol. 45/1 (1984).
Sent. De caelo	*Sententia super librum De caelo et mundo.* Busa.
Sent. De gener.	*Sententia super libros De generatione et corruptione.* Busa.
Sent. De sensu	*Sententia libri De sensu et sensato.* Leonine vol. 45/2 (1985).
Sent. Ethic.	*Sententia libri Ethicorum.* Leonine vol. 47 (1969).
Sent. Metaph.	*Sententia super Metaphysicam.* Busa.
Sent. Meteora	*Sententia super Meteora.* Busa.
Sent. Phys.	*Sententia super Physicam.* Busa.
Sent. Politic.	*Sententia libri Politicorum.* Leonine vol. 48 (1971).
Summa theol.	*Summa theologiae.* Leonine vols. 4–12 (1888–1906). I collate this with *S. Thomae de Aquino Ordinis Praedicatorum Summa Theologiae,* ed. Institut d'Études médiévales d'Ottawa, rev. edn. (Ottawa: Commissio Piana, 1953).
Super De causis	*Super librum De causis.* Busa.
Super De div. nom.	*Super librum Dionysii De divinis nominibus.* Busa.
Super De Trin.	*Super Boetium De Trinitate.* Leonine vol. 50 (1992).
Super Ieremiam	*Super Ieremiam.* Busa.
Super Threnos	*Super Threnos.* Busa.

Chapter One

St Thomas and the Police

If only we could read Thomas Aquinas without encountering some other of his readers – especially the police.

"The police" refers literally or figuratively. Figuratively we use the term to describe self-appointed guardians of social norms, as in "the decency police" or "the style police." Literally we use it to refer to the forces that keep internal order – municipal or state officers, the army on civic duty, and every other monitor or enforcer with the power of approved violence. Here I have both meanings in mind, beginning with the literal. It is a remarkable fact about Thomas Aquinas's texts that they have been quoted so regularly by the police of various regimes – by papal or local inquisitors, of course, but also in service of Franco's victory in Spain or of the Argentine security forces during the 1970s and 1980s.

Here is a single case. In 1971, the Argentine writer Carlos Alberto Sacheri published and widely distributed his broadside, *The Clandestine Church*.[1] Sacheri had been a student of the eminent Thomist Charles de Koninck at Laval in Québec, but in this book his aim was not academic. He accused prominent priests associated with liberationist groups of direct links to Communist cells, and he called for action against them by the state and the Catholic church.[2] The book became famous – infamous – as justification for more brutal repression. Sacheri himself was assassinated in reprisal during December 1974. The year following his death, a series of his essays was published under the title, *The Natural Order*.[3] This collection has a

[1] Carlos Sacheri, *La Iglesia clandestina* (Buenos Aires: Ediciones del Cruzamante, 1970). The book is a collection of journalistic pieces originally published during 1969 (p. 7).

[2] Sacheri, *Iglesia clandestina*, pp. 93–98 (on the Communist connections of Ramondetti, Borzani, Paoli, and Viscovich) and pp. 136–140 (on "conclusions" and the call for action, noting the mentions of the "social order" and the final invocation of "Christ the King").

[3] Sacheri, *El orden natural* (Buenos Aires: Instituto de Promoción Social Argentina, 1975).

eulogy-prologue by the Archbishop of Paraná that opens with an epigram from Aquinas (p. v).[4] In the body of the posthumous book, Sacheri cites Aquinas to establish "the origin and function of authority" from the notion of the common good.[5] Thomas appears again to underwrite the critique of liberal democracy, to restrict any right of revolution, and to subordinate state to papacy.[6] In context, given Sacheri's martyrdom, Aquinas must seem to endorse the increasingly violent reaction of the Argentine authorities, civil and religious, against real or imagined revolutionaries.

More often Thomas has been the darling of figurative "police," of the forces of one or another orthodoxy who have wanted his authority. Thomas has been an authority within his own Dominican order since shortly after his death.[7] He has been favored at the papal court at least since his canonization. He has towered over the Catholic church of the Counter-Reformation from its creation at the Council of Trent until its attempted redirection at the second Vatican Council. If his authority waxed and waned during those centuries, if it varied by religious order and by academic field, Thomas was still the common doctor to such an extent that his opponents too had to speak something of his language. Hence the Thomas industry. Hence the sad fact that the largest readership for Thomas has most often been coerced. Thomism as policy hands Thomas to the figurative police.[8]

This official past confronts most readers of Thomas before they reach his texts. A lucky few may begin to read him without having heard about his authority – though I know of no edition of Thomas that doesn't register it in some way. Many more readers will reach Thomas's texts after they hear of his authority – and perhaps only under its impulse. However one arrives at these texts, the old fondness for them among the police, once discovered,

---

[4]   The front matter also reproduces an earlier letter from the nunciature in Buenos Aires, which quotes in turn an approving letter from the Vatican's Secretariat of State (p. viii), both significant to the book's framing.

[5]   Sacheri, *El orden natural*, parenthetical back reference on p. 154 to the chapter that begins on p. 149 with references to the exposition of Aristotle's *Politics* and the *Summa theologiae*.

[6]   Sacheri, *El orden natural*, pp. 178–179, 181–184, 185–186, respectively. The passage quoted from "De regime principum" 1.14 is in fact not by Thomas Aquinas. For the system of citing works by Aquinas, see "Abbreviations and Editions."

[7]   See most recently Elizabeth Lowe, *The Contested Theological Authority of Thomas Aquinas: The Controversies between Hervaeus Natalis and Durandus of St Pourçain* (New York and London: Routledge, 2003).

[8]   The word "police," as Foucault insisted, is cognate with "policy." Indeed, in eighteenth-century German *Polizeiwissenschaft* meant not the methods of a particular agency, but comprehensive state regulation. See Michel Foucault, course summary for "Security, Territory, and Population" [1976–1977], in Foucault, *Ethics, Subjectivity and Truth*, ed. Paul Rabinow (New York: New Press, 1997), pp. 70–71.

may push a reader to pose sharp questions. If these texts are good teaching, how could they give rise to such a violent posterity? Is there something in them that aids or abets the police?

In this introduction, I consider responses to such sharp questions, but chiefly in order to make the questions sharper still. My timeline is odd. First I tell a story backward, from the present to the early modern period. Then I tell another story forward, from the death of Thomas to the early modern period. By that point you will have gathered that I am not interested in narrating a continuous Thomism. Rather the opposite: I break through continuous narratives to make room for the sharp questions about Thomas's authority. The questions do not fall neatly onto a timeline because they require a curious simultaneity, the simultaneity of a rhetorical structure and its remembered receptions. On the one hand, I suspect that what makes Thomas most attractive to contemporary police is not something *in* him, but rather the circumstances of his having already been abused for the purposes of coercion. On the other hand, I want to pursue the sharp question, whether something in Thomas might have solicited the attention of the police – or failed to prevent it. Behind both suspicion and provocation lies the confidence that Thomas's books lead us to think about theology and power.

For as long as possible, I will set aside another sort of narration as well: the chronicle of when Thomas's texts authorized particular acts of physical violence. It would be a grim task – and a long one – to list assaults committed after invoking Thomas. Of course, the list would not establish a causal relation of readings to crimes. As Sacheri's assassination shows, hatred of official Thomism can be used as easily as official Thomism itself to authorize killing. Leaving aside the chronicle of crimes, I ask how Thomas's texts have been made to support constructions of *textual* authority and whether his authorship can be blamed for them. Authorship, I say, thinking of Kierkegaard's pseudonyms as fictitious authors known through the operation of texts attributed to them. I am interested in Thomas Aquinas as the author of texts whose "intentions," if we want to retain that word, are discerned by looking to their rhetorical features. I am not interested in authorial psychology; I am interested in rhetorical force, in how the voices of theology become the summons of the police.

The Fantasy of Order

Many contemporary readers testify to finding in Thomas absolute orderliness, irresistible control. This is the testimony, for example, of a youthful poem written by Josef Knecht, the protagonist of Hermann Hesse's novel,

The Glass Bead Game. The poem speaks wistfully of forgetting one's turbulent self in the tranquil "*Summa*-temple" of Thomas's *Against the Gentiles.*[9] Similar testimony is given, in less polished form, by other contemporary readers.[10] Thomas's writings appear as monumental discourses that subsume everything within a single "system" or "synthesis." Indeed, that familiar phrase, "the Thomistic synthesis," records this pattern or prescription for experience.[11] The experience is a fantasy. Thomistic synthesis or system is the fantastic wish for a precise resolution to every philosophical or theological question that can appear.

The fantasy draws energy from the nineteenth-century project of neo-Thomism promulgated (though not invented) by the papal encyclical *Aeterni patris* (1879), which endorsed Thomas as the comprehensive synthesizer:

> Their teachings [i.e., of the patristic authors], like the scattered members of a body, Thomas gathered and joined, distributed in admirable order, and increased with such great additions, that he is rightly and deservedly held to be the unique bulwark of the Catholic faith . . . There is no part of philosophy that he did not treat at once acutely and solidly: he considered the laws of reasoning, God and incorporeal substances, man and other sensible things, human actions and their principles, so that there is lacking in him neither the abundant field of questions, nor the apt disposition of parts, nor the best way of proceeding, nor firmness of principles and strength of arguments, nor clarity and appropriateness of language, nor a certain facility in explaining abstruse things.[12]

Leo XIII even quotes Cardinal Cajetan to the effect that Thomas inherited in his one mind the most important thoughts of his predecessors. He is no simple synthesizer: he is the culmination of the history of reason.

---

[9] "Nach dem Lesen in der *Summa contra gentiles*," in Hermann Hesse, *Das Glasperlenspiel*, from the appendix "Josef Knechts Hinterlassene Schriften: Die Gedichte des Schülers und Studenten."

[10] For a recent example, see François Daguet, *Théologie du dessein divin chez Thomas d'Aquin: Finis omnium Ecclesia* (Paris: J. Vrin, 2003). By way of conclusion, Daguet praises Thomas's teaching on the divine "economy" for possessing "a very great coherence, a firm structure founded on perennial principles" (p. 515). He then links it to the teaching of Pope John Paul II.

[11] The phrase circulated widely enough to become a sort of token of Catholic identity – not least for satirists. In Nathanael West's *Miss Lonelyhearts* (1933), a young woman in a bar attempts to ingratiate herself with a Catholic writer by saying, "Get me a drink and please continue. I'm very much interested in the new Thomistic synthesis." See West, *Novels and Other Writings*, ed. Sacvan Bercovitch (New York: Library of America, 1997), p. 65.

[12] Leo XIII, Encyclical letter *Æterni patris* [August 4, 1879], *Acta Sanctae Sedis*, ed. Iosephus Pennachi and Victorius Piazzesi, vol. 12 (Rome: Typographia Polyglotta, 1894), 97–115, p. 108. There are no paragraph numbers in this edition, but the passage is found in no. 17 of the now standard numbering.

Aeterni patris avows a utopian wish to remedy the problems of the modern world by giving to philosophy an unassailable stability – so that philosophy could, in turn, shore up both civil culture and Christian theology. The wish bears many marks of nineteenth-century Catholic thinking, including a recoil from liberalism and a nostalgia for lost order. Still the Thomistic fantasy of *Aeterni patris* was not fabricated out of thin air. The encyclical invokes centuries of earlier appropriations of Thomas. Leo XIII and his advisers were convinced that they could stand atop a monumental Scholasticism: St Thomas as the sure foundation; then the rising edifice of the approved Thomistic commentators from early modernity on – Capreolus and Antoninus, Cajetan and Sylvestris, Victoria and his school at Salamanca, including Cano, Soto, Bañez; then the Jesuits, especially Suarez; but also the anti-Jesuit teams of Carmelites known as the Salmanticenses and the Complutenses. As Leo XIII imagines it, "the minds of all, of teachers as well as students, rested in wonderful concord under the teaching and the authority of the one Angelic Doctor."[13] The fantasy of synthesis in *Aeterni patris* is a fantasy of progressive unanimity among commentators, of a monument built on and out of authoritative consensus.

The fantasy of concord among Thomists has consequences for Thomas. In his manual, *The Thomist Synthesis*, Reginald Garrigou-Lagrange explains his method immediately after citing *Aeterni patris*: "The purpose of this work is to present an exposition of the Thomist synthesis based on the principles commonly received among the greatest commentators of St Thomas and often formulated by him."[14] Note the order: the unanimous commentators first and only then the formulae of the saint himself. In order to create an illusion of Thomistic fixity, one has to suppose that it is possible to rewrite Thomas over and over again into new forms.[15] I mean "rewriting" literally. If every reading might be considered somehow a rewriting, there remains the much stronger rewriting that substitutes a new text for Thomas's own: rewriting as replacing. To produce the illusion of Thomistic

---

[13] Leo XIII, *Æterni patris*, p. 109 [no. 20]. Consider the long list of religious orders and schools, p. 109 [nos. 19–20].

[14] Reginald Garrigou-Lagrange, *La synthèse thomiste* (Paris: Desclée de Brouwer, 1946), p. 12.

[15] Not to say, by denying any number of dialectical complexities in his teaching. See, for example, Wayne J. Hankey, "Pope Leo's Purposes and St Thomas's Platonism," in *S. Tommaso nella storia del pensiero: Atti dell VIII Congresso Tomistico Internationale*, vol. 8 and Studi Tomistici 17 (Vatican City: Libreria Editrice Vaticana, 1982), 39–52, and Hankey, "Making Theology Practical: Thomas Aquinas and the Nineteenth-Century Religious Revival," *Dionysius* 9 (1985): 85–127. The most perceptive study in English of the speculative anxieties leading up to the promulgation of *Æterni patris* remains Gerald A. McCool, *Nineteenth-Century Scholasticism: The Search for a Unitary Method* (New York: Fordham University Press, 1989).

unanimity, you must suppose that you can copy what is essential in Thomas from one form to another without any important loss: Thomas's essence transmitted without change through a hundred genres. By the time of *Aeterni patris*, any sense that there might be something wrong in claiming to reproduce Thomas by rewriting him could be dismissed by pointing to the long line of predecessors. The encyclical only calls for the familiar when it calls for displacing Thomas instead of reading what he wrote.

The claim of every monumental Thomism is that it is a faithful copy.[16] The fact of every monumental Thomism is that it rewrites Thomas while denying its rewriting, while claiming that the substitute is just as good as the original. Or perhaps even better. By contrast, I hold that rewriting Thomas erases a decisive feature of his texts, namely, their pedagogical structure. But even if I were to succumb to the project of strong rewriting, I could not agree that the generations of rewriting from 1450 to the present could be summed in a single history, as *Aeterni patris* wishes. If there might be successful rewriting of Thomas, the modern rewritings we actually inherit do not make a coherent narrative. It is not helpful to speak of a "Thomistic tradition" as if there were one "system" or "school" or "tradition" passed down through the last seven centuries.[17] There has always been fierce rivalry among claims on Thomas's authority. "Thomist," like "Christian," is a term that stakes a controversial claim, not one that records a neutral designation. Indeed, a principal Thomistic pastime has been casting doubt on the Thomism of one's rivals. And there have been so many rivals! In the decades since *Aeterni patris*, we can distinguish the Thomisms of the Angelicum,

[16] I mean here to echo Nietzsche's notion of "monumental history." See Friedrich Nietzsche, "Vom Nutzen und Nachteil der Historie für das Leben," *Unzeitgemässe Betrachtungen* 2, in his *Werke* 3.1, edited by Giorgio Colli and Mazzino Montinari (Berlin and New York: W. de Gruyter, 1972), especially p. 254.

[17] In saying this, I am not sure whether or not I disagree with Alasdair MacIntyre in *Three Rival Versions of Moral Inquiry: Encyclopædia, Genealogy, and Tradition* (Notre Dame: University of Notre Dame Press, 1990). On the one hand, MacIntyre will write that Thomas's texts were misread almost from the beginning (p. 135) or that the papal announcement of neo-Thomism could only "lead in a variety of alternative and conflicting directions" (p. 73). On the other hand, he will speak of "the tradition which Aquinas reconstituted" as the only site for accurate readings of the *Summa theol.* (p. 135) and regularly uses the analogy to craft to argue for a continuous "tradition" of Thomism (pp. 65, 128, and so on). MacIntyre does not specify the historical community that carries this tradition of Thomism, unless it is the "historical scholars of the [modern] Thomistic movement," identified as "Grabmann, Mandonnet, Gilson, Van Steenberghen, Weisheipl" (p. 77). The list is unhelpful, because the authors named have neither any strong institutional connections nor any deep agreement about the theological or philosophical implications of the historical reading of Thomas. Whatever MacIntyre's meaning, part of the work of this book is to reconstitute the category of tradition by introducing the notion of rhetorical inheritance or posterity (see especially the conclusion).

Louvain, Munich, Le Saulchoir, Toulouse, Salamanca, Laval, River Forest, St Louis, Notre Dame, Navarra, Utrecht, Cornell, and Oxford. Any narrative about a grand tradition of Thomism will be both a selective story and a tendentious one.[18]

Neo-Thomist interpretations have also been rather selective and tendentious with respect to Thomas's texts. They must be if they are to project a monumental Thomism. More importantly, they must be in order to construct Thomas as the sort of authority who can serve as foundation for a monument. Let me illustrate the principles of selection and the procedures of construction from some late medieval and early modern rewritings of Thomas's *Summa of Theology*. For the moment, I will assume what I can argue only later: the structure of the whole *Summa* is decisive for the work's pedagogy. I want then to notice that the structure of the *Summa* was one of the first things to be erased by its readers – I mean, its rewriters.

Rewriting the *Summa*

It is not hard to show, from internal and circumstantial evidence, that Thomas wrote his *Summa of Theology* as an ideal of curricular reform for Dominican theology, that is, for the teaching of his own religious order, and by extension for other Christian priests or religious.[19] The chief accomplishment of the reform is to incorporate moral and pastoral topics within the pattern of the great Christian creeds. (You can begin to appreciate the challenge if you remember that the ancient creeds contain no moral clauses.) Thomas's reform is written into the very structure of the *Summa*, which carefully locates its moral teaching between a first Part that corresponds to the opening of the creeds and a third Part that follows those creeds from the

---

[18] Compare Leonard A. Kennedy, *A Catalogue of Thomists, 1270–1900* (Houston: Center for Thomistic Studies/University of St Thomas, 1987), p. 10: "The most difficult problem has been: who was a Thomist? There are no criteria universally agreed on. The criteria used in this Catalogue are fairly liberal, such as an indication in the title of a work (*ad mentem Divi Thomae*), or the nature of a work (e.g., a commentary on Aquinas's *Summa theologiae*), or a statement of alleged Thomism by an author himself or one of his historians, unless this is contradicted by other evidence." The history of Thomism becomes a list of claims, genres, and rumors. Prouvost puts the underlying difficulty precisely when he writes that "almost all of the essential theses of Thomas were, in the course of history, either contested by or unknown to one or another 'Thomist.'" See Géry Prouvost, *Thomas d'Aquin et les thomismes: Essai sur l'histoire des thomismes* (Paris: Éds. du Cerf, 1996), p. 9. He goes on to show the incoherence of criteria that invoke institutional geography or metaphysical doctrines, even after distinguishing between constructive and exegetical Thomisms (pp. 11–12).

[19] I will present the evidence at several points below, but especially in chapter 6.

incarnation of Christ to his return in glory. The structure is a masterful response to gaps or failures in thirteenth-century curricula of both Dominican houses of study and universities.

How interesting to note, then, that the medieval Dominican reception of the *Summa* repeatedly ignores the work's structure by rewriting it. Consider the most material kind of rewriting, the rates of manuscript copying. From the start, the *Summa* is rarely copied as a whole. There are good material reasons: a codex large enough to hold the whole *Summa* would be a very unwieldy codex. So the text is usually copied as individual units corresponding to the three Parts, with the middle or moral Part, by far the longest, divided into its two sub-parts, the *prima secundae* and the *secunda secundae*. So, for example, in the fourteenth-century Dominican library of the convent in Padua, there were two copies of each unit or eight codices; in the contemporary Dominican library at Mantua, one copy of each unit or four codices.[20] The numbers in these cases are equal, but across hundreds of manuscript collections the striking fact is that units of the *Summa* are copied at very different rates. The most frequently copied unit is the *secunda secundae*, the detailed consideration of lived virtues and vices.[21] Indeed, the *secunda secundae* seems to be the most frequently copied of any of Thomas's works.[22] His effort to integrate moral teaching within a unified theological curriculum was rewritten early on by market forces – by the demand for copies just of the units that were judged most immediately useful.

The medieval Dominican reception provides more striking examples of the stripping out of the *Summa*'s moral teaching and so the rewriting of its structure. As early as 15 years after Thomas's death, John of Vercelli, master general of the Dominicans, commissioned an abridgment of the *secunda secundae* of the *Summa*. The moral matter was not only extracted, but con-

---

[20] Luciano Gargan, *Lo studio teologico e la biblioteca dei domenicani a Padova nel tre e quattrocento* (Padua: Antenore, 1971), pp. 191–220, on the Paduan library inventory of 1390; Thomas Kaeppeli, "Antiche biblioteche domenicane in Italia," *Archivum Fratrum Praedicatorum* 36 (1966) 5–80, pp. 24–26, on the Mantuan inventory of 1417.

[21] Here I use the admittedly imperfect figures in James A. Weisheipl, *Friar Thomas d'Aquino: His Life, Thought, and Works* (augmented edition, Washington: Catholic University of America Press, 1984), pp. 360–361: *prima pars*, 246 copies; *prima secundae*, 220; *secunda secundae*, 280; *tertia*, 213. We will have much more exact figures when we have a completely indexed version of Dondaine and Shooner's catalogue of Thomas manuscripts.

[22] I leave aside the liturgical works, where questions of authorship and circulation are different. The only rival among the authentic writings is the booklet *De art. fid. et eccles. sacr.*, for which Weisheipl lists 277 manuscripts (p. 392). Of the major works, the nearest rivals would be the *Contra gent.* and the fourth book of the *Scriptum Sent.*, with 184 and 167 manuscripts respectively (Weisheipl, pp. 358–359).

densed.[23] A few years afterwards, the Dominican John of Freiburg rewrote Thomas's teaching into a confessor's handbook.[24] The handbook was in turn abridged, simplified, and alphabetized – pieces of Thomas now twice or three times rewritten. The rewritings were more popular than the original: there are between two and three times as many copies of one alphabetized summary, the *Summa Pisana*, as there are of the *secunda secundae* of Thomas's *Summa* itself.[25] In proposing a curricular ideal, Thomas appears to have badly mistaken the wants of his brother Dominicans, who preferred and produced more useful moral manuals.

In some cases, medieval Dominicans wished not only that Thomas had written separate manuals, but that he had conformed to older models for their thematic organization. One of the deliberate structural accomplishments of Thomas's *Summa* is to reject an organization according to the seven capital sins. Thomas treats the seven sins separately, but he explicitly sets them aside as an organizing principle.[26] Yet not a few treatises on the seven capital sins were composed by excerpting Thomas – his deliberately scattered remarks gathered together, just as deliberately, into the treatise he refused to write. More grandly, the masterworks of fifteenth-century Dominican morality cite Thomas's *Summa* respectfully and actively resist its structural innovation. The *Theological Summa* of Antoninus of Florence refers to Thomas ostentatiously for many of its definitions and a few of its arguments, but it rewrites Thomas in two ways. First, Antoninus's entire *Summa* is concerned only with moral matters. Antoninus makes moral teaching a separate species of theology rather than an integral portion of it. Second, more importantly, Antoninus organizes his *Summa* not according to the structure of Thomas's *secunda pars* or either of its sub-parts, but according to a series

---

[23] Martin Grabmann, "De summae divi Thomae Aquinatis theologicae studio," in *Miscellanea Dominicana in memoriam VII anni saecularis ab obitu sancti patris Dominici (1221–1921)* (Rome: F. Ferrari, 1923), 151–161, at p. 157.

[24] Leonard E. Boyle, "The *Summa confessorum* of John of Freiburg and the Popularization of the Moral Teaching of St Thomas and of Some of His Contemporaries," in *Commemorative Studies* (Toronto: PIMS, 1974), 2:245–268. The text is reprinted, along with Boyle's other essays on Thomas, in *Facing History: A Different Thomas Aquinas* (Louvain-la-neuve: Fédération Internationale des Instituts d'Études Médiévales, 2000). Here and in other cases I follow the pagination of the original, which is more accessible.

[25] There are some 600 surviving copies of the *Summa Pisana* as against about 280 copies of the *secunda secundae*. See Boyle, "The *Summa confessorum*," p. 260, on the character of text, and Thomas Kaeppeli, *Scriptores ordinis praedicatorum medii aevi* (Rome: S. Sabina, 1970–1993), 1:158–165, "Bartholomaeus de S. Concordia," item no. 436, where the number of extant manuscripts is given as 602.

[26] See, for example, the important qualification in *Summa theol.* 1–2.84.4 *ad* 5, to which compare *De malo* 8.1 *ad* 1, *ad* 6, *ad* 8.

of older schemata, including both the Ten Commandments and the seven capital sins.

Perhaps Thomas's Dominican successors were right to reject the *Summa* on educational grounds. The work proposes a hybrid genre that is fully suitable neither for university nor for pastoral use because it means to reform both. My point is not to fault medieval judgments about what was institutionally useful. I want to suggest instead that erasing the *Summa*'s structure by rewriting it for institutional ends helps to construct Thomas as a theological authority instead of a theological author. Thomas gains institutional authority only after he is subjected to it. His authorship is taken over by the authorship of others in service of their notions of institutional ends. Thomas changes from the author of particular works with distinctive structures to a floating name above any particular work. The floating name can be attached to little fragments of Thomas's texts as they are mobilized for other uses. Or it can be invoked as a name vaguely connected to certain doctrines or arguments or terms – which are then pressed into any service.

Just here someone might object that breaking up the *Summa* is actually a sign of respect for it and for Thomas. Paul Griffiths argues, for example, that for religious readers "the ideally read work is the memorized work, and the ideal mode of reading is by memorial recall."[27] Memorizing a text requires, among other things, dividing it into what Griffiths calls "gobbets," namely, "bite-sized pieces, short enough for rapid memorization and easy recall" (p. 49). It is hard to imagine anyone memorizing the entire *Summa* verbatim, but someone might imagine that what I have deplored as the rewriting of Thomas is actually a reverent effort to memorize at least his most pertinent sections. I see two difficulties in this objection – and, indeed, in Griffiths's notion that "religious" reading tends towards memorizing gobbets. The first difficulty is the assumption that the text or its parts *can* be divided into gobbets without loss of essential teaching. The structure of the *Summa* does not suggest that it should be cut up and memorized. Its structure may indeed be more like what we call a workbook or even a lab manual. The *Summa* may consist more of a carefully ordered series of instructions or directions than of an accomplished set of propositions. Certainly it offers its most important principles almost tacitly, by quiet habituation rather than by loud assertion. Readers of the *Summa* are expected to learn the most important principles by applying them over and over again across a range of typical topics and select authorities. The typical topics and select authorities may

---

[27] Paul J. Griffiths, *Religious Reading: The Place of Reading in the Practice of Religion* (New York and Oxford: Oxford University Press, 1999), p. 46. Parenthetical references in the rest of this paragraph are to the pages of this same work.

become dispensable once the reader has learned through their sequence the tacit principles they enact – in the same way that the pages of a workbook can be pulled out as you complete them.

The second difficulty with Griffiths's notion of religious reading as reverent memorization is that memorization is no guarantee of understanding. Indeed, it can block understanding. The recalled letter of the text, with its assurance of authenticity, can distract us from posing the critical questions required for learning from it. Cardinal Cajetan, for example, provides painstaking commentary on the whole *Summa* in its proper order, article by article. Still Cajetan and the other sixteenth-century expositors of the *Summa* thoroughly distort its structures in other ways, not only by stretching it with their numbing expositions, but also by inter-cutting topics, procedures, and epistemological expectations contrary to it. The topics often belong to Scotists, Ockhamists, or Albertists. The procedures are those of new logic, moral casuistry, and intra-Christian polemic. The expectations are early modern notions of persuasion or refutation. Cajetan runs through the text of the *Summa* verbatim, and probably had memorized much of it. (The legend is that he began to study Thomas when he was five or six.) Yet Cajetan's "memorial recall" of Thomas's words is a thorough distortion of them according to early modern expectations.

For these reasons, I suggest that Griffiths's description of reverent reading in the authorities conceals the ways in which institutions or institutionally-placed readers compose that authority. Medieval excerpting of Thomas is not a response to Thomas's authority. It creates authority around him in a form that is precisely not the form of his authorship. Creating Thomas as an authority prepares, in the several ways I have been trying to suggest, for the project of a commentator like Cajetan, who does treat the *Summa* whole, but as something like a monument. However different they seem, efforts to make Thomas more useful anticipate fantasies of a monumental Thomism. Excerpting and other practices of rewriting suppose that Thomas *can* be made useful to all sorts of topics, including ones he refused to address. He can be made to speak preemptively across decades, then centuries, to debates he could not have known. His teaching, now conceived entirely apart from his texts, takes on perennial authority in multiple uses by advocates who hold high church office. As the nature of authority begins to change with shifts in the dispositions of church power, the icon of Thomas changes too, but imperceptibly, in its frame and background, in the golden field that backs the figure.

Here my second story rejoins the first. Present Catholic communities are thoroughly conditioned by late modern notions of authority: the authority of the bureaucratic archive or – what is worse – of the comprehensive doctrine for managing human behavior. The kind of authority that pre-occupies contemporary Catholicism is not the authority of medieval Dominican communities – or, for that matter, of the monarchical papacy under Innocent III. To repeat the letter of Thomas uncritically within the contemporary context, to reproduce his words as authoritative without noticing the changed character of authority, is to construct him as an all-too-contemporary authority. If neo-Thomism was promulgated in the nineteenth century to rebut certain state doctrines, its imposition, especially during the Modernist controversy, was just another exercise of modern state power.

Culpable Reading and Culpable Writing

To say the conclusion of the two stories in that way is to suggest that the fault lies once again with Thomas's readers. Is the fault *only* in Thomas's readers? Might there also be faults of authority in Thomas's writing? Is it a fault, for example, that he does not better protect his texts against authorita-tive misappropriation?

One way of handling these sharp questions is to set them aside as not per-tinent to the encounter between a contemporary reader and this medieval text. If the *Summa* really is a "Christian classic," in David Tracy's sense, then what does a long history of misinterpretation matter? Why can't the text be appreciated, be loved, in the intimate space of encounter with an individual reader?[28] I think that it can be – and I would be happy to give personal testi-mony to that effect. I knew almost nothing about Thomism or its history when I first started to read Thomas Aquinas (somewhat after the age of six). I fell in love with the text. Could I then ignore a long tradition of institu-tional misreading on a plea of infatuation? Or, rather, as I began to move out of infatuation into more sober study, and began inevitably to encounter other readers of Thomas, didn't I have to wonder whether the claims on my love were entirely honorable? Might not I have succumbed to whatever it is in the text that also summons the police? Might not my having fallen in love with a text so liable to institutional misappropriation reveal something about me?

Formulated in this way, the questions may still betray infatuation or its aftermath. They show the lover's wish to have the beloved author either

---

[28] David Tracy, *The Analogical Imagination: Christian Theology and the Culture of Pluralism* (New York: Crossroad, 1981), e.g., pp. 111–112, 115–116, 163–164.

exonerated from any fault or clearly blamed for any disappointment. We should be suspicious of the choice between immunity and blame. There is an obvious sense in which a written text is defenseless against misreadings – as the Platonic Socrates warns Phaedrus: "Once a thing is committed to writing it circulates equally among those who understand the subject and those who have no business with it; a writing cannot distinguish between suitable and unsuitable readers."[29] The reception of Plato's own texts is a fine illustration of the danger. His ironic dialogues have long been read as if they were treatises, and Plato himself – who nowhere speaks in the dialogues – is routinely assigned some of the opinions expressed in them. Infatuation encourages readers to insist that an author should either write a text that can resist all misreading or take the blame for being misread. It is more helpful – and more sober – to conceive the decision to write as a moral decision in the face of risks of misreading – especially by those in power. The sharp question for Thomas is whether he has thought sufficiently about the risks of writing an integral Christian doctrine that embeds moral teaching within the creed. More exactly, what evidence do Thomas's texts provide of caution before the risk of violent misreading?

The case looks difficult. Certain rhetorical features of Thomas's authorship seem to make his texts particularly vulnerable to misuse. Some of them are admittedly features of thirteenth-century university theology: the impersonal voice of the stereotyped procedural phrases, the abstraction of technical terminology, the omnivorous appetite for opinions plucked out of context, and the almost legal use of textual precedents. We might try to excuse these features in Thomas's texts as limits scripted into the genres available to him. Unfortunately, other rhetorical features are more properly Thomas's own. He is remarkable among "Scholastic" authors for the evenness of his voice and the muting of controversial opinions. The extraordinary simplicity of his diction further encourages the belief that he is easy to translate, to replicate. For the most part, his arguments are both simplified and compressed. Thomas typically seeks to reduce complications or controversies rather than to increase them. So the texts seem effortless and incontrovertible, perfectly general, and endlessly reproducible.

Indeed, we could map distinctive features in Thomas onto passages from *Aeterni patris* and from there onto some surviving species of neo-Thomism. Pope Leo and his counselors were not ignorant of the letter of the texts. Thomas's rhetorical equanimity and impersonality encourage the supposition that he speaks what is absolutely evident to common sense – that he is the

---

[29] Plato, *Phaedrus* 275e, to which compare his seventh *Letter*, 341e.

supreme codifier of common sense. This first illusion produces intolerant neo-Thomisms, neo-Thomisms for which any disagreement is a sign of the opponent's stupidity or malice. The transparency and compactness of Thomas's arguments encourage the illusion that he speaks with the voice of reason itself – that he is somehow universally persuasive across all centuries and cultures. This second illusion produces unhistorical and anti-pedagogical neo-Thomisms. Finally, the comprehensiveness of Thomas's teaching in the *Summa of Theology* (or *Against the Gentiles*) encourages the illusion that he is the ultimate encyclopedia. (In fact, the genius of both works is how much Thomas manages to leave out.) This third illusion produces all those encapsulated neo-Thomisms that are incurious of everything outside.

So far I have mentioned some features of Thomas's rhetoric that would argue his lack of sufficient care for the risks of writing. What can we put against them in the scales? When we look for evidence of caution about the risks of philosophical or theological teaching through writing, we often look at two clusters of textual devices. A first cluster includes irony, deliberate obscurity, and deliberate self-contradiction.[30] A second cluster contains the devices of writing in multiple voices, in symbols and metaphors, or in parables, allegories, and fables. Thomas does not seem to employ the techniques of either cluster. He defends metaphors and other poetic devices in the Christian Scriptures. Indeed, he argues that "the hiddenness of figures" is useful not only for the exercise of inquiry, but also for protecting holy things from the mockery of unbelievers.[31] But Thomas goes on from this first Question in the *Summa* to write of holy things in strikingly unadorned language. Again, Thomas recognizes that Plato writes indirectly, and so may not actually believe the tenets to which Aristotle objects. But then Thomas argues that readers can only engage the arguments on the surface of the Platonic texts.[32] While Thomas knows the devices of esoteric and figural writing, and sometimes commends them, he does not employ them.

Thomas relied not so much on esoteric or figural devices *in* the texts as on institutional safeguards *around* them. He could write in unprotected prose because he counted on the protections of the communities for which he wrote – chiefly the Dominican houses of study, but also the universities. In the thirteenth century, these were indeed communities with innumerable

---

[30] Compare Leo Strauss, *Persecution and the Art of Writing* (Chicago: University of Chicago Press, 1988), perhaps especially pp. 24–37.

[31] Thomas Aquinas, *Summa theol.* 1.1.9 *ad* 2; compare *Contra gent.* 1.8, on the usefulness of gathering "true likenesses (*verisimilitudines*)" for exercising human minds. I will come back to the text from the *Contra gent.* in chapter 5.

[32] Thomas Aquinas, *Sent. De caelo* 1.22, reporting the disagreement between Simplicius and Alexander.

walls around them, both literal and figurative. Thomas's texts were composed to be copied, taught, applied, and extended in communities closed to many classes of outsiders. The insiders, in their turn, were supposed to be formed in specific ways: by previous education, but also by liturgical practice, shared profession of faith, and vows or other forms of clerical discipline. So we might argue on behalf of Thomas's care as a writer that he entrusted unprotected writings to the protections of closed communities. In the next breath, we would have to admit that it was precisely those closed communities, beginning with the Dominicans, who erased Thomas's textual choices by rewriting them according to the changing dispositions of institutional power.

Faced with this embarrassing contrast, we might go in one of several ways. We could plead institutional prerogative and argue that since Thomas wrote within and for the Dominicans, the order could use him as it wished. Or we could construe Thomas's confidence in the community to which he committed his texts as a sacramental or incarnational act, as a trust in the power of the divine to work through failing flesh.

Each of these possibilities has something in it, but each gives up too quickly on Thomas's authorship. The fact that the texts were rewritten relentlessly can become evidence in favor of Thomas's care in writing. The texts *had to be rewritten* in order to be made into successive figures of authority. As originally written, the major texts were not useful to authoritative constructions. This is at least partly because Thomas has provided, on every page, devices for preventing the excesses of authority. The devices are a micro-dialectic in which competing claims of authority are put into pedagogical sequences that encourage an ongoing learning without the promise of a conclusion. It is an irony that such a dialectical author should have been made into so undialectical an authority. It is also a testimony to Thomas's authorship that making him into an authority of another kind required rewriting his texts – until his authority had increased to such a point that his texts could sound undialectical, because his least utterance sounded final. The long history of rewriting that I have sketched may be the best evidence for Thomas's success as a deliberate writer. So we might turn back upon the wish announced in my first sentence – the wish to read Thomas without encountering the police who are also reading him. Perhaps we might feel some gratitude even for the police, so far as their ceaseless appropriation of Thomas, their aggressive rewriting, makes us wonder what in Thomas's texts requires that they rewrite.

Do we have, then, finally, a happy answer to the sharp questions about Thomas's responsibility for his misappropriation? Can we resolve and so dismiss the questions by replying that Thomas wrote well enough to require

that he be thoroughly rewritten before becoming an authority? We can say
this and still not resolve the questions. The sharp questions posed at the
beginning are not principally about compositional responsibility. They are
rather more about what I can only call the drama of textual authority. We
can marvel at Thomas's thoughtful authorship and still be forced to admit
that something in the texts draws the police. Let me describe the attractant
as an interlacing of hybris and trauma, of impossible ambition and inconsolable betrayal.

The impossible ambition is to think that you could write moral theology,
for example, without attracting the police – as observers and as imitators.
You cannot write a persuasive moral text without giving grounds for violent
misappropriation, because in attempting to reform character or community
you necessarily energize the sources for character-building and community-
formation. Language capable of teaching religious life is language capable of
imposing tyranny – or managing behavior comprehensively. The means of
persuasion, once disclosed, can be abused by those in authority, can be
adapted by the police. The more persuasively you write moral theology, the
more you invite the police. To consider writing theology is to imagine an
ultimate power in language. Such language must be imagined, and then it
must be rejected as both tyranny and idolatry.

Inconsolable betrayal follows. Once the police move in, there are many
betrayals. For example, the pedagogy of a text is betrayed, in ways we have
seen, when its author, title, or principal claims are invoked as floating
authorities for quite alien purposes. But I have in mind another betrayal –
and one that seems inconsolable, in the way trauma does: it is the betrayal of
the reader who has trusted the pedagogy of a text only to find that it is in
the hands of the police. For such a reader, the very words of the text may
become saturated not only with the sense of deception, but with violent
police acts. Imagine someone tortured in Argentina by those who appealed
to what Thomas's *Summa* says about self-defense or political stability.
Imagine what is fused for that person into the *Summa*'s text.

The overly neat distinction between textual authority and the chronicle
of particular crimes now collapses. When it does, particular readers, whole
communities of readers, may find it impossible to hear the text without
recalling – indeed, reliving – certain crimes. I do not regard this as an accidental feature in textual traditions of religious instruction. While it cannot
be blamed on a text's structure or author, this sort of violence is something
that cannot be denied in a text's reception, its rhetorical afterlife. Indeed, it
can take over the text's rhetorical afterlife if it affixes itself by traumatic
juxtaposition to the text itself – to the text and not just to its readers, so far
as the rhetorical force of a teaching text actually takes place in its serious

readers. When readers today are taught by a medieval text, they participate in a curious simultaneity that also opens the text to its reception, for good or ill. If we want to admire the ways in which traditions of commentary or elaboration enrich classic texts, we must also recognize and deplore ways in which traditions of institutional appropriation deform them.

Sharp questions about Thomas. We cannot duck them or dismiss them. We cannot resolve them with happily ingenious answers. We have to hear them – and in their sharpest form. The question is not, could Thomas have written better? (Yes, probably, but he wrote well enough to require the police to rewrite him.) Nor is the question, do Thomas's texts contain something that attracts the police? (Yes, necessarily, because he is trying to write persuasively about the claims of divinity on human lives.) The sharpest question is, have so many betrayals been fused into Thomas's texts that the only readers willing to persist with him are the police? I want to answer, "no," but I see that the answer cannot be given once and for all, because it must be given in the presence of the police – and their victims.

My provisional "no" will be spelled out in what follows as a way of reading Thomas that attends to the practice of writing after and before authority. Some of the more outrageous claims I have already made will be substantiated. Other claims will be added – with their evidence. Fuller answers will be considered and analyzed. Throughout the book, I read Thomas against many of his rewriters as a teacher of the dangers of power in appropriating philosophy and composing theology.

Chapter Two

The Competition of Authoritative Languages

One cliché in the iconography of Thomas Aquinas shows the saint, abstracted, counting off arguments on his fingers.[1] The image plainly represents an effort of memory, but we moderns are liable to mistake what is being remembered. To us, Thomas seems to recollect principles and to excogitate arguments. In fact, Thomas counts off on his fingers terms, topics, and classifications learned from texts that he has inherited.[2] The inherited texts speak a multiplicity of languages that Thomas's theological writing tries to speak again. It is not possible to understand him except by hearing how many languages he remembers.

Modern readers are for the most part deaf to the play of these languages in Thomas. On the one hand, readers are simply ignorant that they are hearing inherited languages: they miss Thomas's gestures of quotation, allusion, appropriation, and correction. On the other hand, they lack ways of understanding how Thomas would have received these languages. Modern readers tend to mistake the reception for eclecticism, for the operation of "sources and influences," or for a diffident masking of a "system" of Thomas's own devise.

---

[1] Representative examples can be found in George Kaftal, *Iconography of the Saints in Tuscan Painting* (Florence: Sansoni, [1952]), no. 297, 1', fig. 1,109; Kaftal, *Iconography of the Saints in Central and South Italian Schools of Painting* (Florence: Sansoni, [1965]), no. 385, 1', fig. 1,277.

[2] The modern equivalent would be Thomas surrounded by books (or databases) of indexed sources. There are a few images of Thomas amid books in the late medieval iconography. See, for example, Kaftal, *Iconography of the Saints in the Painting of North East Italy* (Florence: Sansoni, 1978), no. 294, 8, fig. 1,264. I would put the emphasis on indexed sources ready to hand, rather than on originals read and remembered whole. For evidence of Thomas's research habits, not to say of the speed at which he composed, see Jean-Pierre Torrell, *Initiation à saint Thomas d'Aquin: sa personne et son oeuvre* (Fribourg: Éds. Universitaires de Fribourg, and Paris: Éds. du Cerf, 1993), pp. 351-355. Contrast the depiction of Thomas in Mary Carruthers, *The Book of Memory: A Study of Memory in Medieval Culture* (Cambridge: Cambridge University Press, 1992), pp. 2–6.

There is a more helpful way to conceive Thomas's inheritance of theological languages. It demands specificity or concreteness – even when using the term "language" to describe the objects of Thomas's concern and the means of his composition. I use "language" to cover three features of theological discourse that are connected in Thomas, but not named by him with a single term. The first feature, the most evident in theological composition, is what Thomas calls the "manner of speaking" (*modus loquendi*). Manner of speaking comprises technical terminologies, but also argumentative procedures, typical metaphors or tropes, and tested rhetorical strategies. The second feature named by "language" is the incorporation of textual pieces that fix patterns and set limits for the deployment of technical terms – what Thomas calls *auctoritates* or "authorities" in the slang of the Schools. A Latin-speaking theologian of Thomas's time did not just receive the word "*substantia*" (substance) and a set of procedures, metaphors, or strategies for deploying it. He (the restrictive pronoun is appropriate) also received authoritative examples showing permitted and prohibited uses of "*substantia*." The third feature of theological "language" is the natural language (*lingua*) within which a manner of speaking can be constructed. On Thomas's understanding, different possibilities for theological expression are offered by the different national languages, say, by patristic Greek and medieval Latin.

By grouping these features together under the English "language" I confess to having read Wittgenstein. The confession is lexical, not philosophical. I mean to assert no doctrinal similarities – or possibilities of similarity – between Wittgenstein and Aquinas. I do suggest that Aquinas would have agreed with at least this remark from *Philosophical Investigations*:

> Our language can be seen as an ancient city; a maze of little streets and squares, of old and new houses, and of houses with additions from various periods; and this surrounded by a multitude of new boroughs with straight regular streets and uniform houses.[3]

Better to begin reading Thomas with this picture than with assumptions about eclecticism, absorbed "sources," or masked "systems." If Thomas would complicate Wittgenstein's optimistic chronology, if he would multiply the architectural styles needed for a habitable city, he would agree emphatically that theology is knowledge about an ancient city of Christian discourses.

---

[3] Ludwig Wittgenstein, *Philosophical Investigations*, tr. G. E. M. Anscombe (New York: Macmillan, 1970), p. 8, no. 18.

On Recovering Thomas's "Sources"

The term "source" is a sedimented metaphor of origin: it hints that the text using sources is secondary, derivative, belated. Originality and purity lie further back, upstream. To speak of "sources" is for this reason much like speaking of a "sincere" manuscript – A. E. Housman's instance of badly misplaced "moral sympathy."[4] Manuscripts cannot be sincere, and sources are not origins. We rarely suffer scruples over our category because the effort to identify what appear to us as Thomas's "sources" looks so venerable. Readers have been inserting citations into Thomas's texts for seven centuries in the effort to learn them and to teach them. As one generation of readers succeeded another, more and other citations were needed. Indeed, two different sorts of citations must now be added to Thomas's texts as to other works of medieval academic theology. The first sort fills in an incomplete allusion or quotation. The second, by far the more important, marks off and identifies implicit or invisible references.

To take the easier first: Thomas assumes that his readers are roughly as familiar as he is with the available authorities attached to standard theological topics. He cuts his references to the minimum, especially when dealing with a famous or reiterated text. Where Thomas does provide a brief citation, it may be according to a scheme of numeration – or even of titles – far from schemes familiar to his latter-day readers. After filling in the citation, an annotator must find the version of the text that Thomas cites. Few texts are lucky enough to have modern editions of their medieval versions. A reader can consult John Damascene almost as Thomas would have found him or can read, with some patience, Saracenus's rendering of Pseudo-Dionysius, the translation Thomas took as his main text.[5] Still the reader is far from having anything like the Dominican library at Paris as it would have been in 1255. She could not with any assurance reconstruct even the catalogue of that library.[6]

---

[4]   A. E. Housman, "The Application of Thought to Textual Criticism," in *The Classical Papers of A. E. Housman*, ed. J. Diggle and F. R. D. Goodyear (Cambridge: Cambridge University Press, 1972), 3:1,058–1,069, at pp. 1,063–1,064.

[5]   John Damascene, *De fide orthodoxa: Versions of Burgundio and Cerbanus*, ed. Eligius M. Buytaert (St Bonaventure, New York: Franciscan Institute, 1955); *Dionysiaca: Receuil donnant l'ensemble des traductions latines des ouvrages attribués au Denys l'Aréopage*, ed. Philippe Chevallier et al. (Paris and Bruges: Desclée de Brouwer, 1937). By saying that we have Thomas's versions, I do not mean to say that we have them in the way that he did. The difference between reading a modern edition and a medieval manuscript is great, and not all to the credit of the former. A manuscript forces one to read slowly, and many manuscripts intended for reference use encircle the main text with a marvelous array of exegetical aids.

[6]   Most inventories so far published for Dominican houses date from around 1400. No

To remark this ignorance is not pedantry. A reader cannot judge Thomas's literal commentaries on Aristotle, on Pseudo-Dionysius, or on Scripture unless she has his *littera*, the text he comments on. Thomas was esteemed by many early readers, including those not otherwise sympathetic, precisely for his exegetical attention to detail. A reader cannot appreciate his attentiveness, his teaching as an exegete, if she holds a different text. The failure of appreciation is troublesome because the center of theological procedure in Thomas is disputative exegesis. Almost any article in the *Summa*, in the *Scriptum* on Peter Lombard's *Sentences*, or in the disputed questions turns upon dialectically stressed interpretations of textual authorities.[7] Unless a reader can begin to share Thomas's passion for rigorous readings, in which single words and phrases very much matter, she will hardly make progress in reading what theology he writes.

It is all the more awkward, then, to realize that there are towering authorities to which modern readers hardly have access. Obvious examples are the *Standard Gloss* (*Glossa ordinaria*) on Scripture and the Dominican liturgy. There is no edition of the *Gloss* in the version(s) Thomas consulted, yet dozens of arguments in his most important texts turn on citations to that Scriptural supplement.[8] The lack of a Dominican liturgy may seem less painful at first glance, since Thomas makes relatively few arguments from liturgical texts.[9] Still those arguments are not the only or chief reason for wanting to know more of Dominican liturgy as he prayed it. I suspect that many of Thomas's citations to Scripture are framed or conditioned as much by their liturgical as by their Scriptural contexts. For the moment, this must remain a hypothesis. There are few helps for discovering how Thomas

---

systematic study has been made of the earlier materials. For samples of the later inventories, see Kaeppeli, "Antiche biblioteche domenicane," with a 1417 inventory from Mantua beginning on p. 24; Gargan, *Lo studio teologico*, with a 1390 inventory, pp. 191–220.

7   I have tried throughout to translate recurring book titles into English, but "scriptum" is one title-word that I cannot render convincingly. The word means any piece of writing, regardless of genre. So a "literal" translation of *Scriptum super libros Sententiarum* would be *Writing on the Books of Sentences* [namely, *of Peter Lombard*]. This translation has the merit of emphasizing the act of writing and the multiplicity of genres it traverses. Unfortunately, using *Writing* as a short-title tends to trip up English readers, especially when the word is being used so often in other ways. So I have chosen instead the Latin short-title.

8   The *Biblia latina cum glossa ordinaria . . . et interlineari . . .* printed by Adolf Rusch in Strasbourg about 1480 does reflect the text and arrangement of some twelfth-century copies of the *Glossa*. It has been reprinted in facsimile under the direction of Karlfried Froehlich and Margaret T. Gibson (Turnhout: Brepols, 1992). The Strasbourg version is not always what Thomas reads in his *Glossa*.

9   For example, *Summa theol.* 1.31.4 *arg.* 4, 1.52.1 *sed contra*, 1–2.113.9 *sed contra*, 2–2.82.3 *ad* 2, 2–2.82.4 *sed contra*, 2–2.83.17 *corpus*, 2–2.124.2 *corpus*, 2–2.154.5 *corpus*, 2–2.176.2 *arg.* 1, and so on.

would have heard a text in his community's public prayer. For the period before about 1256, one would have to go from house to house, manuscript to manuscript, according to Thomas's (presumed) biography. For the standardized Dominican liturgy after 1256, there are several exemplary copies, including one made at St Jacques during Thomas's first regency there.[10] These exemplars remain almost entirely in manuscript.

Next to be hunted are implicit or unnamed sources. There are the notorious "some say" references (*quidam dicunt*), by which Thomas's gestures towards interlocutors he will not name. Then a reader must try to recognize invisible allusions – passages in which nothing suggests that Thomas is quoting or paraphrasing when he is in fact doing so. It was known, for example, that Thomas depended on Raymond of Peñafort's *Summa of Penance* for citations of canon law, but it had not been widely recognized that there are unmarked quotations of another of Raymond's compilations, the *Summa of Cases*, in Thomas's *Summa* 2–2.[11] Then there are the implicit intermediary sources. Many of Thomas's authorities, often the most important, come to him through other authorities, including theological works of reference. For most quotations, Thomas's authority is not the full text of an author he is quoting, but only the quotation itself, taken at second hand from an earlier theologian.

Let me give a single example.[12]

The topic is whether and in what way it is true to say that all human wills converge on one last end. The problem appears prominently in the crucial first Question of *Summa* 1–2, where it serves to cap the doctrine of the teleology of human willing.[13] The explicit authority is Augustine's *On the Trinity* 13.3. Yet Augustine's doctrine there is not exactly on point. Augus-

[10] London, British Library, Additional MS 23,935. Part of the lectionary from this manuscript is edited in Maura O'Carroll, "The Lectionary for the Proper of the Year in the Dominican and Franciscan Rites of the Thirteenth Century," *Archivum Fratrum Praedicatorum* 49 (1979): 79–103. Humbert's liturgical reforms have been discussed in comparison with earlier Dominican rites by Ansgarius Dirks, especially in his "De liturgiae dominicanae evolutione," *Archivum Fratrum Praedicatorum* 52 (1982): 5–76; 53 (1983): 53–145; 54 (1984): 39–82; 55 (1985): 5–47; and 57 (1987): 25–30. We still do not have an edition even of the whole of Humbert's norms.

[11] The earliest printed remark known to me is that of Leonard Boyle, *The Setting of the Summa theologiae of Saint Thomas* (Toronto: PIMS, 1982), p. 7. Ignatius T. Eschmann had also noticed the resemblances and left some collations of them in his papers.

[12] I was alerted to this example when I was working on I. T. Eschmann's lecture notes on the passage in Thomas, preserved among his papers at the library of the Pontifical Institute of Mediaeval Studies (PIMS), Toronto. For a printed version, see Ignatius Theodore Eschmann, *The Ethics of Saint Thomas Aquinas: Two Courses*, ed. Edward A. Synan (Toronto: PIMS, 1997), pp. 44–46.

[13] *Summa theol.* 1–2.1.7.

tine seems to hold, not for a single external end, but for a shared will psychologically discoverable in each human agent. Is Thomas simply mis-reading Augustine? He is not, but we can learn this only from the parallel Question in Thomas's *Scriptum*, which puts the issue rather differently: Is there only one end for all right wills?[14] This formulation of the issue is lifted out of Peter Lombard,[15] who also cites an Augustinian authority, *On the Trinity* 11.6. The Lombard does misread or misapply Augustine's text. Augustine speaks not of a single end for the wills of different individuals, but of a single end within various acts of the will of a single individual. The Lombard's misreading not only fixes the formulation of the issue, it gives Thomas confidence in construing Augustine's mind on the matter. What is decisive in reading the passage at the beginning of *Summa* 1–2 is not to be led back to *On the Trinity* 13.3, though that is the "correct" citation, but to be led back to Peter Lombard and his misconstrual of *On the Trinity* 11.6.

It would be possible to go on with other cases and other kinds of implicit intermediaries, but let me break off to reframe the issue. When readers begin to notice the multiplicity of languages in Thomas Aquinas, they should want to discover what these languages are and how he used them. Contemporary readers do not yet know even that much. If they did, they would still not have grasped Thomas's practice of the multiplicity of theological languages.

Thomas's Teaching on Multiple Languages

For those trying to retrace Thomas's conception of linguistic inheritance, there is at least one longer way and one shorter way. The longer way is to begin from Thomas's teaching on the nature of language, to apprentice oneself to the liberal arts of language as Thomas receives them in the *trivium*, to ascend through the variously self-limiting languages of his arrangement of speculative sciences, and then to grasp, at last, his theological transformations and delimi-tations of all the previous stages.[16] The shorter way, which is just now the only practicable way, is to take up Thomas's explicit remarks on the multiplicity of languages and then to watch his handling of that multiplicity in the structure of his main works. I begin with the explicit remarks, but not before a warning.

---

[14] *Scriptum Sent.* 2.38.1.1.

[15] Peter Lombard, *Sententiae in IV libris distinctae* 2.38.1.1, ed. Patres C. S. B. (Grottaferrata: Editiones C. S. B., 1951), 1:548.

[16] I attempted the first part of this ascent in *Ordering Wisdom: The Hierarchy of Philosophical Discourses in Aquinas* (Notre Dame: University of Notre Dame Press, 1986). I had intended to write a sequel completing the ascent in theology. This book is that sequel – or, rather, a com-mentary on the impossibility of writing the sequel as I originally envisioned it.

One product of the covert entry of Cartesianism into Scholastic circles was the fantasy of a Thomistic method. Some Thomists hoped that affixing a proper statement of this method as prologue would save the whole corpus from Cartesian doubt or its sequel in Kantian critique. The project met immediate resistance in Thomas's texts. Thomas nowhere speaks for more than a few dozen lines about his procedure. He lets his "method" be read off from his practice. When I say that there are explicit remarks on the multiplicity of languages, I do not mean that the remarks can substitute for an acquaintance with Thomas's handling of particular languages in particular cases. Theological procedure is learned by habituation. The scattered remarks I gather here serve best as invitations to appropriate Thomas's teaching practices at proper length.

Thomas discovers contrary manners of speech in the national languages.[17] Within each, there are "common" or "customary" manners of speaking, then technical or special manners (where "technical" translates "*artificialis*").[18] The most prominent technical modes are found in the pedagogically ordered bodies of knowledge, the "sciences" or *scientiae*.[19] The manners of speaking proper to each science are distinguished from the rest in many ways, but chiefly by degree of certainty. Other distinctions of the *modus loquendi* must be attended to in theology. The circumstances of human embodiment demand extraordinary care when making assertions about the divine.[20]

There is more than one way of speaking in each science, since different authorities speak differently about the same objects. Sometimes the differences are in the manner of speaking only. Dionysius the Areopagite will speak in a way that is opposed to the Aristotelian, and yet will speak to the same point.[21] At other times, a difference in manner of speaking betrays a difference in doctrine. So Aristotle must argue against the Platonic habit of speaking about "Ideas," though he himself will also sometimes speak "in the manner of the Platonists (*more Platonicorum*)."[22] The manner of speaking in philosophy can become a matter of style – which is not to say merely a

---

[17] For example, *Summa theol.* 1.39.3, with regard to plural expressions in Greek and Hebrew for God. Compare *Sent. Ethic.* 5.7, "according to the manner of speaking among the Greeks (*per modum loquendi apud Graecos*)." The point is also made at length in the prologue to the *Contra err. Graec. pars prior*, which will be discussed below.

[18] So, for example, the philosophical poems of Empedocles, "which, since they were written metrically in Greek, possess a certain difficulty and are different from the common way of speaking (*a communi modo loquendi*)" (*Sent. Metaph.* 3.11).

[19] The *modus* of each science is both its procedure and the limitations on its speech. See especially *Super De Trin. expositio cap.* 2 and 6.1.

[20] *De verit.* 23.3 *corpus*; *Contra gent.* 4.9.6 (no. 3,445).

[21] *Super De div. nom.* 4.2.

[22] *Sent. Ethic.* 1.6, to which compare *Sent. Politic.* 1[a].1.

matter of style. Thomas reproves the obscure style of the Platonists and justifies Aristotle in attacking the misunderstandings to which such a style
inevitably gives rise.[23]

The complexities of parsing the manner of speaking in a given passage
can be illustrated by Thomas's use of the allied notion of condescension
(*condescensio*). The conception is applied to passages of Scripture in which
literally false locutions are explained as concessions to the weakness of the
first readers.[24] So, for example, the account of creation in Genesis 1 appears
to contain scientific and philosophical errors, but they are excused as divine
condescension to the cosmological (mis)understanding of the ancient
Israelites. *Condescensio* figures not just in Scripture: every careful teacher
employs it. The teacher does not give a student the whole of an art at once,
"but slowly, condescending to his capacity."[25] Thomas mentions *condescensio*
specifically when noting Aristotle's dialectical acceptance of false views.[26]
He relies on it implicitly when setting forth the considerations of prudence
that limit theological speech in front of those with weak faith or none.[27]

Thomas does not want to abolish multiple manners of speaking. He
means instead to enter into many of them, to adjust them one to another,
and to correct them where they are misleading or false. His own favored
terms and tropes do not replace other ways of speaking so much as supplement them. Thomas's whole practice as exegete and dialectician is to
preserve the multiplicity of inherited languages, even under translation. A
translator in particular must appreciate exactly the distinguishing characteristics of any language, and so translation becomes a second point at which
Thomas reflects explicitly on inherited languages. His solicitude for translation is famous. Although he did not direct or collaborate with the great
Dominican translator, William of Moerbeke, as legend wishes, Thomas was
eager to acquire Moerbeke's translations as quickly as they appeared.[28]
Thomas himself initiated translations of Greek texts needed in compiling his
Gospel gloss, the *Golden Chain* (about which more in a moment).[29] Whenever he had to content himself with extant translations, he collated them
assiduously.

---

[23] *Super De div. nom. prol.*; *Sent. De anima* 1.8.
[24] So the primitive cosmology in Genesis, on which see *Summa theol.* 1.68.3 *corpus*, 1.70.1
ad 3. For the *condescensio* of Scripture generally, see *Super De div. nom.* 1.2.
[25] *Summa theol.* 2–2.1.7 *ad* 2.
[26] *Sent. De sensu* 1.5.
[27] Consider *Super De Trin. expositio proemii*; *Contra gent.* 1.8.
[28] See the summary of the negative evidence in Torrell, *Initiation*, pp. 255–258.
[29] Thomas says, "I had certain of the expositions of the Greek teachers (*doctores*) translated
into Latin" (*Catena aurea: in Marcum epist. dedic.*).

Thomas writes about translation most extensively in *Against the Errors of the Greeks* (that is, of Greek-speaking or other eastern Christians). He means to explain why certain passages in ancient authorities strike later readers as doubtful.[30] Thomas gives as one reason the difference between Greek and Latin as languages. "[M]any things that sound right (*bene sonant*) in the Greek language often do not sound right in Latin, since Latins and Greeks confess the same truth of faith with different words." Thomas's example is the mistranslation of the Trinitarian term "hypostasis" by "substance." One can say "rightly and with the catholic [or universal] faith" that there are in God three hypostases, but not that there are three substances. Thomas draws a general consequence: "it belongs to the task of the good translator, in translating what belongs to the catholic faith, to preserve the thought (*sententia*), while changing the manner of speaking (*modus loquendi*) according to the particularity (*proprietas*) of the language into which he translates." If a speaker of Latin cannot properly understand every Latin locution with word-for-word literality, how much less can she translate from another language in such a fashion.

Thomas sees clearly that translation is not a mechanical task. It requires, beyond erudition, the virtues of prudent interpretation. In calling for these virtues, Thomas may seem to commit himself unreflectively to the possibility of translation in every case. While he insists that Greek and Latin will diverge "literally,"[31] he does not seem to qualify – or to question – the confidence that some translation is always possible. Thomas appears to have eluded one false optimism about translation only to be trapped by another. This is only an appearance. Thomas's confidence in the possibility of translation is a theological confidence. It extends just to the essentials of faith. He does hold that translation can preserve the *sententia* of essential theological teachings, that is, the act of judgment or resolution registered by their words. Still the words of any text are not transparent. On Thomas's general account, any mental act is refracted when it is written or spoken.[32] A meditated theological doctrine is refracted even more in its authoritative formulations. Thomas reiterates the dispensability of particular theological utterances with regard to the truths they announce or recall. The letter of

---

[30] *Contra err. Graec. pars prior prol.* The references in the rest of this paragraph are also to this passage.

[31] At the end of the discussion on the differences between *hypostasis* and *substantia*, Thomas adds, "Nor is it to be doubted that it is also similar in many other [instances]" (*Contra err. Graec. pars prior prol.*).

[32] I have argued this from Thomas's texts in *Ordering Wisdom*, pp. 31–39. What I give here as statement is there formulated as conclusion (p. 39).

the New Testament, for example, is fully subordinate to the law of grace announced through it. Its words are instruments for disposing believers to the inward dictates of the Holy Spirit.[33] Again, the church establishes creeds in response to pedagogical needs, but they are always open to qualification and further interpretation in the face of other needs.[34] The church gives authority to the words of great theological teachers according to the rule of faith – and only so far as the words serve faith's up-building.[35]

Each of these teachings emphasizes the subservience of particular words to saving truths. It must be possible to articulate truths essential to faith in every language. There is no language in which salvation cannot be preached. At the same time, there is no guarantee that a preacher or teacher in one linguistic tradition will recognize appropriate formulations of saving truths in another tradition. The capacity for judging translations is an acquired erudition exercised contingently. It is not a form of second sight.

Translation leads to doxography or the tabulation of positions. Translation in the ordinary sense makes doxography possible across linguistic traditions by representing alien views in the prudently chosen equivalents of some common language. Translation in a metaphorical sense is required every time one moves from one manner of speaking to another within the same national language. Having remarked on both these kinds of translation, Thomas considers doxography as well. It would be surprising if he did not, since most of the academic genres within which he writes are doxographical.

Doxography is practiced everywhere in Thomas, but the principles of the practice are nowhere summarized. They cannot be summarized. The doxography of Christian teaching, in particular, provokes controversial questions about the hierarchy of binding authorities. The hierarchy of authoritative texts in theology not only controls doctrinal development, but also enacts a reverse chronology. The most authoritative texts within the church come from the church's beginnings, and so the history of theology can seem a fall from authenticity. Yet Thomas is clearly aware of theological development in the ordinary sense. He insists that the faith must be formulated more explicitly in response to new questions or errors.[36] Thomas also knows – how could an author of disputed questions not? – that interpretation must refer to context, including the circumstances of the author. So, for example, Thomas frequently remarks on Augustine's use of Platonic

---

[33] *Summa theol.* 1–2.106.1 *corpus.*
[34] *Summa theol.* 2–2.1.10 *corpus* and *ad* 2.
[35] See the striking formulation in *Summa theol.* 2–2.10.12 *corpus.*
[36] *Summa theol.* 2–2.1.9 *ad* 2, 2–2.1.10.

vocabulary and Platonic argument, and he supplies what he can in order to make that use understandable.[37]

The most sustained remarks on theological doxography come once again in *Against the Errors of the Greeks*.[38] They are the first reason Thomas gives for our having trouble with certain passages in older authoritative texts. The emergence of new errors with regard to the faith has given occasion for the Church's teachers to formulate contested points "with greater circumspection."[39] Aquinas gives as examples the changes wrought in fighting Arianism and Augustine's increasing care with the Pelagians. So Thomas's immediate predecessors, faced with fresh errors, "speak more cautiously (*cautius*) and almost more selectively (*quasi eliminatius*) about the teaching of the faith." If certain locutions in the ancients appear incautious, one ought not to despise, reject, or rewrite them. One ought rather to "interpret them reverently (*exponere reverenter*)."

We are obliged to take this passage in good faith and not to dismiss it as an excuse for exegetical violence in the service of a presumed orthodoxy. Thomas does not mean by "*exponere reverenter*" imposing a later theological consensus backwards. His point is just the opposite: the earlier writers could not have known the later consensus. Thomas counsels the doxographer to affirm that earlier Christian writers wrote truly even where their remarks now seem incautious or ambiguous. This counsel assumes a ground of faith outside its possible articulations. Community of faith can be meaningfully asserted behind literally discordant articulations. The doxographer is responsible precisely for making the unity of faith manifest through the history of changing articulations. Since changes will never end so long as history continues, theological articulations must continue to multiply. Under multiplication, the doxographer's task is not to cancel earlier formulations, but to save them. Theology ought never to be an *abolitio memoriae*, the kind of history-unwriting favored by violent orthodoxies. It ought be an act of gratitude towards one's predecessors acted out as charitable attention to them.

Thomas's attention is animated and directed by the needs of the Christian faithful around him. The needs cannot be met by piecemeal reinterpretation. They require that an integral theological truth be spoken anew, in the present. They require, in other words, that Thomas take up reinterpreted authorities into new patterns of theological persuasion.

---

[37]   See especially *De spir. creat.* 10 *ad* 8.

[38]   These are not the only remarks on patristic doxography. For surveys of a much larger selection, see Walter H. Principe, "Thomas Aquinas' Principles for Interpretation of Patristic Texts," *Studies in Medieval Culture* 59 (1976): 111–121.

[39]   *Contra err. Graec. pars prior prol.* The references in the rest of this paragraph are also to this text.

Rhetorical Structures for the Multiplicity of Languages

Thomas's explicit remarks on manners of speaking, on translation, and on doxography are parts of a program that is carried out in the construction of his major works. His most famous works explicitly propose reorganizations of inherited languages, where "languages" comprise at once manners of speaking, authorities, and national languages. Readers ought to expect this of a thirteenth-century Dominican. The reorganization of sources was a principal preoccupation of mendicant learning.[40] Among Dominican productions in the decades immediately before Thomas's career as teacher – and leaving aside such genres as the commentaries on Peter Lombard – there are famous instances: the Scriptural annotations (*postillae*), emendations (*correctoria*), and alphabetical concordances produced by the Parisian team under Hugh of St Cher;[41] the parts of the *Greater Mirror* of Vincent of Beauvais, in their many redactions; the *Summas of Vices and Virtues* by William Peraldus;[42] and both the digest of decretals and – more importantly for Thomas – the *Summa of Cases* by Raymond of Peñafort.[43]

To the list of Dominican reference works, there should be added at least one by Thomas, the *Continuous Gloss* or *"Golden Chain"* (*Catena aurea*). It was among Thomas's most popular writings, to judge from the surviving manuscript evidence,[44] and it was regularly plundered by Thomas's early readers.[45] The *Chain* is a running gloss on the four Gospels, composed of short passages from patristic authors, Latin and Greek, as well as from the

---

[40] Many of these were the products of teams of researchers. On the importance of these collaborations, see Yves Congar, "*In dulcedine societatis quaerere veritatem*: Note sur le travail en équipe chez S. Albert et chez les Prêcheurs au XIIIe siècle," in *Albertus Magnus, Doctor Universalis: 1280/1980*, ed. C. Meyer and Albert Zimmermann (Mainz: Matthias-Grünewald, 1980), pp. 47–57.

[41] On the genesis of this text, see Richard H. and Mary A. Rouse, "The Verbal Concordance to the Scriptures," *Archivum Fratrum Praedicatorum* 44 (1974): 5–30, at pp. 7–13.

[42] For an introduction, see Antoine Dondaine, "Guillaume Peyraut: Vie et oeuvres," *Archivum Fratrum Praedicatorum* 18 (1948): 162–236.

[43] For a survey of Raymond's works, with much emphasis on the manuscript evidence, see Laureano Robles, "Escritores dominicos de la Corona de Aragón (siglos XIII–XV)," in *Repertorio de historia de las ciencias eclesiasticas en España*, vol. 3 (Salamanca: IHTE, 1971), 11–[177], at pp. 12–53.

[44] According to Weisheipl's figures, the *Catena aurea* is the most widely copied of all of Thomas's Scriptural works, and except for Thomas's other expository innovation – the literal commentary on Job – it is far and away the most widely copied. Torrell, following Conticello, confirms Weisheipl's numbers for manuscripts of the complete text. See Torrell, *Initiation*, p. 204.

[45] In John of Paris's *On Royal and Papal Power* (written between 1302 and 1303), for example, Gospel authorities invoked by the papal party are reinterpreted by copying out sections from Thomas's compilation.

Standard Gloss. It is, in fact, something like the *Gloss* revised to the stricter standards of thirteenth-century patristic erudition. The *Chain* is justly famous for its ample use of Greek material, but Thomas's contribution is not just the importation of unfamiliar authorities. The whole of the *Chain* is remarkable for its clarity of organization, its precision of citation, and even its revision of confused or corrupted texts.[46] The *Chain* is more than a comprehensive patristic anthology neatly arranged. It is a continuous clarification of patristic passages, that is, a commentary on salient texts of patristic exegesis.

The *Chain* is hardly Thomas's most compelling rhetorical invention for uniting and applying authorities. That invention comes in the large-scale structures for teaching theology that he devised throughout his authorship. The structures suppose at least three things. They suppose, first, that responsible pedagogy cannot take place except by entering into the multiplicity of languages. They hold, second, that multiple languages can be made to correct and supplement one another topic by topic. They affirm, third, that a topically-arranged multiplicity of languages can lead to a single pedagogical end. If a conviction of the unity of theology gives warrant for these suppositions, it hardly renders them self-evident. I would like to end by trying to supply some evidence – which is to say, by trying to answer the question, why Thomas thinks that a multiplicity of languages must be preserved in the teaching of theology. How does a contemporary reader explain Thomas's ways of inheriting the multiplicity of theological languages? How does she translate his principles for constructing large-scale works?

For Thomas, the first step in speaking about the divine is an act of renunciation. The speaker must renounce the familiarity of the mother tongue. We are accustomed to call this demand for renunciation a "doctrine," the "doctrine of the divine names." The tag is superficial. The "doctrine of divine names," as Thomas learns it from Pseudo-Dionysius and Maimonides among others, is a critique of linguistic immediacy and so precisely not a doctrine. What is most familiar to human beings in their language – daily uses, functions in the economy of human desires, "fit" onto the world – must be denied. The speaker who would speak about God must replace familiarity with strangeness, immediacy with irony.

The denial is not uniform. It operates distinctly on different classes of locutions. Thomas affirms with Pseudo-Dionysius that the classes can be pedagogically arranged. The theological speaker can then perform a sequence of renunciations. Thomas reads in Pseudo-Dionysius and learns in

---

[46] *Catena aurea: in Matt. epist. dedic.*

theological disputation that ordered linguistic renunciation is fostered by apprenticeship to a multiplicity of authoritative languages. Linguistic multiplicity is honored in the form of Scripture itself – with its multiple authors, modes of speaking, genres, and audiences. So far as theology remains for Thomas the teaching of the "sacred page," it enacts the speaking of a series of languages. It leads those who hear it or read it to loosen their unreflective grip on one language. With Scripture, it depicts the ways in which languages shatter against the divine; it leads its appropriate readers to a less untrue activity of speaking about God.

I say "activity of speaking," because linguistic renunciation is not inscribed in single words or phrases. It is not a typographical convention for deploying words "under erasure." Some accounts of theological language treat it as a heap of cold, leaden lumps that must be warmed and reworked before they can have effect. A reader as rhetorically-minded as Thomas will insist that theological language is hardly inert. It has its own purposes, projects its own pedagogies, and constitutes its own posterities. To enter a pedagogy is to lend one's lived time to the retelling of the text's narrative, to the reenactment of its teaching. The rhetorically minded reader sees that to read theology well is to be invited in as protagonist in a curriculum that is a narrative, in a school of comprehensive persuasion.

For most Christians, the privileged curriculum is traced out by the sequence of languages in Scripture. If there is to be anything spoken or written besides Scripture, and Scripture itself demands that there must be, then theological speakers will have to make rhetorical forms that incorporate Scripture or mimic it, while leading to the end that is also Scripture's end. Thomas sees Pseudo-Dionysius as a theologian who builds a curricular narrative out of multiple Scriptural locutions. The curriculum ends by pointing to union with God. Because he comes later in the swelling sound of Christian texts, Thomas composes a curriculum out of both Scripture and the generations of speaking descended from it. This is Thomas's enactment of the Dionysian pedagogy.

Thomas does not expect that a single language can be imposed universally on all. He does not try to impose one. He takes a multiplicity of theological languages as inevitable given human diversity and human history. He takes the multiplicity as desirable given the weakness of human understanding and the consequent poverty of speech. Thomas does trust that a reader can move among languages with understanding and be moved through them to a single end. In this way, hierarchies of inherited theological languages begin to imitate the plenitude of Scriptural rhetoric, though they never equal it.

The criterion for judging the success of Thomas's constructions is not the criterion of propositional picturing. It is the criterion of helpful persuasion. The end of his authorship is to orchestrate the multiplicity of theological languages in order to persuade a reader to step back from the idolatry of one familiar language. To step back is to free oneself for a whole curriculum of persuasions, a narrative of sequential faith.

Chapter Three

Imaginary Thomistic Sciences

Readers of Thomas miss the importance of his plurality of languages for a variety of reasons, including the kinds of ignorance or misapprehension just traced. Equally powerful motives can be found in some readers' wish that Thomas should supply a single language covering the entire realm of knowledge as they conceive it. The wish demands that there be a Thomistic teaching on every topic, even those that Thomas could hardly conceive or about which he had little to say. The ideal map of the realm of knowledge changes with time, of course, and so different Thomistic sciences are made up from one century to the next. The claim in each century is that Thomas had already mapped out any new realm.

In this chapter, I recall two efforts to make up Thomistic sciences despite the absence of textual support in Thomas. The first is a relatively obvious case, though one that a few zealots in the nineteenth century attempted to project backwards into the texts: medicine on Thomistic principles. The second case of a manufactured Thomistic science seems more plausible. It is certainly more durable: some readers of Thomas are still trying to make it up. It is the case of a Thomistic politics. In both cases, I mean to show that every wish to turn Thomas into an encyclopedic authority not only leads to ridiculous overstatements of his originality, but also fundamentally distorts his relation to those who were authorities for him. The (mutable) craving for Thomistic universality endows Thomas with a kind of authority he never claimed and that he deliberately rejected in his own practice of intellectual inheritance.

The juxtaposition of medicine and politics is particularly apt for showing how the craving mutates in relation to changes in the fields of knowledge — in what Thomas would conceive as hierarchies of knowledge. The search for a Thomistic medicine and politics may be attributable in part to the neo-Thomist rehabilitation of Thomas, but must be attributed as well to the nineteenth-century alliance between the two fields. Neo-Thomists needed Thomas to speak in every field, but particularly in medicine and politics, because they wrote under the double monarchy of those disciplines. Knowledge is tangled up with power. The "retrieval" or "restoration" of old knowledge inevitably alters it by bringing it under the currently prevailing dispositions of power. The conjunction of medicine and politics in Thomas is not their alliance in nineteenth-century programs of comprehensive state management. Even had he taught much about those bodies of knowledge, he would not have been teaching them with their modern disciplinary force. In fact, he did not teach them. Modern readers insist that he did because they need his power in the field of contemporary disciplines.[1]

Wishing for a Thomist Medicine

One episode in what might be called the legendary history of the medieval medical school at Salerno features a role for Thomas Aquinas. For Salvatore De Renzi, Aquinas is "the most complete synthesis and the most exact expression" of Salernitan medical teaching through the thirteenth century.[2] Andrea Sinno invokes the tradition that Aquinas taught theology in the Cathedral of Salerno for a time, apparently in close cooperation with the Masters of medicine.[3] Both authors cite what they consider to be instances of Aquinas's borrowing from Salernitan treatises, not to say quoting them.[4] Capparoni adds to the evidence a passage "from Thomas" that praises Salernitan expertise.[5] Unfortunately, the passage comes from a spurious text.[6] If the textual evidence in De Renzi and Sinno is not so obviously misleading,

[1]   This paragraph contains many invisible references to Michel Foucault. I have in mind particularly his *Surveiller et punir. Naissance de la prison* (Paris: NRF/Gallimard, 1975), pp. 303–315; compare the English of *Discipline and Punish: The Birth of the Prison*, tr. Alan Sheridan (New York: Vintage/Random House, 1995), pp. 296–308.
[2]   Salvatore De Renzi, *Storia documentata della Scuola medica di Salerno*, 2nd edn. (Naples 1857), p. 482. See pp. 481–490 for De Renzi's collation of Salernitan matter in Thomas.
[3]   Andrea Sinno, "Determinazione della sede della scuola medica di Salerno: Diplomi di laurea dell'Almo Collegio Salernitano," *Archivio storico della Provincia di Salerno* 1 (1921): 29–57, at pp. 45–47.
[4]   De Renzi, *Storia documentata*, pp. 487–490; Sinno, "Determinazione," pp. 45–56, with reference to De Renzi.
[5]   Pietro Capparoni, *Magistri Salernitani nondum cogniti* (London: Wellcome Institute for the History of Medicine, 1923), p. 8.
[6]   The treatise appears as Opusculum 64 in the Parma-Vivès edition. It was counted as inauthentic by Mandonnet and Grabmann, who have been followed by later writers, such as Weisheipl and Torrell.

it does not show that Thomas was a member of the Salernitan school – much less, that he was its supreme embodiment.

The legends do pose a question: what is the role of medical doctrine, Salernitan or not, in Aquinas? For believers in the explanatory power of biography, there are several reasons to find the question suggestive. Thomas learned his liberal arts at the university in Naples, Salerno's near neighbor and administrative center.[7] Norman Naples is known to have been much concerned with the new natural philosophy and its medical contexts.[8] Again, Aquinas first studied physics there under Peter of Ireland, from whom there survives a later disputed question on the teleology of organ-formation.[9] More substantively, medicine would seem to offer Thomas a detailed supplement to certain parts of Aristotelian biology. (Aristotle himself frequently gives examples from medicine, but there is no Aristotelian treatise on it.) There are many references to medicine throughout Thomas's writing that point beyond Aristotle. Surely Thomas must have contributed importantly to medicine, even if he was not associated with a legendary medieval medical school.

As soon as one begins to read the texts, these biographical probabilities dissolve. Many of Thomas's mentions of medicine are not pertinent. Medical metaphors appear, for example, throughout his discussion of the sacraments, but the metaphors are both traditional and perfectly general. The same holds for medical examples in illustration of other points, such as the Aristotelian doctrine of analogy. Finally, and again following Aristotle, Thomas frequently uses the physician, the *medicus*, as typical of those who know by habit some body of knowledge. Thus the *medicus* appears in discussions about learned error. In each of these cases, the mention of medicine implies no learned views about it.[10]

Other passages do contain substantive medical doctrine but, on closer examination, the doctrine will appear to be both derivative and rudimentary. Since it is impracticable to survey all the passages, I will concentrate

[7] See the early biographies of Peter Calo and William Tocco in *Fontes vitae S. Thomae Aquinatis*, ed. Dominicus Prümmer (Toulouse: Revue Thomiste, 1935), pp. 20 and 70, respectively.

[8] Martin Grabmann, "Kaiser Friedrich II. und sein Verhältnis zur aristotelischen und arabischen Philosophie," in his *Mittelalterliches Geistesleben* (Munich: M. Hüber, 1926) 2: 103–137.

[9] The disputation was published by Clemens Baeumker under the title *Petrus de Hibernia, der jugendlehrer des Thomas von Aquino und seine Disputation vor König Manfred*, SB Bayer. Akad. Wissenschaften, Philos.-philolog. u. hist. Klassen, J. 1920, Abh. 8, with the text on pp. 41–49.

[10] Compare Nancy Siraisi's remarks on the three kinds of medical lore in Albert, "The Medical Learning of Albertus Magnus," in *Albertus Magnus and the Sciences*, ed. James A. Weisheipl (Toronto: PIMS, 1980), 379–404, at p. 394.

just on three: Thomas's definitions and authorities for medicine, his description of human reproduction, and his mentions of root (or original) moisture.

Definitions and Authorities

Thomas nowhere stops to construct or defend a definition of medicine in the way that he does with physics, metaphysics, or theology. Still he several times quotes definitions of medicine on the way to some other point. Three times he gives the formula, "medicine is the science of the healthy and the sick"; in a fourth text, he says that medicine is by definition "about the healthy and the sick."[11] The phrases might be taken as echoes of the short definition that Galen himself calls the "old account" of medicine.[12] Something like it also figures in the works of Albert the Great from the time Thomas was with him in Cologne.[13] Alternately, Thomas's formula might be taken as an abbreviation of the tripartite definition offered in Galen's *Art of Medicine*, which states that medicine concerns the healthy, the sick, and what is neither.[14] This definition is widely echoed in the Latin tradition, both in medical texts and in compendia of the sciences.[15] Of course, it might be simpler to suppose that Thomas's definition comes from Aristotle, who offers quite similar formulations as examples or analogies.[16]

Thomas spends more attention on the question, whether medicine is practical or theoretical. He poses it in his early exposition of Boethius's *On the Trinity*, when he is trying to defend the Aristotelian division of speculative science. The objection holds that while medicine is divided into

---

[11] Respectively, *Sent Phys.* 8.2; *Sent. Metaph.* 5.17; *Sent. Ethic.* 6.9.

[12] *De sectis* cap. 1, ed. Georg Helmreich in *Claudii Galeni Pergameni Scripta minora*, ed. Johann Marquardt et al. (Leipzig: Teuber, 1884–1893), 1:1.8–9.

[13] Albert the Great, *Super Dionysii epistulas* 7, as in his *Opera omnia ad fidem codicum manuscriptorum edenda*, ed. Institutum Albertus Magnus Coloniense (Munster: Aschendorff, 1951–), 37/2:502. I will refer to this edition as "Cologne *Opera omnia.*"

[14] *Ars Medica* 1, in his *Opera omnia*, ed. Karl G. Kühn et al. (Leipzig, 1821–1833; rptd. Hildesheim: G. Olms, 1964), 1:307.

[15] See, for example, Constantine the African, *Pantegni* 1.2, as in *Constantini Africani . . . Opera conquisita undique magna studio . . .* (Basel: Heinrich Petri, 1536–1539), 2:2, and Gundissalinus, *De divisione philosophiae*, ed. Ludwig Baur, BGPhM 4/2–3 (Munster: Aschendorff, 1903), 83.14–15.

[16] See, for example, *Topics* 6.4 (141a19–20), 6.5 (143a3–5); *Nicomachean Ethics* 1.1 (1094a7), 6.10 (1143a3). It might also come from Thomas's thinking that Aristotle's *Parva naturalia* included a treatise "De sanitate et aegritudine." See *Sent. De sensu prol.* and the notations in *Opera omnia* (Leonine) 45/2:4 for ll. 38–54.

theoretical and practical, the same might be true of any other knowledge ordered to skilled activity. Every skill, then, deserves to be counted as theoretical science. Thomas's reply depends on a citation to the opening of Avicenna's *Canon of Medicine*, which explains the distinction between theoretical and practical medicine.[17] Following Avicenna, Thomas holds that the distinction is only one between principles and their particular application. Practical medicine teaches that certain remedies are to be used, say, in treating certain tumors ("apostemes"): theoretical medicine teaches the kinds and numbers of vital powers or fevers. Both the distinction and the illustrations are from Avicenna, to whom Thomas explicitly refers when invoking them elsewhere.[18] Can we assume he knew the whole of Avicenna's *Canon* directly? On the contrary, this single reference is precisely the kind learned from public disputation or as part of a tradition of commentary.

Other explicit citations to medical authorities are few in Thomas. Galen is cited several times for his views on the soul.[19] The ultimate source here is Nemesius of Emesa, but the proximate source may be Albert.[20] Perhaps it was neither. Galen's view on these matters was notorious. Thomas's contemporary and fellow Dominican Raymond Marti quotes Algazel as saying that Galen was the prince of those natural philosophers who held for the soul's mortality.[21] Certainly Thomas refers to Galen elsewhere. He cites the *Book on the Action of Simple Medicines* in favor of the principle that all bodies are consumed by fire.[22] A general allusion reports Galen as teaching that "abstinence is the best medicine."[23] Both of these are again the sort of aphoristic locus easily learned at second hand. The only other medical authority named by Thomas is Constantine the African. Constantine is cited not for his systematic works or translations – which were enormously influential in the twelfth century at Salerno, at Chartres, and in England – but for the little treatise *On Coitus*. His authority is needed by Thomas only to

---

[17] *Super De Trin.* 5.1 *ad* 4.

[18] *De ver.* 2.8 *corpus* and, without the reference, 3.3 *arg.* 2.

[19] *Contra gent.* 2.63–64, 68.

[20] Nemesius of Emesa, *Premnon physikon* 2. For Albert's role, see the passages considered below.

[21] Raymond Marti, *Pugio fidei* 1.2.7, ed. Joseph de Voisin (Leipzig: haered. Friderici Lanckisi, 1687), p. 94.

[22] *Scriptum Sent.* 2.15.2.2 *ad* 1, 4.44.3 *ad* 3. The bit of Galen occurs together with a quotation from the pseudo-Aristotelian *Liber de proprietatibus elementorum*: "no animal can live in fire." For a similar appearance of the question of the salamander, see Albert, *Sent.* 2.15 C *ad aliud* . . ., as in his *Opera omnia*, ed. Auguste Borgnet (Paris: Vivès, 1890–1899), 27:278. I will refer to this edition as "Borgnet *Opera omnia*."

[23] *Scriptum Sent.* 4.15.3.1.2 *ad* 3.

explain the teleology of sexual pleasure.[24] Since the citation refers to the very beginning of Constantine's work, and since the phrase is once again of the sort that circulates in sayings-collections and public debates, it is hard to argue from it for any prolonged reading on Thomas's part.

The question of authorities is more complicated in Thomas's epistolary extract *On the Motion of Heart*. The editors of the critical edition think that Thomas's tract is something of a reply to Alfred of Sareshel.[25] Alfred's own *On the Motion*, written before 1217, had a fairly wide circulation in the thirteenth century.[26] It is cited by Albert the Great, for example, in his *Questions on Animals*.[27] Since Thomas wrote his little treatise after 1260 and perhaps as late as 1273 (if one follows Mandonnet),[28] he could have garnered some knowledge of Alfred's position from any number of sources. Moreover, his explicit point is to justify and perhaps clarify the *Aristotelian* model for the heart. There are 12 explicit citations to Aristotle and four to unnamed interlocutors. Perhaps the latter prove a direct use of Alfred or, indeed, of the medical sources Alfred outlines in order to reject. The unattributed views claim that cardiac motion derives from an extrinsic universal cause, that it comes from heat, and that man is a microcosm, a "lesser world."[29] Certain "physicians" are further credited with distinguishing vital from animal operations.[30] Of course, Man as Microcosm is a well worn image and needs no specific source. The Leonine editors do find a specific echo of Alfred in the claim that cardiac motion comes from heat. Yet the doctrine also figures in Constantine the African and even in Cistercian anthropology.[31] The distinction between animal and vital forces is indeed a medical doctrine, found in Constantine and Johannitius, for example.[32] Of course, it also enters into such tracts as the Cistercian *On Spirit and Soul*, which Thomas cites elsewhere.[33] The claim for a universal extrinsic causality is common enough in

[24] *Scriptum Sent.* 4.33.1.3a; compare *Summa theol.* Suppl. 65.3. There is a textual difficulty here, since Busa reads only "as Augustine says." Elsewhere in the *Scriptum* on the *Sentences*, the opinion is attributed just to the *medici*; see *Scriptum Sent.* 2.38.1.2 *ad* 6.
[25] See the editorial remarks in Leonine *Opera omnia*, 43:96.
[26] Baeumker, *Petrus de Hibernia*, p. 1, n. 4.
[27] *Quaestiones de animalibus* 3.5 (Cologne *Opera omnia*, 12:126–127).
[28] See the summary in Leonine *Opera omnia*, 43:95–96.
[29] *De motu* (Leonine *Opera omnia* ll. 24–27, 151–152; 43–45; and 59, respectively).
[30] *De motu* (ll. 209–210).
[31] Constantine, *Pantegni theor.* 4.19 (Basel [1539] 92): William of St Thierry, *De natura corporis et animae* 1 (Migne *PL* 180:700D).
[32] Compare Constantine, *Pantegni theor.* 4.1 (Basel [1539] 79); Johannitius, *Isagoge* 9. For the Galenic context, see Owsei Temkin, "On Galen's Pneumatology," *Gesnerus* 8 (1951) 180–189.
[33] *De spiritu et anima* 20–22 (Migne *PL* 40:794–795); compare *Scriptum Sent.* 4.44.3.3 *sol.* 2 *ad* 1, where Thomas comments on its reputed composition by "a certain Cistercian."

the philosophical tradition and appears elsewhere in biological discussions – for example, with regard to the origin of the human soul. An editor's impulse to provide an exact source once again leads us astray.

I conclude that neither explicit nor implicit authorities demonstrate that Thomas had any extensive acquaintance with medical authors. If this is a trial for his editors, it is a boon for ambitious readers who want to project missing sciences onto him. Had Thomas referred in detail to a large library of medieval medical authorities, it would be more difficult for later readers to project their versions of medicine onto him. The very generality of Thomas's references to medicine provide a relatively blank slate onto which other conceptions of the disciplinary power of medicine can be written. Moreover, and crucially, later readers who wanted to manufacture a Thomist medicine did not go even so far as I have already gone in noticing the details of medieval medicine that do appear. They were content – they were required – to snatch up a few "principles" of the utmost generality so that they would not be distracted by even the few details that the texts offer. Take this as a parable for the construction of Thomistic sciences. The gaps in Thomas's interest or erudition are the points at which his authority can be most easily appropriated for later disciplinary struggles.

Human Reproduction

Human reproduction is a famous crux of Aristotelian biology. Aristotle must explain not only how higher and higher states of actualization are brought about in the fetus, but also how an immaterial intellect (if it is immaterial) comes to be produced from or associated with an animal body. Thomas grapples with these issues in numerous places, but mostly from Aristotelian sources and in contention with Aristotelian interpreters. There are only a few other sources, and they had entered Aristotelian discussion in a previous generation. For example, Thomas quotes a verse on the periods of gestation that is known from Salernitan writings, but it is also found in Michael Scot and in Albert's *Sentences*-commentary.[34]

Thomas treats human reproduction in four texts that are extensive enough to invite chronological reading. The main doctrinal lines are laid down in the *Sentences*-commentary, while discussing the creation of Eve. The two pertinent articles ask whether parents transmit the human soul as a whole and the

---

[34] *Scriptum Sent.* 3.3.5.2. See also C. M. Joris Vansteenkiste, "'Versus' dans les œuvres de Saint Thomas," in *St Thomas Aquinas 1274–1974*, 1:77–85, at p. 80.

sensible soul in particular.[35] Thomas holds that the rational soul is *not* received from the parents: being immaterial, it cannot be transmitted by material means. Thomas's argument here takes the form of a schematic doxography that contrasts the views of Plato, Avicenna, and Themistius with those of Aristotle and Averroes. The Platonic group, says Thomas, holds for a separate cause in human reproduction; its adherents are misled both by the limited properties of bodies and by a general prejudice in favor of separate causes. The Aristotelian camp holds more generous views about natural causality, making an exception only for the intellect itself. Thomas defends the Aristotelian causal view and then inserts a longish description of the processes of human generation.

The description follows Aristotle on disputed points: the origin of human seed from the last residue of unassimilated food, the presence in the seed of an indistinct potency, and the failure of the female to contribute formally to generation.[36] Human seed contains "formative power" (*virtus formativa*), a diffuse vital energy deriving from the father. The formative power uses the vital spirit enclosed in the seed as its "instrument," its "subject," and its "organ." To this bodily spirit there is joined a threefold heat: the consuming "elementary heat" (*calor elementaris*), the life-giving "heat of the soul" (*calor animae*), and the species-bearing "celestial heat" (*calor caeli*). By means of these three, the fetal material is formed into the embryo's cerebral membranes. Thomas seems here to allow some material contribution from the seed to the embryo, though this contribution is denied by Aristotle.[37] The activation of the potential soul in the embryo requires the assistance of the power of the celestial sphere. A series of forms is acquired and then lost until the whole rational soul is created by God.

I said that the treatment was largely Aristotelian, but it would be more precise to call it Albertist. Albert's long treatments of reproductive physiology come in the "paraphrases" of the *Books on Animals* and related questions. On the current chronology, these would fall in and after 1258, that is, after even the final redaction of Thomas's *Scriptum* on the *Sentences*.[38] But there is already a substantial treatment in Albert's *Summa of Creatures*, which he completed before 1246 and which represents his teaching at or before the time

---

[35] *Scriptum Sent.* 2.18.2.1, 3.

[36] *Scriptum Sent.* 2.18.2.3.

[37] *Scriptum Sent.* 2.18.2.3 and *ad* 4; compare 2.30.2.1 *ad* 3, which is more fully discussed below. Compare Aristotle, *De generatione animalium* 1.21 (729bl–730a32), 1.22 (730b9–31).

[38] See the editorial remarks by Ephrem Filthaut in Cologne *Opera omnia*, 12: xlv–xlvi; compare Weisheipl, *Friar Thomas*, pp. 358–359.

when Thomas joined him in Paris.[39] The *Summa of Creatures* provides the key to Thomas's treatment in the *Scriptum*. Three of the objections in the first article correspond exactly to the first three of Albert's arguments after Apollinaris.[40] The doctrine of the triple heat serves as the centerpiece of Albert's mechanical explanation.[41] Albert also speaks of heat as the instrument of generative power.[42] But the most important dependence is structural: Thomas's grouping of previous opinions corresponds to the dialectic in Albert, who contrasts the view of "Plato, Avicenna, Theodorus and others following them" with those of Aristotle.[43] If the dialectic is the same, so is the line of resolution. Thomas's ambiguity about the material contribution from the male seed is borrowed from Albert, who distinguishes the material seed from the efficient and who describes the use of the seed's humidity in generating the embryo.[44] The most striking change Thomas makes is to simplify the textual structure of the treatment by condensing arguments and *eliminating* authorities, especially medical ones. Albert alludes, for example, to the history of the quarrel between Aristotle and Galen.[45] Thomas passes over the controversy in silence, preferring to concentrate on philosophical controversies concerning the embodiment of intellect.

So far I have dealt with Thomas's commentary on the *Sentences*. His three other texts can be reviewed much more quickly, with an eye only to significant differences. The treatment in *Against the Gentiles* spreads over four chapters within a polemical defense of Thomas's views on the intellect.[46] Much is familiar.[47] The noticeable changes are rhetorical: Thomas is moving

---

[39]   James A. Weisheipl, "The Life and Works of St Albert the Great," in *Albertus Magnus and the Sciences: Commemorative Essays 1980*, ed. Weisheipl (Toronto: PIMS, 1980), 13–41, at pp. 22–23 and 25.

[40]   Compare *Scriptum Sent.* 2.18.2.1 *arg.* 2–3 and 7 with Albert, *Summa de creaturis* 2.1.17.3 objs. 1–3 (Borgnet *Opera omnia* 35:148).

[41]   Albert, *Summa de creaturis* 2.1.17.3 *ad* 14 and *ad* 22–24 (Borgnet *Opera omnia* 35:157, 159–160).

[42]   *Summa de creaturis* 2.1.17.4 (Borgnet *Opera omnia* 35:161–162).

[43]   *Summa de creaturis* 2.1.17.3 *arg.* 26 (Borgnet *Opera omnia* 35:152).

[44]   *Summa de creaturis* 2.1.17.2 *ad* 2 and 2.1.17.3 *ad sed contra* 11–13 (Borgnet *Opera omnia* 35:145, 161). The deeper authority is probably Avicenna; see Thomas S. Hall, "Life, Death, and the Radical Moisture," *Clio Medica* 6 (1971): 3–23, at p. 4.

[45]   *Summa de creaturis* 2.1.17.3 *sed contra* 15 (Borgnet *Opera omnia* 35:155).

[46]   *Contra gent.* 2.86–89.

[47]   There are familiar references to bisected worms and triple heat in *Contra gent.* 2.86 (nos. 1,708 and 1,738; 1,710). The three counter-positions against which Thomas constructs his own view are borrowed from Albert: *Contra gent.* 2.89 (no. 1,736) = *Summa de creaturis* 2.1.17.3 *sed contra* 15; *Contra gent.* 2. 89 (nos. 1,737–1,738) = *Summa de creaturis* 2.1.17.3 *sed contra* 14. The double view on the material role of the seed persists, though Thomas approaches the more strictly Aristotelian position in *Contra gent.* 2.89 (nos. 1,742–1,743).

further from sources in physics and medicine. Here he emphasizes arguments against the view that the human soul can be transmitted by material means, but the argument is now also directed against more explicitly theological authorities. One of the most prominent in these chapters of *Against the Gentiles* is "Gregory of Nyssa," that is, both Gregory of Nyssa's *On the Making of Man* and Nemesius of Emesa's *Premnon physikon*.[48] Nemesius already stood behind Albert's treatment, of course, but now appears explicitly (albeit pseudonymously) in Thomas.

Thomas shifts even further towards theological authorities in the questions *On Power*. The issue is whether rational souls are created or transmitted. Thomas invokes the collection *On Ecclesiastical Dogmas* twice in order to set aside opposing views as heretical.[49] The most striking passage is the reply to the ninth objection. Longer even than the body of the article, it might seem (at last) to supply a technical discussion of the human seed's progressive actualizations. In fact, the reply is an amplified version of the parallel in *Against the Gentiles*. Its five counter-positions, for example, are variations on the three main views rejected in the earlier text.

Thomas's final treatment of human generation appears in two questions at the very end of *Summa* 1. The large context here is the distinction of creatures; the small context, certain special questions about the actions of bodies. Thomas is now more strictly Aristotelian about the material contribution of the male seed.[50] Alternative opinions about embryonic actualization, so lengthily considered in *Against the Gentiles* and *On Power*, are passed over with a single reply.[51] The authority of *On Ecclesiastical Dogmas* reappears prominently,[52] together with a host of familiar authorities from Aristotle and Averroes. The only structural achievement is to clarify the origin of seed by interposing an article on nutrition (the doctrine of which I will consider below).

The textual transit from the *Sentences*-commentary to the *Summa* suggests some general observations. Thomas begins by simplifying the medical and physical material contained in Albert. This simplification is accompanied by a shift to philosophical authorities and issues. At no point is the issue an

---

[48]   *Contra gent.* 2.88 (nos. 1,728–1,733), 2.86 (no. 1,713). The textual parallels to the *De opificio hominis* cited by Marc are not compelling. For the availability of the Latin versions of that work, see the essay by Helen Brown Wicher in *Catalogus Translationum et Commentariorum* 5 (1984), 1–250, at pp. 120–127.

[49]   *De potentia* 3.9 *corpus* and *ad* 9.

[50]   *Summa theol.* 1.118.1 *ad* 4.

[51]   *Summa theol.* 1.118.2 *ad* 2.

[52]   *Summa theol.* 1.118.2 *sed contra*, 3 *sed contra*.

empirical one for Thomas, as it sometimes is in Albert.[53] Thomas is concerned, rather, with the twin questions of generation by actualization and the unity of substantial forms. So his treatment is brought increasingly under the control of theological authorities. Over the transit, Thomas comes to correct himself at the one point where he had sided with the medical tradition, the material contribution of human seed. This correction must be placed in the larger context of the teaching about "root moisture."

Root Moisture

Thomas alludes to the doctrine of root moisture (*humidum radicale*) in seven works spread over his career. The notion is linked generally either to the discussion of digestion or to that of reproduction.[54] More specifically, the notion is regularly introduced when deciding whether anything is added to human nature by digestion or what will figure in resurrected bodies.[55] The second locus depends on the first, as Thomas makes clear by cross-reference within the *Scriptum* on the *Sentences*.

The most detailed treatment comes in the *Scriptum* as a pendant to the discussion of the transmission of original sin. A first article asks whether food is assimilated into human nature; a second, whether human seed is derived from food.[56] The first article proposes a trichotomy of received views that will become standard for Thomas. The first view holds that true human nature consists in whatever is received from the parents, which is multiplied either miraculously, or by presence of the "fifth essence," or by reversion to dimensionless prime matter. This view is taken directly from the Lombard's text. The second view holds that there is a certain quantity of matter that remains constant throughout human life, though supplementary matter is added to it. This second view Thomas attributes to Alexander of Aphrodisias on the authority of Averroes. The third position holds that only the form of humanity remains constant during life, taking on and losing matter by physiological processes. This view, which Thomas attributes to

---

[53] Compare the passages collected in James Rochester Shaw, "Scientific Empiricism in the Middle Ages: Albertus Magnus on Sexual Anatomy and Physiology," *Clio Medica* 10 (1975): 53–64, though Shaw over-states the conclusion.

[54] So the general examples in *De anima* 9 *arg.* 16, *Sent. Metaph.* 5.6.

[55] For additions to human nature, see *Scriptum Sent.* 2.30.2.1 *ad* 3, *Summa theol.* 1.119.1; for resurrected bodies, *Scriptum Sent.* 4.44.1.2, *Lect. Matt.* 10.2, *Contra gent.* 4.81 (no. 4,158). For an expert treatment of the question, see now Philip Lyndon Reynolds, *Food and the Body: Some Peculiar Questions in High Medieval Theology* (Leiden: E. J. Brill, 1999), pp. 357–395.

[56] *Scriptum Sent.* 2.30.2.1–2.

Aristotle and Averroes, he himself chooses "without prejudice to others."[57] The last phrase is worth underscoring, because it helps to mark Thomas's disengagement from technical discussions of medical matter.

The doctrine of root moisture appears at several points in the discussion of these views. It figures first in an objection, where it is linked to the doctrine of fevers. The third degree of hectic fever destroys the power of nutrition by drying out root moisture.[58] The phrase appears again in Thomas's clarification of the second position; he notes that it assumes the distinction between nutritional and root moisture.[59] Only in replying to the third objection does Thomas consider any medical detail. "According to the physicians," he says, original root moisture does not remain distinct in matter and property from the moisture that the human body generates by digesting food. On the contrary, that first moisture is the root (*radix*) of all later moisture. It is assimilated equally to old and new matter; it is never destroyed by adding matter, but only by corrupting the human form itself.[60] Thomas seems to accept the medical doctrine once properly understood, but without strong attachment to it.

The second article confirms this reading. In it, the same three positions are extended to explain the production of male seed. The first view holds that the seed is derived from the substance of the members and that its substance is wholly composed of the father's root moisture.[61] Thomas argues that this view implies various absurdities, including the progressive diminution of root moisture with each new generation. The second view argues that human seed is a mixture of radical and nutritional moisture. The third view, which Thomas shares with Aristotle, explains that the seed is derived only from the excess of unassimilated food.

Several times in these two articles Thomas refers the doctrine of root moisture to "the physicians." He is right. The doctrine belongs to Galen, though it reaches the Latin West through a series of intermediaries: Constantine's *Pantegni*, Isaac Israeli's *Book of Fevers*, and Avicenna's *Canon*.[62] The last is most important for Thomas. The particular relation of hectic fever to root moisture, for example, is treated several times in the

---

57 *Scriptum Sent.* 2.30.2.1.
58 *Scriptum Sent.* 2.30.2.1 *arg.* 3.
59 *Scriptum Sent.* 2.30.2.1.
60 *Scriptum Sent.* 2.30.2.1 *ad* 3.
61 *Scriptum Sent.* 2.30.2.2.
62 See Michael McVaugh, "The 'Humidum Radicale' in Thirteenth-Century Medicine," *Traditio* 30 (1974): 259–283, at pp. 260–268; and Joan Cadden, "Albertus Magnus' Universal Physiology: The Example of Nutrition," in *Albertus Magnus and the Sciences*, ed. Weisheipl, 321–339.

Canon.[63] Here again Thomas does not show any direct acquaintance with the text of Avicenna, but only with Avicenna as rehearsed by Albert the Great. Albert mentions root moisture in many places.[64] He describes the connection with fever in *On Death and Life.*[65] There is no need to look further for Thomas's learning. He got it from his principal teacher – and he felt no intellectual urgency to go further.

Medicine and Natural Philosophy

The conclusion about Thomas's use of medical doctrines and their sources would so far look to be entirely negative. There is no convincing evidence that Thomas knew much medicine beyond what was mediated by Albert or taught by Aristotle and his commentators. The few details of Galenic doctrine that figure in Thomas's earlier works are removed later on in favor of Aristotle. The preliminary argument for expecting detailed medical doctrine in Thomas was misleading – which ought to offer yet another caution against interpretation from supposed intellectual biography.

Various kinds of consequences follow on the negative conclusion. One of the most interesting concerns the sequence or hierarchy of learning in Thomas. When he adopts the Aristotelian or Boethian hierarchy of speculative knowledge, Thomas affirms the indispensability of natural philosophy on the way to metaphysics. He makes the argument explicitly both in commenting on the received hierarchy and in constructing his major works. But does Thomas really follow the hierarchy? How much of physics or of its component sub-sciences is required as a stepping stone to higher knowing? To judge from the case of medicine, the answer would seem to be, "Rather little."

Readers cannot skirt the question by pleading that Thomas was only a professional theologian.[66] On Thomas's account, it is especially the theologian who both depends on and presides over the hierarchy of sciences. Still there are obvious limitations in his use of sources in physics. Unless he is to be convicted of gross inconsistency, Thomas must answer that the student of metaphysics or of theology need not be formed in physics so far

---

[63] *Canon* 1.1.4.1, 1.3.3 single chapter; 4.1.3.1.

[64] *Summa de creaturis* 2.1.17.3 *ad* 13 (Borgnet *Opera omnia* 35:161); *De generatione et corruptione* 1.3.8 (4:383–384); *De aetate* 2.2 (9:318); *De morte et vita* 2.6 (9:360); *Quaestiones de animalibus* (Cologne *Opera omnia* 12:184–185).

[65] *De morte et vita* 2.6 (Borgnet *Opera omnia* 9:361).

[66] The Leonine editors suggest such an argument when they summarize the straitened sources of the commentary on *De sensu et sensato*; see Leonine *Opera omnia* 45/2:87★.

as to acquire a thorough acquaintance with medicine. Aristotle provides enough. Indeed, to judge Thomas's own corpus of commentary, even the more technical works of Aristotelian biology do not need much attention. The hierarchy requires from physics both a general knowledge of principles and detailed knowledge of topics in which speculatively significant errors have been made. In both cases, natural philosophy should lead to the higher stages of the hierarchy. Its principles and its cases must be means of intellectual ascent. Technical doctrines can be endorsed "without prejudice" to their alternatives because there is no need to settle every question before ascending to the next step of the hierarchy.

This conclusion might seem to lend aid and comfort to those who wish to subordinate Thomas's own medical or physical learning to the higher ends of whatever Thomistic metaphysics or theology they are trying to construct. In fact, it does not. Thomas's practice as a writer suggests that the theologian needs to know only enough medicine or biology to treat theologically significant topics, but he (not alas she) does need to know that much. If Thomas displays "rather little" medical erudition drawn from a handful of sources, he presses that specific erudition into important use. The medicine he knows is not a blank slate. It cannot be casually displaced by modern accounts or modern disciplinary arrangements – not, that is, if one has any respect for the coherence of Thomistic intellectual projects. There is no complete Thomistic medicine, but there are a few specific doctrines on medical points in Thomas. They cannot ground a modern medicine. On the contrary, they belong to a medicine long since rejected. Their alien specificity can serve to remind a reader that Thomas is not infinitely elastic. He writes in history.

Wishing for a Thomistic Politics

During the last century, fragments of a booklet by Thomas served as charter for a Catholic politics. The text has the form of a letter to the king of Cyprus and bears the short title *De regno, On Kingship*. The fragment is puzzling, especially because it appears sometimes to contradict what Thomas teaches in his exposition of Aristotle's *Politics* or in the *Summa of Theology*.[67] Still some

---

[67] Many of the troubles over *De regno* are ably narrated in J. M. Blythe, "The Mixed Constitution and the Distinction between Regal and Political Power in the Work of Thomas Aquinas," *Journal of the History of Ideas* 47 (1986): 547–565. Blythe himself repeats some of the misunderstandings that he describes. Since he ignores the genres of the Thomistic texts, he claims to find in Thomas "a truly original synthesis of Greek political theory and medieval thought" (p. 564).

readers did not hesitate to enlist *On Kingship* in support of one or other project of Thomistic political philosophy. The puzzles and the projects can be resolved by a careful discrimination of what is invented and what inherited in Thomas's texts. Without the claim that *On Kingship* is an original political "treatise," there would be little reason for imagining that Thomas had ever wanted to offer a self-contained discourse of political philosophy. To borrow teaching is not to fail at teaching; originality is not the principal excellence in intellectual tradition. But if Thomas's teaching on politics begins to look more like a quick collation of commonplaces than a deeply meditated inheritance, the claim for a "Thomistic" political science fails to convince. If a careful exegesis of *On Kingship* shows that it was not intended as an original treatise in Thomas's own voice, then the textual warrants for a project of Thomistic political philosophy shrink or vanish.

In what follows, I show that in *On Kingship* Thomas appropriates and transforms sets of inherited texts, their patterns and authorities. My reading begins with discrete authorities and then proceeds to the structures for organizing them. I conclude from this double reading that *On Kingship* cannot warrant the construction of a freestanding Thomistic political philosophy. The place of political thinking in Thomas is not as an autonomous philosophic treatise, but as an excursus within the moral part of theology. That conclusion might have offered Thomas's readers a radical alternative to modern notions about both political thought and governmental practice. The attempt by some of them to extract from Thomas a political philosophy according to twentieth-century disciplinary notions refuses the alternative.

Authorities in *On Kingship*

For *On Kingship*, as for most of Thomas's works, there is little internal evidence about the date or the circumstances of composition. By combining citational and doctrinal evidence, Eschmann argued that *On Kingship* had to be written between 1260 and 1267.[68] The Leonine edition corrects Eschmann on one detail, but concurs with the main conclusion: the text was written while Thomas was in Italy during the 1260s.[69]

The date is suggestive for a study of the pattern of authorities in the

---

[68] I. T. Eschmann, "Introduction," in Thomas Aquinas, *On Kingship to the King of Cyprus*, tr. G. B. Phelan (Toronto: PIMS, 1949), pp. xxvi–xxx.

[69] Leonine *Opera omnia* 42:424–425. In what follows, I will cite *De regno* according to the textual divisions and line numbers of this edition.

unfinished work. During his Italian sojourn, Thomas was experimenting with new ways of using authorities. Indeed, we possess three products of his experimentation: *Against the Gentiles*, *Against the Errors of the Greeks*, and the *Golden Chain*. The proximity of these experiments should prompt a reader to look more carefully at the selection, arrangement, and manipulation of authoritative texts in *On Kingship* – the more so, since *On Kingship* quotes the *Book of the Faith of the Trinity* that occasioned *Against the Errors of the Greeks*.[70]

On Kingship explicitly addresses a king.[71] All of the early catalogs and some of the manuscript titles assert that he was the king of Cyprus.[72] For a medieval reader, then, the text would take its place immediately in the genre of mirrors for princes. It does not stand out in that genre. *On Kingship* treats traditional topics briefly and with few embellishments. Although Thomas promises in its prologue to treat the origin of kingship and the kingly office "according to the authority of divine Scripture, the teachings of philosophers, and the examples of famous princes," he is in fact sparing of both authorities and examples. The treatise offers nothing like the profusion of classical admonitions or episodes to be found in its more famous antecedents or its contemporary rivals. Among the older works, John of Salisbury's *Policraticus* displays much more Roman erudition and explicit reflection on the relation of philosophy to statesmanship. Among Thomas's Dominican contemporaries, Vincent of Beauvais is by far the more ambitious compiler. The several sections of Vincent's *Doctrinal Mirror* on political topics bristle with classical and Scriptural quotations.[73] Vincent's incomplete *Universal Work on the Princely Office* invokes dozens more authorities than Thomas's *On Kingship*.[74] Comparison with works by Thomas's students will deliver the same lesson. Even for the abbreviated opening chapters of *On Royal and Papal Power*, John of Paris feels compelled to supplement the source apparatus of *On Kingship* when he draws from it.[75]

---

[70] *De regno* 2.3 (114–116), recalling the passage from *Contra err. Graec.* 2.35.

[71] *De regno prol.* (1–2).

[72] See the editorial remarks in Leonine *Opera omnia* 42:424.

[73] See especially *Speculum doctrinale* 5.1–7, on the character of rulers and subjects, and 7.1–33, on regimes and rulers.

[74] The completed portions of the *Opus universale* were written in two periods, 1247–1249 (Book 4) and 1261–1263 (Book 1). *De morali principis institutione* 1 is thus almost exactly contemporary with *De regno*. Since it is also a work of Dominican learning, *Opus universale* 1 offers a precise comparison with *De regno*. For the dating, see Serge Lusignan, *Préface au Speculum maius de Vincent de Beauvais: Réfraction et diffraction*, Cahiers d'Études Médiévales 5 (Montreal: Bellarmin, and Paris: Vrin, 1979), 52–53.

[75] See, for example, John of Paris, *De potestate papali et regale* 5, with two pagan authorities from *De regno* augmented by three Christian authorities.

The slightness of Thomas's address to the king is confirmed by noticing how many powerful authorities do not appear in the portions he chose to complete. The absence of the Pseudo-Plutarchian *Instruction of Trajan*, which informs so much of the *Policraticus*, may be due to Thomas's ignorance of it or to suspicions about its authenticity. Still Gregory the Great's *Pastoral Rule*, well known and indubitable, is mentioned by Thomas only once and then for its admonition that a king should cultivate calm.[76] Thomas does not so much as gesture towards *Pastoral Rule* 2, which served some of his contemporaries as a cornerstone for teaching about political virtue. Two other absences among the authorities are more startling still. *On Kingship* nowhere adverts to Bernard of Clairvaux's *On Consideration* or to Seneca. Bernard had already become indispensable to other authors on many questions of just rule. Seneca had been in the twelfth century, and was still for some of Thomas's contemporaries such as Roger Bacon, a precious guide to civic virtues and vices.[77]

The range of authorities in *On Kingship* is narrow, and the authorities that do appear most likely derive from previous treatises or anthologies. So, for example, many of Thomas's important allusions figure in Vincent of Beauvais's *Doctrinal Mirror* or *Universal Work*.[78] Others can be found in published medieval anthologies or *florilegia*.[79] Others still probably come from unstudied *florilegia* or from the informal lists of authorities circulated among mendicant scholars. Again, some passages appropriated by Thomas had long genealogies in Latin traditions. Deuteronomy 17 is the object of detailed commentary in *Policraticus* 4.4–12. John of Salisbury's exegesis passes through

---

[76] *De regno* 1.9 (72–78), where Gregory is cited and paraphrased.

[77] Bacon was so delighted by the belated discovery of the rarer works of Seneca that he copied long extracts from them into the moral section of the *Opus majus*. See *Opus majus* 7.3.5.1. *prol.* 4 and 7.4.1. *prol.* 1, in *Rogeri Baconis Moralis Philosophia*, ed. F. Delorme and E. Massa (Turin: Thesaurus Mundi, 1953), 133.1–8 and 187.1–4.

[78] I give samples of the shared texts, listing for each the authority first, next its appearance in Thomas, then its appearance(s) in Vincent. Job 34:30: *De regno* 1.6 and 1.10; Vincent, *Opus universale* 1.5, to which compare Augustine, *De civitate Dei* 5.19.48. Gregory, *Regula pastoralis* 1.9: *De regno* 1.1; Vincent, *Opus universale* 1.9. Isidore, *Etymologiae* 9.3.19: *De regno* 1.1; Vincent, *Speculum doctrinale* 7.8. Eusebius, *Chronicles* 2 and Jerome, *De viris illustribus* 9 on Archelaus: *De regno* 1.6; Vincent, *Speculum historiale* 7.103–104. Sallust, *Bellum Catilinae* 7.2: *De regno* 1.3; Vincent, *Speculum doctrinale* 5.4.

[79] Some versions of both the *Florilegium Gallicum* and the *Florilegium Angelicum*, for example, contain excerpts of classical authors used by Thomas. For brief descriptions of the contents of these versions, see Anders Gagnér, *Florilegium Gallicum: Untersuchungen und Texte zur Geschichte der mittellateinischen Florilegienliteraur* (Lund: H. Ohlssons, 1936), 121–123, with other *florilegia* at pp. 30–31; M. A. and R. H. Rouse, "The Florilegium Angelicum: Its Origin, Content, and Influence," rptd. in their *Authentic Witnesses: Approaches to Medieval Texts and Manuscripts* (Notre Dame: University of Notre Dame Press, 1991), 101–152, at p. 135.

Helinand to Vincent's *Doctrinal Mirror*.[80] Two verses of the passage are invoked in Innocent III's *Per venerabilem* in support of the jurisdictional claims of the Apostolic See and the bishops.[81] Little or none of this complexity registers when Thomas mentions the passage.[82]

Why would Thomas want to contribute so laconic a survey of such well-mapped territory? The main motive could have been circumstantial: the Dominicans may have needed a strategically impressive gift for the Cypriot king. Such a motive cannot be proved from the available evidence. It is also problematic as a guide to Thomas's text. Thomas elsewhere reinvents commissions as he fulfills them. Two of the clearest examples are found among those reference works Thomas composed just before *On Kingship*. *Against the Errors of the Greeks* was commissioned as an expert opinion on a little book of supposedly patristic citations. In fact, as we have seen, Thomas used the occasion to delineate general tasks of responsible theological exegesis in the face of historical change. More famously, as we will see below, *Against the Gentiles* is supposed to have been written in response to a request for a missionary manual by Raymond of Peñafort. If such a request was made, *Against the Gentiles* is hardly a missionary manual by Dominican standards of the thirteenth century. It seems rather a fundamental classification of the grounds for rational persuasion towards Christianity. Suppose then that Thomas was commissioned to write a learned gift for a strategically important ruler: he need not have delivered what was expected.

A reader must imagine better compositional motives for taking up well-worn topics and their familiar authorities. If we continue to follow the authorities deployed in *On Kingship* as a guide to that treatise's motivation, two further motives appear. Thomas's motive could be to supplement the largely Latin erudition of the mirrors for princes with the newly available teaching of Aristotle's *Politics*. Alternately he might want to balance political prudence drawn from pagan authors with the narratives of the Christian Scriptures, especially the Old Testament. There is some truth in each of these motives, but neither explains enough.

Aristotle does figure prominently in *On Kingship*. The critical edition counts some 18 passages recollected by Thomas from the Aristotelian corpus. If you sum implicit allusions, explicit references, and quotations, *On*

---

[80] Helinand, *Chronicon* (Migne *PL* 212:735–739); Vincent of Beauvais, *Speculum doctrinale* 7.16, as in *Speculum quadruplex* (Douai: Baltazaris Belleri, 1624; rptd. Graz: Akademische Druck- u. Verlagsanstalt, 1965), cols. 568–570.

[81] *Decretales* 13.19.4, as in *Corpus iuris canonici*, ed. E. L. Richter and E. Friedberg (2nd Leipzig edn., rptd. Graz: Akademische Druck- u. Verlagsanstalt, 1955), 2:714.

[82] *De regno* 2.4 (34–40).

Kingship recollects a total of eight passages from *Politics* 3, 5, and 7.[83] The distribution and detail of the allusions show that Thomas had a full text of Moerbeke's Latin translation of the *Politics* when he wrote *On Kingship*. It is easy to imagine, then, that *On Kingship* was written to apply Aristotle's *Politics* to the traditional topics of the mirrors for princes. If so, the application was not wholly successful. The *Politics* appears neither as a frequent nor as a central interlocutor in *On Kingship*. For example, the critical edition first cites the *Politics* in support of a maxim: "in all things that are ordered to one, something is found to rule another."[84] The principle and its consequences are commonplaces of the Latin political handbooks. Thomas uses the maxim just to introduce an analogy between a political regime and the human body. This analogy is developed at length by John of Salisbury with references to Pseudo-Plutarch. Moreover, the principle is not exactly abstruse. Thomas did not need Aristotle's *Politics* to learn it. The same can be said about three other of the apparent recollections of the *Politics*.[85] Even when the *Politics* is used as a source for more technical material, its contribution is difficult to assess. Sometimes its lessons are not peculiarly Aristotelian. Thus when Thomas describes the repressive policies of the tyrant, he paraphrases much that is in Aristotle.[86] But he could have learned the same in Augustine's *City of God* 19 or John's *Policraticus* 8.16–20. From them too he could have learned the brevity of a tyrant's rule.[87]

The only important borrowing from Aristotle's *Politics* in *On Kingship* would appear to be the classification of six types of regime, three unjust (tyranny, oligarchy, democracy) and three just (polity, aristocracy, monarchy).[88] The classification pertains directly to the matter of *On Kingship*. How surprising to notice, then, that Thomas uses the division only on the way to defining a king or monarch. He does not draw subsequent arguments for the superiority of monarchy from the *Politics*. When Thomas

---

[83] References to the *Politics* are as follows: *Politics* 3.5 anonymously in *De regno* 1.1 (100–114), 3.6 anonymously in 1.1 (121–153), 3.9 by paraphrase in 2.3 (58–73), 5.3 (or perhaps 7.6) explicitly in 2.7 (41–46), 5.11 anonymously in 1.3 (89–106), 5.12 explicitly in 1.10 (125–131), 7.2 anonymously in 2.3 (45), and 7.7 by quotation in 2.5 (57–59). As Weisheipl notes, the passages from Aristotle's books 5 and 7 were not subsequently commented on by Thomas. See Weisheipl, *Friar Thomas*, 381.

[84] *De regno* 1.1 (88–89).

[85] The remarks in *De regno* 1.1 (100–114) on just and unjust regimes are perfectly general and bear no linguistic relations to Moerbeke's Latin version of *Politics* 3.5 (1279a17–20), for which see Thomas, *Sent. Politic.* 3.5. So for the recollections in *De regno* 2.3 of *Politics* 7.2 and 3.9.

[86] *De regno* 1.3 (89–106).

[87] *De regno* 1.10 (125–128), with the explicit mention of Aristotle.

[88] *De regno* 1.1 (121–153), with apparent reference to *Politics* 3.6 (1279a22–b10).

actually quotes the *Politics*, he does so not in support of some grand principle of political philosophy, but in order to establish a relation between
climate and aptitude for civil life.[89] *On Kingship* cannot be considered a
thorough or revolutionary appropriation of the newly recovered text of
Aristotle's *Politics*. One could as easily claim that the fragmentary booklet
records Thomas's full appropriation of Augustine's *City of God*, just as other
works of the Italian years do.[90]

Consider then the second motive, which reverses the first. Perhaps
Thomas undertook to write *On Kingship* because the existing mirrors for
princes were too attached to pagan sources instead of Scriptural ones.
Vincent of Beauvais quotes Augustine's teaching that pagan and Christian
political doctrine must differ, but the stuff of his political teaching in the *Doctrinal Mirror* is almost wholly pagan.[91] The only Scriptural citations occur in
Vincent's quotations from Augustine and Helinand. By contrast, the Scriptural quotations in Thomas's *On Kingship* outnumber non-Scriptural quotations more than three to one. Thomas quotes from 30 books of the Christian
Bible, 23 of them in the Old Testament.

Here again qualification is required. If *On Kingship* is a Scriptural text, its
use of Scripture is neither uniform nor self-explanatory. The most frequently cited books are Proverbs (12 times), Ezekiel (7), Sirach (6), Isaiah
(5), and Psalms (4). In sum, Thomas quotes principally from moralizing passages of the wisdom and prophetic books, not from narratives about the
kings of Israel. He employs Scripture here, as he often uses Aristotle, more
for its moral maxims than for its concrete political illustrations or dispositions. Perhaps this should not surprise us. Thomas learned from previous
generations of homilists the usefulness of the wisdom books for the
preacher of morals. He shows his fondness for those books in many parts of
his corpus. If the prevalence of Scriptural citations in *On Kingship* is notable,
it cannot be considered distinctive of Thomas's political thought.

Again, Thomas makes no particular distinction between non-Scriptural
and Scriptural examples or cases. He freely intermingles Greek or Roman
tales with episodes from Old and New Testaments.[92] He does not segregate

---

[89]   *De regno* 2.5 (57–59).

[90]   Congar has written that the *De civitate Dei* figures in Thomas's political thought for its
eschatological teaching on the church, not for what it teaches about the earthly city. Still
Thomas does learn from Augustine about the breadth of ancient reflection on politics, as
about the details of ancient philosophic teaching. Compare Yves Congar, "Orientations de
Bonaventure et surtout de Thomas d'Aquin dans leur vision de l'Église et celle de l'état," in
1274 — Année charnière: Mutations et continuitiés (Paris: CNRS, 1974), p. 697.

[91]   Vincent, *Speculum doctrinale* 7.3 (cols. 557–558), from Augustine, *De civitate Dei* 19.

[92]   So Dionysius, Eglon, the Theban Legion, and Joash in *De regno* 1.6.

them as John of Salisbury does in some of the chronologically-arranged sections of the *Policraticus*. Nor does Thomas place any particular emphasis on what Scripture teaches in opposition to paganism, though he sometimes distinguishes the apparent sense of the Old Testament from the apostolic doctrine of the New.[93] Thomas depends more and more on his pagan sources when he treats statecraft. So, for example, *On Kingship* 2.5 and 2.6 discuss the kind of site to be chosen for a new city. The percentage of quotation is higher here than for any other chapters; the quoted authorities are Vegetius, Aristotle, and Vitruvius.

The two compositional motives derived from *On Kingship*'s actual use of authorities are suggestive, not conclusive. We need to look elsewhere in the text for its motives.

The Structure of *On Kingship*

What is original in Thomas is often an order, an arrangement, or a hierarchical subordination. He illuminates received materials by displaying their pedagogical sequence, causal connections, or cognitive dependencies. So too with *On Kingship*: its compositional motive may wait to be discovered in its structure. The discovery will not be easy. By all accounts, *On Kingship* is incomplete, and there is no agreement as to the order even of the extant parts.

Thomas indicates in a preliminary way the intended structure for *On Kingship*. It will treat, he promises, two topics: the origin of the kingdom and the things that pertain to the office of the king.[94] The second topic is explicitly recalled and specified at the beginning of Book 2: "Next there should be considered the office of the king and how the king ought to be."[95] The discussion of the royal office is begun in the following chapters, though most of the extant text is taken up with the royal founding of cities. What then of the first book? It is described retrospectively in 1.12 as "on the king . . . what he is and that it is useful for a multitude to have a king."[96] The description covers 1.16. The remaining chapters, 1.7–11, treat of the reward of the good king and the sufferings of the tyrant. If the inquiry about the king can be considered a part at least of an inquiry on the origin

---

[93] In *De regno* 1.6 (60), Thomas explicitly corrects the example of Ehud and Eglon by appeal to the "apostolic teaching" of 1 Peter 11.18–19.

[94] *De regno prol.* (4–5).

[95] *De regno* 2.1 (1–2).

[96] *De regno* 1.12 (10–11).

of kingship, the discussion of the reward of the king cannot. Something is out of order.

Eschmann, finding this and a number of other "ruptures" in the present disposition of *On Kingship*, proposed to regard the text as "a collection of fragments."[97] The conclusion is extreme. There are certainly lacunae in our text, but the largest displacement is not hard to remedy. The discussion of the rewards of a good king would fit quite nicely as the conclusion of a teaching on what kind of character the king should have. In other words, 1.7–11 can be seen as the end of the discussion promised in 2.1.[98] Hence 1.7–11 must be moved from the end of the first book at least to the end of the second. With this transposition, the order of topics in *On Kingship* becomes: the origin of the kingdom explained (at least partly) through the natural grounds for kingship; the office of the king, beginning with his role as founder; the reward for the virtuous exercise of that office. The pattern can usefully be contrasted with three others.

The first alternate pattern figures in Hugh of St Victor's *Didascalicon*; it derives from Boethius and Isidore.[99] According to Hugh, politics is the third of three practical sciences, which are variously called solitary, private, and public, or ethical, economic, and political, or private, economic, and managerial, or public, political, and civil. The third science of each triplet – the public, political, managerial, civil science – concerns itself with governors of states, and it ministers to the commonweal of cities. Hugh says nothing further about its parts.

A second pattern for comparison appears in Vincent's *Doctrinal Mirror*.[100] As Vincent says, it derives from al-Farabi, who divides political science into three parts. The first part discriminates what is true and false in the actions and customs of cities and peoples. The second part studies the kinds of royal virtue and how they can be acquired, as well as the cultivation of corresponding citizen virtues. The last part of al-Farabi's science treats of the interpretation of legislation, especially in teaching the discernment of the legislator's intent.

A third comparison can be made with the order of topics that Thomas presents, a few years after writing *On Kingship*, while expounding Aristotle's *Politics*. Thomas interprets Aristotle's table of contents as follows: the house-

---

[97] Eschmann, "Introduction," *xiv–xxi*.

[98] Indeed, there are textual signs in 1.7 and 1.9 that Thomas intended just that placement. Both chapters refer back to a conclusion about the office of a king – they refer back, that is, to matters broached in 1.12 and 2.1. See especially *De regno* 1.7 (1–4), then compare 1.9 (1–4).

[99] Hugh of St Victor, *Didascalicon* 2.19.

[100] Vincent of Beauvais, *Speculum doctrinale* 7.5 (col. 559).

hold as comprising elements of the city (Book 1), the teaching of Aristotle's predecessors about the city itself (2), the division of kinds of regimes (3), the characteristics of each kind (4–6), and the best regime (7–8).[101]

The results of the comparison are surprising. The pattern of Thomas's *On Kingship* is closest, not to Aristotle's *Politics*, but to Vincent's tripartite political knowledge. There are, of course, correspondences between the structures of the opening of Thomas's Book 2 and the middle of Aristotle's Book 7. It is even possible to suppose that Thomas would have carried on the correspondences further if he had kept writing. Still the pattern for the whole of *On Kingship* would not be an Aristotelian one. It is the pattern of a more traditional science of kingly rule. The chapters on the reward of the good king suggest that Thomas appropriated not only the order, but also the rhetorical purposes and limits of traditional mirrors for princes. So that his own teaching will be most effective rhetorically, Thomas seals it with a tale of rewards. The teaching, even if it were complete rhetorically, cannot be complete doctrinally. The prince must be taught both his own virtue and how to foster virtue in others. He must be taught a whole doctrine of morality. The rhetoric of a mirror is only hortatory because it cannot enact by its words the long and personal teaching of morals that is required for just rule. This might suggest yet another reason for Thomas's abandoning *On Kingship* in favor of more adequate structures for ethical teaching.

Political Philosophy in Aquinas

On Kingship is not an independent treatise on political philosophy composed by Thomas from his own reflections. Analyses of its choices among authorities and structures show that *On Kingship* is a clarification of inherited topics, arguments, and materials. Its novelties are novelties of balance and selection, not of doctrine or discovery. Thomas subordinates even the newest Aristotle, the Aristotle of a more complete *Politics*, to traditional themes and ends. Those themes and ends carry with them, among other implications, an important limitation of pedagogical rhetoric.

If this characterization is right, *On Kingship* cannot serve as a source for a specifically Thomist political teaching, especially according to the modern sense of that discipline. Indeed, it cannot warrant an effort to construct such a teaching as a separate "treatise." So far as *On Kingship* is Thomas's skillful

---

[101] *Sent. Politic.* 2.1, 3.1.

reworking of the inherited genres, it gives no evidence for supposing that Thomas had any alternative structure for political teaching in view. You could more plausibly call it "medieval Latin" than "Thomistic." The incompletion of *On Kingship* may be due as much to a reflective decision by Thomas as to the accident of the Cypriot king's death. Thomas may have judged his essay in writing a mirror for princes too familiar in its limitations. Or he may have failed to make the kind of pedagogical discoveries he wanted for thinking about kingship. In short, the incompletion of *On Kingship* could be a wise choice rather than a lamentable accident. Thomas may have chosen, soberly and rightly, not to undertake the writing of a Thomist political philosophy.

These speculations gather support, though certainly not the forcefulness of proof, when one places *On Kingship* back into Thomas's corpus. Within some five years of its composition, and perhaps within as few as three, Thomas would twice return to political topics. He would do so once in writing a literal exposition of Aristotle's *Politics*. He would do so again in the discussion of the judicial precepts of the Old Law at the end of *Summa of Theology* 1–2. Both works confirm what the condition and character of *On Kingship* suggest: Thomas was skeptical of independent treatments of political topics, as of pretensions to an autonomous political science.

Thomas's exposition of *Politics* is also incomplete. It breaks off at 3.6, about a third of the way through Aristotle's text. More than a few of Thomas's expositions of Aristotle break off before finishing, but the exposition of the *Politics* covers the least percentage of any Aristotelian text that Thomas took in hand.[102] The break is not due to Thomas's final silence or death. The exposition was undertaken and set aside in Paris, before Thomas's return to Italy for his final stay. Thomas apparently chose to stop with the *Politics* after proceeding into it only a short way. Why? Thomas may well have stopped expounding the *Politics* because he judged its project too alien or too incomplete for his own purposes as a Christian theologian. This hypothesis gains some credibility by looking at the most complete expression of Thomas's theological purposes. The *Summa of Theology* disposes the discussion of political matters quite differently than either the exposition of the *Politics* or *On Kingship*.

Of course, the first difficulty in approaching the *Summa* is to locate the

---

[102] The exposition of *Peri hermenias* ends in chapter 10 (19b31), about 50% of the way through the text. The exposition of *De celo* ends at 3.3 (302b9), about 75% of the way through the text. The exposition of *De generatione et corruptione* ends at 1.5 (322a3), about 37% of the way through the text. The exposition of *Meteora* ends at 2.8 (369a9), about 66% of the way through the text.

discussion of political matters in it. Virtues and vices important to political life are scattered throughout the second half of the moral part.[103] Each of these sections must always be read back into the overarching plan of *Summa* 2–2, which makes no special place for political virtues. Indeed, the only specifically political Questions in the *Summa* concern human dominion in the state of innocence (1.96) and the judicial precepts of the Old Law (1–2.104–105). Only the latter two Questions can be considered anything like an extended discussion. Together they are just a little longer than the single Question on moral precepts. They are less than half as long as the three Questions on the ceremonial precepts, which comprise the longest individual articles in the *Summa*. No structural prominence is given, then, to the judicial precepts. Thomas proceeds with them as with the others. His purpose is to show that the Old Law was not irrational. Hence Thomas begins his discussion of the Israelite regime with the issue, "Whether it is fitting that the Old Law establish ordinates for princes" (1–2.105.1).

It is important to be precise about this purpose. Thomas wants to argue that the judicial precepts are rational, not that they are universally binding. They do not bind in virtue of God's command, since the legal force of the Old Law was abrogated with the new. A king in Thomas's time could choose without sin to imitate Israel's regime; he would sin if he pretended that the regime was obligatory because legislated by God.[104] The judicial precepts do not bind by rational self-evidence. They represent a prudent disposition in view of the character and historical situation of the Jewish people.[105] They do not reveal universally applicable constitutional principles. There is for Thomas no "best regime" simply speaking. The wise legislator disposes offices and powers in view of the character and the historical maturity of the people.

Any real enactment of a regime depends on moral diagnosis and therapy. Thomas shows this by embedding his few political remarks within a treatment of law, which itself falls near the center of the extended moral teaching that is the second part of the *Summa*. No section of the *Summa* has been abused so regularly as the discussion on law, and no abuse of it is so regular as the refusal to see the discussion whole and in place. Thomas's discussion does not stop with the last article on human law (102.107.4). On

---

[103] The most obvious instances are the following: 2–2.10.8–11, on political relations to unbelief; 2–2.40, on war; 2–2.42, on sedition; 2–2.60, on judicial judgment; 2–2.104, on obedience.

[104] *Summa theol.* 1–2.104.3.

[105] *Summa theol.* 102.105.1 *ad* 2, on God's concessions to the alleged cruelty and avariciousness of the Israelites.

the contrary, he treats natural law and human law on the way to divine law and grace. A reader can understand what Thomas means by law only after she has read at least up through the Questions on the New Law – and, preferably, the Questions on grace and merit. Those Questions, in turn, take their full sense only when read as the culmination of *Summa* 1–2 and the opening for the more particular discussion of virtues and vices in 2–2.

I conclude that the treatment of political matters in the *Summa* confirms what was suggested by the analysis of *On Kingship* and the exposition of the *Politics*. Thomas thinks about political matters only within the larger project of a Christian morality. His view on politics is eminently theological, but he hardly intended to construct a separate political theology. Writing the *Summa*, he fractures the discourse of politics in order to distribute it within a meticulously elaborated moral teaching. The moral teaching is then framed by the great mysteries of Christian creed.

Disappearing Sciences

The second of two wished-for sciences has just disappeared. It vanished, as did the first, under textual scrutiny. Thomas's scattered remarks on medicine say too little to found a medieval science, but thus invite a contemporary one to be inserted. *On Kingship* is no charter for Catholic politics, and Thomas's other treatment of political questions suggest that he would be suspicious of a free-standing political theory. He conceives political discourse as the education of rulers in virtue, and he comes to understand that education to require the integral discourse of a Christian theology.

Someone might well say, even if Thomas provides no separable discourse of politics, we contemporary Thomists can construct one on Thomistic principles. The suggestion is worth rebutting – and not just by pointing out that it begs the question of what principles should be counted "Thomistic" when Thomas had little original to say about a body of knowledge. It is important to reverse the question and to ask back, what makes you so certain that Thomas wants to lend principles for new sciences that he considered either incidental to discourses he did pursue or else inseparable from them? So far as I can tell, the confidence of some Thomists before this question rests on a tacit model for Thomas's authorship. The model is that of the (modern) "system." It supposes that the thought of any "great" thinker is actually or virtually an encyclopedic whole. This is one view of human thought, but hardly the only one. It is a distinctively modern notion of intellectual coherence and completeness, much indebted to the Enlightenment (as I will show below).

Enlightened models of mind determine wishes for Thomistic sciences in other ways. They encourage the conviction that disciplines are stable across time – more, that the idea of discipline itself, of "disciplinarity," remains the same. A little intellectual history will show otherwise. The alignments and relations of disciplines change rapidly. The idea of discipline changes more slowly – but also more consequentially. Even if Thomas had wanted to offer a self-contained medical or political science, why should a reader think that it could survive retrieval into a modern disciplinary regime in which a historically specific alliance of medicine and law plots comprehensive management? Why trust that his authorship could function within our dispositions of epistemic power?

Thomas held other notions about philosophic and theological authorship. As a superb dialectician and astute interpreter of intellectual succession, he would have found it untrue and unhelpful to imagine that any human author (or authors) could settle every important question once for all, even by way of principles. As a believer in a rule of faith passed down through a sacramental community in anticipation of heavenly vision, Thomas would have judged it outrageous to claim that any philosopher or theologian could possess complete truth in this life. To assert that Thomas wanted a system in the modern sense is to confuse Thomas with his philosophical and theological opposites. Wishing for Thomistic sciences denies Thomas's practices of knowing, teaching, and writing.

Chapter Four

Thomas's Alleged Aristotelianism *or* Aristotle among the Authorities

Wishes that Thomas had provided sciences he could not, or had written texts that he decided against, are nowhere denser than around the topic of Thomas's Aristotelianism. The same topic provides the best site for thinking about his relation to philosophic authority in general. The quest to extract a discrete philosophy from Thomas, quite distinct from his theology and supposedly more credible before secular audiences, has expressed itself time and again in efforts to make Thomas a pure Aristotelian. At the same time, and curiously, if Thomas's philosophical contribution is pure Aristotelianism, then his relation to philosophical authority must seem rather abject – as abject, say, as the relation certain modern Thomists want to establish with Thomas as philosophical arbiter. How one describes Aristotle in Thomas reveals how one situates Thomas's thought with regard to philosophy, how one narrates the historical life of philosophy or justifies the usefulness of pagan science after the preaching of the Gospel. At the same time, strong claims about Thomas's relation to Aristotle often reveal most about how the claimant imagines Thomas's authority for the present. To resist allegations of Thomas's "Aristotelianism," then, is not only to resist certain misreadings of Thomas, it is also to insist on a more helpful conception of intellectual inheritance, not least in philosophy. The conception makes for a large difference. A false conception about intellectual inheritance will misdirect one's reading anywhere in Thomas, since his genres are above all genres for inheriting intellect well.

The first defect of the allegations is their employment of the term "Aristotelianism," and the simplest way to expose the defect is to recall certain features of that term's genealogy. In pointing to the form and history of this term, I might seem to be quibbling. I am actually beginning from the assumptions built into the allegations about Thomas's relation to Aristotle before moving on to examine their evidence and their consequences.

The term "Aristotelianism" and its philosophic siblings are unattested in ancient Greek or Latin.[1] Beginning with the patristic authors, there are such terms as "Arianism" or "Sabellianism," terms drawn from religious polemic.[2] The polemical extension to a term like "Platonism" or "Aristotelianism" is made in neo-Latin and the early modern vernaculars.[3] With the Enlightenment, the polemical intent is only amplified. Once the ancient schools of philosophy are pictured as no different than (heretical) sects, once philosophy and religion are both treated as manipulable dogmas, then the Enlightened *Philosophes* can begin to speak of every (other) philosophic doctrine as an "ism."[4] Such terms enter academic writing with Enlightenment historiography of philosophy, most influentially in Jakob Brucker's *Critical History of Philosophy*.[5] Brucker organizes his works, in the ancient manner, by schools (*sectae*), but one finds sprinkled throughout a whole family of "-isms": *Platonismus*, *Peripateticismus*, *Averroismus*.[6] Brucker imagines that there is an essence of pure Aristotelianism, adulterated in the Middle Ages, purified at the Renaissance.[7] Unfortunately, the modern academic study of medieval philosophy began under the sway of Brucker's imaginings. Its first proponents accommodated themselves all too easily to the jargon prevailing in

---

[1]   There is one fragment from the scarcely preserved comic poet Alexis that speaks of "Pythagorisms" (as quoted by Athenaeus in the *Deipnosophists* 4.52 [=161], ed. Georg Kaibel, 3 vols. [Leipzig: Teubner, 1887–1890], 1: 363.25–364.1). Alexis's jibe refers to the involved locutions affected by Pythagoras's followers.

[2]   These Christian coinages are to be distinguished from the earlier forms, such as *Attikismos*, *Kanôbismos*, *Kilikismos*, or *Mêdismos*, that refer to linguistic or cultural idiosyncrasies. The only ancient warrants for the sectarian use would be terms like *Korubantismos* or *Manichaismos*, though even here the emphasis is on shared cultic practice, not doctrine.

[3]   In an English rhyming dictionary of 1570, both "Platonisme" and "Platonismus" appear in a list of names of "sectes and fashions, whom we call after the masters and beginners of opinions and doctrines." See Peter Levens, *Manipulus vocabulorum* (1570; rptd. Menston, England: Scolar Press, 1969), s.v. *Isme*.

[4]   Thus, in the first volume of the great *Encyclopédie*, there is a facetious and condescending article "Aristotélisme" (1:652–673), while the 1771 edition of the *Dictionnaire de Trévoux* offers this charming definition: "Aristotelianism. The teaching of Aristotle and his partisans which was in vogue in the schools until the time of Descartes." See the *Dictionnaire universel françois et latin, vulgairement appelé Dictionnaire de Trévoux*, 8 vols. (Paris: Compagnie des librairies associés, 1771), s.v. "Aristotélisme."

[5]   Iacob Brucker, *Historia critica philosophiae a mundi incunabulis ad nostram usque aetatem deducta* (1742). I cite from the second edition in six volumes (Leipzig: Weidemann and Reich, 1766–1767).

[6]   For example, Brucker, *Historia critica*, 4:149–151 ("Platonismus"), 3:882 and 4:162 ("Averroismus"), and 4:200 ("Peripateticismus"). Brucker is addicted to technical terms of dubiously Greek origin. In one place, for example, he speaks of the "Aristotelomania of the Scholastics" (*Historia critica* 3:885–886).

[7]   For example, Brucker, *Historia critica* 4:156.

historiography.[8] Beyond historiography, the category of "Aristotelianism" was written into some programs of "neo-Thomism" or "neo-Scholasticism."[9] Thomas's philosophic standard-bearers may have thought they were in a war against the Enlightenment or Kant or Hegel, but they had already absorbed the enemy's vocabulary and table for the organization of knowledge. The philosophical charter of "neo-Thomism" counted against a philosophically adequate reading of Thomas.[10]

Whatever else might be said of it, a term like "Aristotelianism" does not accord with Thomas's view of philosophy in history. For Thomas, "philosophy (*philosophia*)" names primarily a hierarchy of bodies of knowledge that can be built up as intellectual virtues in human souls. Philosophy is, second, a pedagogy for building intellectual virtues that is enacted in teachings and textual traditions. A philosophical teaching is not principally a set of propositions shared by several minds; it is a series of like statements formulated in the several minds that teach it and learn it, that write it and read

[8] The Enlightenment usages can be heard in Victor Cousin's Introduction to the *Ouvrages inédits d'Abélard* (Paris: Imprimerie Royale, 1836), pp. lxii–lxiii, where he discusses the perpetual opposition between Plato and Aristotle. The link with Brucker is through Tennemann, who is explicitly cited at the beginning of Cousin's Introduction. A few years later, Barthélemy Hauréau ends his prize-winning memoir on medieval philosophy by meditating on "péripatétisme" and its relation to the triad "réalisme," "nominalisme," "conceptualisme." See his *De la philosophie scolastique*, 2 vols. (Paris: Pagnerre, 1850), 2:499. In the augmented version, Hauréau adds remarks on "péripatétisme" to the preliminary discussion of Scholastic philosophy; see his *Histoire de la philosophie scolastique*, 3 vols. (Paris: Durand et Pedone-Lauriel, 1872–1880), 1:33–35. The usage is ubiquitous by the century's end. See, for example, Salvatore Talamo, *L'Aristotelismo della scolastica nella storia della filosofia* (1873; 3rd exp. edn., Siena: S. Bernardino, 1881), *passim*; and Th. Heitz, *Essai historique sur les rapports entre la philosophie et la foi de Bérenger de Tours à S. Thomas d'Aquin* (Paris: Victor Lecoffre, 1909), pp. 87–91. Even very fine historians picked up the usage. So, for example, Franz Ehrle not only deploys the "-ism" terms, but justifies them by appeal to differentiating core-insights; see his "Beiträge zur Geschichte der mittelalterlichen Scholastik, 2: Der Augustinismus und der Aristotelismus in der Scholastik gegen Ende des 13. Jahrhunderts," *Archiv für Literatur- und Kirchengeschichte des Mittelalters* 5 (1889): 603–635.

[9] Obviously the question of Thomas's relation to Aristotle is much older than Enlightenment historiography. It is as old as the reading of Thomas, being debated already in the controversy of the *Correctoria* just after the condemnations of 1277. The question was also taken up repeatedly in Renaissance or early modern criticisms and defenses of Thomas. It had become fixed enough by the sixteenth century to merit a separate chapter in Melchior Cano's methodological reflections; see his *De locis theologicis* 10.5, which both pleads for balance and provides a short list of Aristotle's errors. Admitting all of this, I do still argue that the language of "Aristotelianism" and its presuppositions of method misdirected even sympathetic study of Thomas from the nineteenth century on.

[10] See Anton C. Pegis, *The Middle Ages and Philosophy: Some Reflections on the Ambivalence of Modern Scholasticism* (Chicago: H. Regnery, 1963); and, more recently, Hankey, "Pope Leo's Purposes and St Thomas' Platonism," pp. 42–44.

it.[11] So it is not helpful to ask about Thomas's relation to Aristotle in terms of "Aristotelianism," because to do so implies either the reduction of philosophy to ideology or the sublimating of philosophy into subsistent bodies of propositions. Thomas held neither view. Indeed, he rejected both. The task, then, is to find a more adequate way of conceiving philosophical inheritance, a way more consonant with Thomas's own views of his relation to Aristotle.

One alternative suggests itself immediately, even in Brucker: the ancient divisions among "schools" of philosophers. Here the school is not a retrospectively constructed grouping of thinkers who are held to have subscribed to a body of propositions. It is the historically unfolding community, constituted by genealogies of teachers and students, by shared ways of life mutated over time, by evolving languages, topics, and procedures. If there is no mention of "Aristotelianism" in the ancient texts, there are abundant mentions of the "Peripatetics," conceived as a community of inquirers into which one can choose to enter – or not.

While talk of schools is a much more adequate way of describing philosophy, it is hardly adequate to the relation between Thomas and Aristotle. For Thomas, membership in a school of philosophy does not befit Christians. One can see this both in his terminology and in the forms of some of his historical arguments. Thomas speaks about philosophy, of course, as a habit of knowing needed by an educated Christian believer. When he speaks of the schools of philosophy or of philosophers, he means the condition of wisdom under paganism. I cannot find that the epithet "philosopher" is ever deliberately applied by Thomas to a Christian.[12] Again, Thomas never includes Christians in his doxographies of philosophy, even when he does include philosophic writers beyond those mentioned

---

[11] This becomes a technical issues in the disputes over the unity of mind; see *Contra gent.* 2.75 (nos. 1,547, 1,557–1,559).

[12] One apparent counter-example seems to involve textual corruption. In the received text of *Expos. Pery*, Thomas refers to a "Joannes Grammaticus" as "philosophus" (1.6, para. 4). In *Sent. De caelo* 1.8 and throughout Averroes, "Joannes Grammaticus" is John Philoponus, a Christian. But Gauthier proposes now to read "Philonus" for "philosophus," thus removing the puzzling epithet and positing a mis-association by Thomas; see *Expos. Pery* 1.6 (Leonine *Opera omnia* 1★/1:34.85–87). In any case, Thomas would not have known of Philoponus's faith, since he learns of him only at second hand as an Aristotelian commentator. More will be said below about the sense of *philosophus*, but it should be noted at once that Thomas's refusal to use it of Christians is not uncommon in thirteenth-century authors. For a very suggestive survey of passages, especially in Albert, see M.-D. Chenu, "Les 'Philosophes' dans la philosophie chrétienne médiévale," *Revue des sciences philosophiques et théologiques* 26 (1937): 27–40.

in the ancient or patristic narratives from which he draws.[13] Thomas is quite ready to posit that the compiler of the *Book of Causes* was one of the Arab philosophers.[14] He is not willing to name a similar group of Christians. "Philosophers" properly so-called are not always ancient, but they seem always to be unbelievers. I will come back to this telling usage below, but it serves for the moment to warn against holding that Thomas might understand himself as a member of an Aristotelian school.[15]

Thomas's positive conception of his relation to Aristotle can be inferred more successfully from the kind of evidence that he had before him – and that we have before us. He had texts of Aristotle; we have texts of Aristotle and Thomas. The relations of Aristotle to Thomas, whatever else they might be, will be at least relations to and among texts. The texts of Thomas can take up towards the texts of Aristotle any of the local relations that texts have to each other – including quotation, allusion, annotation, revisionist imitation, eclectic incorporation, tense repression, direct refutation, or silent correction. Local textual relations are then qualified by the textual wholes within which Thomas places them and by the other textual relations with which he juxtaposes them. This is what Thomas understands as the proper use of a philosophical "authority" (*auctoritas*), of a textual precedent deserving attention. Almost every text in Thomas enacts an arrangement of pertinent authorities. He disposes them in constellations. His texts cannot be well understood without noticing the interpretations, valuations, and omissions in these constellations. Thomas appropriates the content of Aristotle in the first instance through Aristotelian text-pieces. Wherever it may end, any inquiry about Thomas and Aristotle must begin with them.

The simple-sounding admonition is quite difficult to obey, because it prohibits us from doing what contemporary Thomists like to do best –

---

[13] Some of the passages are open to question. In *Summa theol.* 1.44.2, for example, Thomas speaks of "some" who managed to consider "being so far as it is being." There is no textual warrant, I think, for following the Ottawa editors in construing this as a reference to "Christian teachers" (note on 1:281).

[14] *Super De causis prol.*: "so that it seems to have been excerpted from the aforementioned book of Proclus by someone among the Arab philosophers."

[15] Brian Davies writes that this kind of argument supposes an artificially strict sense of the term. By contrast, "if we take philosophers to be people prepared to try to think clearly without necessarily invoking religious doctrines as premises in their arguments, Aquinas is unquestionably a philosopher." See Davies, *Aquinas* (London and New York: Continuum, 2002), p. 12. This is puzzling. Surely any number of people whom we would not ordinarily call "philosophers" are prepared to think clearly without invoking religious doctrines as premises: consider astrophysicists, legal historians, and poets. In any case, the telling thing remains that Thomas, who knew the Greek texts from which our contemporary philosophers also claim descent, was unwilling to call himself or any other Christian a philosopher.

either constructing "systematic" paraphrases at some great height above the texts or burying themselves in philological details without worrying about sense. The admonition proposes instead a series of local readings in which the handling of textual precedents is watched closely, in context and in relation to previous handlings. It requires, in other words, a rather "Scholastic" reading of these "Scholastic" texts.

The Expositions of Aristotle

Where would be a more likely place to begin than in Thomas's sustained engagement with Aristotle as authority, that is, with his so-called Aristotelian "commentaries"? No choice of starting-place is more liable to mislead. Thomas's expositions of Aristotle are the one group of texts in which the Aristotelian authorities are systematically isolated. The expositions attend just to Aristotle and traditions of commentary on him. They can in principle offer little help in understanding how Aristotelian authorities enter into larger structures of argument. In fact, contemporary readers are better off setting the expositions aside if they want to understand Thomas's relation to Aristotle. I recognize that the suggestion will sound merely provoking without further justification.[16]

The isolation of authorities within Thomas's expositions of Aristotle can be appreciated by looking to the kinds of works they are. Their kind can be inferred, in turn, from several types of evidence. There is the evidence of circumstance. With each new critical edition, there is more evidence that Thomas subordinated the expositions to more important works. All of the expositions, except perhaps that on the *Metaphysics*, followed the exposition of *On the Soul*, which was written between December 1267 and September 1268.[17] In other words, at least 11 of the 12 expositions were undertaken

---

[16] The suggestion has provoked my readers in the past. Some of them have been kind enough to reply in detail. See especially Christopher Kaczor, "Thomas Aquinas's Commentary on the *Ethics*: Merely an Interpretation of Aristotle?," *American Catholic Philosophical Quarterly* 78 (2004): 353–378.

[17] On *Sent. De anima*, see the prefatory remarks by Gauthier in Leonine *Opera omnia*, 45/1: 283*–288*. According to the Leonine editors, other expositions would be dated as follows: *Sent. De sensu*, 1268–1269 at Paris (45/2:128*); *Expos. Pery*, in the first half of 1271 at Paris (1*/1:85*–87*); *Sent. Ethic.*, 1271–1272 at Paris (48:B55); *Sent. Politic.*, during the second Parisian regency (48:A8); *Expos. Post.*, 1271–1272 at Paris and Naples (1*/2:73*–76*). Torrell would insert *Sent. Phys.* and the exposition of the *Meteors* early in the list, at Paris before 1270. *Sent. Metaph.* poses other problems, but it was completed before *Sent. De caelo*, that is, before 1272–1273. *Sent. De gener.* is probably the last of the series to be undertaken, in Naples at the end of Thomas's writing. See Torrell, *Initiation*, pp. 498–503.

during the last six years of Thomas's active authorship, the time in which he composed the *Summa*. Five of the expositions were left unfinished by Thomas.[18] It seems unlikely that he was working on the five texts simultaneously at the moment he stopped writing, so I conclude that Thomas had already set aside some of them with no intention of finishing any time soon.[19] The dates of the expositions and, in many cases, their unfinished state suggest that Thomas considered them less important than the *Summa* and perhaps preparatory to it.

One may dismiss circumstantial arguments about the relative importance of the expositions, but the evidence of the corpus remains. Taken together, Thomas's expositions of Aristotle make up something just over a tenth of his finished writings.[20] The whole lot of them is significantly shorter than either the *Scriptum* on Peter Lombard's *Sentences* or what was finished of the *Summa*. Thomas composed twice as much by way of commenting on Scripture and did so over a much longer period of time. By contrast, Albert the Great's enormous project of explaining Aristotle to Latin readers spanned two decades – that is, almost four times as long as Thomas's expository writing, while Albert's finished commentaries and paraphrases fill up one-third of his corpus – that is, about three times the percentage in Thomas.[21] The exposition of Aristotle was a large and long portion of Albert's authorship, but not of Thomas's. Nor can the mere fact that Thomas decided to expound Aristotle count as an argument for some unique doctrinal affinity. If writing commentaries on Aristotle makes one an Aristotelian, then the great neo-Platonists Porphyry, Ammonius, and Simplicius are Aristotelians of the first rank – not to speak of Ezra Pound.

The character of Thomas's expositions can also be inferred from their style. Thomas did not learn this style from Albert, who wrote either commentaries with questions or else paraphrases, never merely expositions.

---

[18] I follow the traditional enumeration of commentaries. If the exposition of *On Memory and Reminiscence* is included in *Sent. De sensu* (see, for example, Leonine 45/2:127★), then the total of expositions drops to 11, or which four are incomplete.

[19] Indeed, Thomas's preface to the exposition of the *Peri hermenias* refers to the body of the text in the past tense ("expositionem adhibere curaui"). This suggests, as Weisheipl concludes, that the work was sent along to Louvain incomplete. See Weisheipl, *Friar Thomas*, p. 374, no. 36; compare Gauthier's assessment in Leonine *Opera omnia*, 1★/1:87★. If Thomas were willing to dedicate the text in such condition, he did not count himself in the middle of writing it. He must have decided that the text would never be finished – or that he had finished with it.

[20] I use the word counts of the *Index Thomisticus*. The Aristotle commentaries, including that on the first book of *De anima*, come to 1,165,000 words or just over 13% of the corpus.

[21] The calculation for Albert is very inexact, being based on the relative number of pages in Borgnet's edition of the *Opera omnia*.

Albert does provide careful divisions of the Aristotelian texts and does raise exegetical difficulties about them, but he is always on the way to or from ampler inquiries. Thomas's models in the genre come immediately from styles of reading in university faculties of the Arts, more remotely from the "great commentaries" of Averroes. Averroes's stylistic influence was particularly strong on literal expositions. His *magna commentaria*,[22] as they were known to the Latins, fix many standards for close reading.[23] Among these are the regular alternation of short quotation and exposition, each part introduced by a stereotyped formula, all parts held together by exact textual divisions meant to disclose logical order. More broadly, the Latins learned from the "great commentaries" that one could write an exposition of Aristotle within the horizon of the Aristotelian tradition, that is, by invoking materials consonant with a pagan philosophy and engaging commentators who stand within its tradition. If Averroes's epitomes contain allusions to the ordinary experience of Islamic readers, his "great commentaries" exclude such mentions and confine themselves almost entirely to Aristotle's texts and their posterity.[24] So Averroes speaks, through the Latin of the proemium to the *Physics*, of "glossing" the text precisely because no one has yet composed "a continuous gloss on the single words of Aristotle."[25]

Thomas's expositions share many of these features, whatever their differences and however much they depend on other models from the Arts

---

[22] In asserting a remote dependence on Averroes, I do not mean to make his *magna commentaria* the only or the closest forerunners to Thomas. This was Ernest Renan's claim in *Averroes et l'averroïsme: Essai historique* (1852; 4th rev. edn., Paris: Calmann-Levy, 1925), p. 237, repeated by Léon Gauthier, *Ibn Rochd (Averroes)* (Paris: Presses Universitaires de France, 1948), p. 16. The claim has been rejected by René-Antoine Gauthier in *L'Éthique à Nicomaque*, ed. and tr. Jean-Yves Jolif, 2 vols. in 3 (Louvain: Publications universitaires; Paris: Béatrice-Nauwelaerts, 1958), 1:82★–83★, n. 247, and Clemens Vansteenkiste, "San Tommaso d'Aquino ed Averroes," in *Scritti in onore di Giuseppe Furlani = Rivista degli studi orientali* 32 (Rome: G. Bardi, 1957), 585–623, at p. 622. If it is extravagant to claim that Thomas could have learned the procedure only from Averroes, it is unconvincing to assert that Averroes's procedure had no influence on Thomas, especially since the available Arts commentaries are less clear about procedure than Averroes.

[23] There was some confusion in the Latin texts over the names of the levels of Averroes's commentaries. So, for example, there is a confusion between *paraphrasis* and *commentarium medium*. See George Lacombe's remarks in *Aristoteles Latinus*, 1: *Codices* (Rome: La Libreria dello Stato, 1939), p. 100. There seems to have been less confusion over the highest level, that of the "great commentaries."

[24] Abdurrahman Badawi, "Averroes face au texte qu'il commente," in *Multiple Averroes: Actes du colloque international organisé à l'occasion du 850e anniversaire de la naissance d'Averroés (Paris, 2–3 decembre 1976)*, ed. Jean Jolivet (Paris: Les Belles Lettres, 1978), 59–89, at p. 60.

[25] In the version of the "antiqua translatio" printed in *Aristotelis de physico auditu libri octo cum Averrois Cordubensis variis in eosdem commentaris* (Venice: Iunctas, 1572), fols. 1r–BC.

faculty. He takes up the program of "glossing" the "single words of Aristotle" at a time when many other masters were turning to more intrusive commentaries, with sprawling sets of tangential questions.[26] Thomas's expositions are old fashioned so far as they respect the Aristotelian text's concerns and borders.[27] Thomas insists that his readers build up a sense for the habits of delimitation in Aristotle's authorship.[28] He requires equally that they do not distort the natural meaning of the text, and so he provides any number of detailed contextual arguments at points of difficulty.[29] Where Thomas's procedure differs from that of Averroes, it does so under the influence of alternate models of literal commentary. So, for example, the exposition of *De caelo* has an unusual pattern of objections and replies under each of the lemmata. The reason for this is Thomas's borrowing from Simplicius.[30] In the exposition of the *Ethics*, again, there is an abundance of philological and

[26]   The lesson about the literal motive of Thomas's expositions is an old one – so old that it ought by now to have been received universally. See, among others, Charles Jourdain, *La Philosophie de saint Thomas d'Aquin* (Paris: Hachette, 1858), pp. 81–96; Matthias Schneid, *Aristoteles in der Scholastik: Ein Beitrag zur Geschichte der Philosophie im Mittelalter* (Eichstätt: Krüll'sche Buchhandlung, 1875), pp. 72–73; Mandonnet, *Siger de Brabant*, 1:42; Martin Grabmann, "Les Commentaires de saint Thomas d'Aquin sur les ouvrages d'Aristote," *Annales de l'Institut Supérieur de Philosophie* 3 (1914):231–281, at pp. 248–254; Réginald Garrigou-Lagrange, "Saint Thomas, commentateur d'Aristote" [1946], in *Dictionnaire de théologie catholique* (Paris: Librairie Letouzey et Ané, 1908–1951), 15:641–651, cols. 642 and 650; M.-D. Chenu, *Introduction à l'étude de saint Thomas d'Aquin* (Montreal: L'Institut d'Études Médiévales; Paris: J. Vrin, 1950), pp. 177–178, 188–190; Daniel A. Callus, "Les Sources de saint Thomas: État de la question," in *Aristote et saint Thomas d'Aquin*, Chaire Cardinal Mercier 1955 (Louvain: Publications universitaires; Paris: Béatrice-Nauwelaerts, 1957), 93–174, at pp. 98–103, after Grabmann; Joseph Owens, "Aquinas as Aristotelian Commentator," in *St Thomas Aquinas, 1274–1974*, 1:213–238, at pp. 216, 228, 234; F. Edward Cranz, "The Publishing History of the Aristotle Commentaries of Thomas Aquinas," *Traditio* 34 (1978): 157–192, at pp. 157–158. To say that Thomas intended mainly to discover Aristotle's sense is not to say that he succeeded everywhere in excluding his own philosophical reoccupations. See, for example, Georges Ducoin, "Saint Thomas commentateur d'Aristote: Étude sur le commentaire thomiste du livre Λ des Métaphysiques d'Aristote," *Archives de Philosophie* (new ser.) vol. 20 (1957): 78–117, 240–271, and 392–445; Simon Decloux, *Temps, Dieu, liberté dans les "Commentaires aristotéliciens" de saint Thomas d'Aquin: Essaie sur la pensée grecque et la pensée chrétienne* (Paris: Desclée de Brouwer, 1967), and Owens, "Aquinas as Aristotelian Commentator."

[27]   Respect for Aristotle's boundaries can take many forms. Sometimes Thomas insists on the scope of an Aristotelian inquiry, as in holding that the *Ethics* is concerned only with the natural happiness of the present life. Sometimes Thomas wants to keep within the measure of an Aristotelian discussion, rejecting digressions.

[28]   *Sent. De caelo* proem., 1.2, 1.7. Thomas is also much concerned to understand the kinds of writing in ancient philosophy; see, for example, *Sent. De caelo* 1.21 and *Sent. Phys.* 1.1.

[29]   *Sent. De caelo* 1.21, *Expos. Pery* 2.2.

[30]   D. J. Allan, "Medieval Versions of Aristotle, *De caelo*, and of the Commentary of Simplicius," *Mediaeval and Renaissance Studies* [London] 2 (1950): 82–120, at pp. 84–85.

historical material. The source is a body of Greek commentary and annotation made available by Robert Grosseteste.[31]

If Thomas had wanted to lay out an Aristotelian philosophy, or to declare one of his own, he could have quoted a slice of Aristotelian text, tersely divided it or glossed it, and then headed off to determine issues suggested by it, using a full range of authorities and elaborating or refuting positions far beyond those in the letter. Thomas did not do that in his expositions. He chose instead to compose clarifying explications of the Aristotelian text in which he restrained his full teacher's voice. The dedicatory epistle to the exposition of the *Peri hermeneias* is in most respects a slim selection of commonplaces, but Thomas does twice refer to the work that follows as an "exposition."[32] His usage is exact. He has written an *expositio* – not a "paraphrase" or "abbreviation" or "summa," not a commentary with introjected disputations, not a table or a concordance. Thomas's exposition is a close reading of the Aristotelian text – nothing less, nothing more – and thus much like Averroes's continuous glosses, so far as any works of such diverse genius can be alike.[33]

Literal exposition is always liable to be misunderstood in the way that diffident teaching is. Which is the voice of the original, which of the expositor? The uncertainty is increased when Thomas changes expository position. It is obvious that in any given section or *lectio* Thomas will have some paragraphs of division, some of exposition, and some of amplification. I mean something more. It is not easy, for example, to tell what audience Thomas means to address. Perhaps there are different audiences for different expositions or multiple audiences for each one of them. He seems to assume different levels of learning and different capacities for attending to technical argument.[34] Again, the self-identification of the voice, of Thomas's expository "we,"

---

[31] See H. Paul F. Mercken's introductory remarks in *The Greek Commentaries on the Nicomachaen Ethics of Aristotle in the Latin Translation of Robert Grosseteste* . . . (Leiden: E. J. Brill, 1973), 1:30*–60*.

[32] *Expos. Pery epist. dedic.*, "*expositionem* adhibere curaui," "*expositionis* munus exiguum." Compare *Sent. De caelo proem.*, "apud antiquos expositores Aristotelis," and 1.29, "Sed quantum pertinet ad expositionem huius libri . . ."

[33] It is important to remember that Aristotle's meaning, his *intentio*, had been and would remain heatedly controversial on important points. See, for example, Luca Bianchi, *L'errore di Aristotele: La polemica contro l'eternità del mondo nel XIII secolo* (Florence: La Nuova Italia, 1984), pp. 19–39.

[34] One way of tracing the different expectations is to notice the kinds of identifications that Thomas provides for his readers. At times, he seems to explain things repeatedly that require little explanation – for example, that the *Iliad* is a book about Troy: see *Sent. Metaph.* 7.3, 7.4, and 8.5. What kind of reader would require such repeated glosses? Is it the same reader who would be able to follow the more technical arguments of the Aristotelian corpus?

sometimes refers differently even within a single section. It is variously "we interlocutors of Aristotle," "we remote descendants of Aristotle," "we embodied intellects experiencing the world," and (most rarely) "we Christian believers."[35] Such rhetorical complexities require a scrupulous discernment that is not possible when reading the expositions in bits. It is a vice to consult Thomas's works as if they were statistical tables, plucking out one discrete datum after another. The accomplishment of Thomas's expositions of Aristotle is that they read Aristotle continuously. Shifts of audience or of voice are notable in view both of that continuity and of Thomas's presumption that Aristotle wrote unified works.[36]

Continuity and unity are reinforced by a set of exclusions in the expositions. Thomas excludes for the most part Christian references, even such as might arguably be just philosophical or historical.[37] He then puts aside textual authorities and disputed topics outside the Aristotelian texts and traditions of commentary on them. Here we can repeat the contrast with Albert. Albert's paraphrases of Aristotle deploy the full range of available authorities, and they cover the entire corpus of Aristotelian science, even where no Aristotelian treatise is extant. So, for example, Albert inserts in its proper place a treatise *On the Intellect and the Intelligible*, even though the Aristotelian original is lacking, and he composes his insertion from materials much later than Aristotle and quite different from

[35] For examples of "we" taken directly from Aristotle, see *Sent. Politic.* 2.6, "As we now see happen in cities," but the "now" and the observation are in the original; 3.2, "as we see in those who sing songs in choruses," with reference to ancient comedies. For the "we" in agreement with Aristotle's (false) starting points, see *Sent. Metaph.* 12.7: "since we suppose that motion is eternal." For the "we" of Christian believers, see *Sent. Politic.* 2.12, "So that we do not believe that man can be made naturally from earth, but only by divine power," and "just as we assert that Noah was saved in the ark during the time of the general downpour"; compare *Sent. De caelo* 1.29.

[36] Thomas is quite insistent that the Aristotelian texts as he receives them are well-crafted wholes. See, for example, *Sent. Phys.* 8.1.

[37] There are some Christian references, of course. Scriptural citations, especially to the Wisdom books, are sometimes adduced in illustration of a point: 1 Corinthians 14:11 and Ecclesiastes 10:7 cited at *Sent. Politic.* 1.1a; Proverbs 11:29 cited at 1.3; Proverbs 12:24 and 1 Kings 2:30 cited at 1.4; Ecclesiastes 10:19 cited at 1.8; and Sirach [Ecclesiasticus] 30:11 and 1 Corinthians 14: 34–35 cited at 1.10. Christian authors do occasionally appear, though they are not theological authorities so much as speculative thinkers or historiographers: Augustine at *Sent. De anima* 1.3; Boethius at *Sent. De anima* 1.7 and 2.17 and at *Sent. De caelo* 2.1; Pseudo-Dionysius at *Sent. Ethic.* 2.7; Isidore at 5.12 (47/2: 304.16–17); and "Bede" at *Sent. Politic.* 1.1a, although the citation seems spurious. Figures of Scriptural or ecclesiastical history are introduced to explain or replace pagan examples: St Lawrence at *Sent. Ethic.* 3.2; the Israelite judges at *Sent. Metaph.* 1.4; Christmas and Epiphany at 2.3; John the Baptist and Anthony the Great at *Sent. Politic.* 1.1b. Other references seem casual, as if by spontaneous association; see, for example, the mention of angels at *Sent. Politic.* 1.3 and of duels at 2.12.

him.[38] To find that kind of comprehensive consideration in Thomas, a reader must go to *Against the Gentiles*, the disputed questions, or the *Summa*. When he exposits Aristotle, Thomas attends only to a given text and controversies he knows to have arisen among its readers.[39] He trims even these controversies with an eye to pedagogy, asking that his readers notice only the most important ones.[40] Thus no section of Thomas's expositions, including the amplifying remarks introduced by such phrases as "Note that . . ." or "Know that . . ." can be taken as the full explanation that Thomas would offer in his own voice.[41]

Sometimes in the expositions Thomas will demur in his own voice.[42] It is well known that he dissents from Aristotle's assumption of the eternity of the world.[43] Just as regularly, he corrects mentions of gods or divinities, as he

---

[38] Albert the Great *De intellectu et intelligibili* 1.1.1 (Borgnet *Opera omnia* 9:478a). The authorities explicitly invoked in the text include Alfarabi, Algazel, Apuleius, Pseudo-Dionysius, Hermes, Isaac Israeli, John Damascene, and Ptolemy. More importantly, the topics in large sections derive from Avicenna and Averroes on prophecy.

[39] As with the mentions of Christian material, Thomas will sometimes adduce a classical Latin author in the Arts. So, for example, Cicero and Virgil at *Sent. De sensu* 2.1; Cicero at 2.2 and 2.6; Vegetius at *Sent. Ethic.* 3.16; Cicero on Caesar at 4.10; and Cicero at 5.12; Palladius at *Sent. Politic.* 1.9, but the source is Albert's commentary; and Vegetius at 2.13. Thomas will also supply Latin examples. Thus, he uses Cicero in an example of nominal definition in *Sent. Metaph.* 7.15 and adds the Romans to the Heraclids as an example of a race at 10.10.

[40] In this respect, the Aristotelian commentaries also share in the pedagogical project of the *Summa*, namely, as caring for what beginners must learn from among the disordered masses of traditions.

[41] I say this even of such paragraphs as those in *Sent. Metaph.* 11.2 where Thomas announces several times "the truth is." So I must disagree with those who hold that such locutions show that Thomas meant in the Aristotle commentaries to demonstrate a number of final conclusions. See, recently and among many others, the methodological assumptions in Guy-François Delaporte, *Lecture du commentaire de Thomas d'Aquin sur le* Traité de l'âme *d'Aristote: L'âme, souffle de vie* (Paris and Montreal: L'Harmattan, 1999), p. 9.

[42] I distinguish demurrals both from technical corrections and from friendly additions. Thomas does note possible corrections of Aristotle in technical matters, as in the postulation of epicycles and the discovery of the precession of the equinoxes. See, for example, *Sent. De caelo* 1.1; *Sent. Metaph.* 12.9, 12.10. Thomas also makes a number of verbal additions so that Aristotle's conclusions become friendlier to Christian readers. See, for example, *Sent. De caelo* 2.4 on divine will over celestial motion; *Sent. Metaph.* 9.9 on divine will; 10.2 on divine knowledge as causative; 10.12 on miraculous preservation of corruptible substances; 12.7 on divine will.

[43] *Sent. De caelo* 1.6, 1.26, 1.29, 2.1; *Sent. Metaph.* 9.9, 12.5. Thomas held different views on the exact intention behind Aristotle's demonstrations of eternity and some traces of ambivalence can be detected in the passages cited. For the larger changes in Thomas's views, see John F. Wippel, "Did Thomas Aquinas Defend the Possibility of an Eternally Created World? (The *De aeternitate mundi* Revisited)," *Journal of History of Philosophy* 19 (1981): 21–37; Weisheipl, "The Date and Context of Aquinas' *De aeternitate mundi*," in *Graceful Reason: Essays in Ancient and Medieval Philosophy Presented to Joseph Owens, CSSR*, ed. Lloyd P. Gerson (Toronto: PIMS, 1983), 239–271.

does references to an animated celestial sphere.[44] Other objections are more particular. When Aristotle seems to deny providence, Thomas rehabilitates it and points to the limitation of Aristotle's purview.[45] Aristotle mentions the endowing of civic cult as an instance of magnificence. Thomas says: "The Philosopher speaks here according to the custom of the Gentiles, which has been abrogated by truth made manifest. So that if someone were now to spend something on the cult of demons, it would not be magnificent, but sacrilegious."[46]

Still there are surprising silences by which Thomas appears to acquiesce in an objectionable teaching. When reviewing Cretan legislation that encouraged same-sex acts as a means of population control, Thomas cannot stop himself from inserting the adjective "wicked" (*turpis*) in naming the acts, but he then agrees to Aristotle's postponement of the question, whether the legislative provision for them was well or ill made.[47] Rehearsing Aristotle's arguments against an actual infinite, he does not mention the important sense of intensive infinity that he himself will apply to God.[48] Contrasting the Platonists with Aristotle on the corruptibility of forms, Thomas elides one respect in which the Platonists were right – namely, that there are incorruptible patterns for creatures in the divine Ideas.[49] There are silences even in small things. For example, Thomas explains what the Areopagus was, but does not remind his Christian readers that they have heard of it in the Acts of the Apostles.[50] Again, he notes that some pagans attributed the number three to God as a perfection, but makes no allusion to the Trinity.[51]

What did Thomas hope to achieve by writing literal expositions of central works in the Aristotelian corpus? The question may mislead so far as

---

[44] For general corrections or diagnoses of pagan views: *Sent. De anima* 1.13, 3.2; *Sent. De caelo* 2.1; *Sent. Ethic.* 1.14, 3.13, 5.12, 10.12; *Sent. Metaph.* 12.4, 12.8. For deprecations of Olympian deities: Jove, Juno, and Ixion at *Sent. De caelo* 2.1; Vulcan and Jove at *Sent. Politic.* 1.2, 1.10 respectively; and Mars and Venus at 2.13. At *Sent. De caelo* 2.1, however, Thomas allows the myth of Atlas holding up the world to be allegorized to the point that it contains "something divine." On the Gentiles' "error" of calling great rulers or heroes "gods," see *Sent. Ethic.* 7.1, *Sent. Politic.* 1.4. On Aristotle's sometimes speaking "in the manner of the Platonists" or "of the gentiles," see *Sent. De caelo* 2.4, *Sent. Ethic.* 8.7, *Sent. Politic.* 1.1a.

[45] *Sent. Metaph.* 6.3. I take the backwards reference at 11.8 as a way of recalling these demurrals without repeating them.

[46] *Sent. Ethic.* 4.7. For other mentions of errors about cult, see *Sent. Ethic.* 5.12 and *Sent. Politic.* 2.10.

[47] *Sent. Politic.* 2.15.

[48] *Sent. Metaph.* 11.10; compare the deliberate expansion of the term in *Contra gent.* 1.43 and even its "negative" use in *Sent. Metaph.* 12.8.

[49] *Sent. Metaph.* 8.3, to which compare *Contra gent.* 1.54, *Summa theol.* 1.15.1, especially *ad* 1.

[50] *Sent. Politic.* 2.17.

[51] *Sent. De caelo* 1.2.

it assumes that there is one intention. Thomas's expositions on Aristotle accomplish different tasks depending both on the subject-matter of the underlying text and the received interpretations of it. The purview, procedure, and detail of the expositions vary with the sources at Thomas's disposal, the history of the work's reception, and the theological importance of its doctrines. Any generalizing remarks about the intention of all of the expositions risk false abstraction. Still, if the question about intention is posed to the expositions in general, three general answers are ready at hand. The first, which dates back in modern interpretation at least to Mandonnet, is that Thomas meant to combat false readings of Aristotle arising in university circles from the baneful influence of the "Latin Averroists" or heterodox Aristotelians.[52] This view of intention has the merit of explaining why most of the expositions were written during Thomas's second regency at Paris and why many of them engage Averroistic readings. Unfortunately, the view contradicts at least one chronological fact. The exposition of *On the Soul* was begun and finished before Thomas returned to Paris, that is, before he would have been thrown back into the intellectual turbulence of the controversies. Thomas's return to Paris may have had as much to do with the defense of his own teaching as with troubles over Aristotle.[53] If these circumstantial claims should be discredited, engagement with heterodox "Aristotelianism" would not be a sufficient explanation for the writing of the Aristotle expositions as we have them.

Thomas had begun refuting incorrect readings of Aristotle long before he took up continuous exposition. His habit in controversy is to provide both exegetical and dialectical arguments. Thus, in the latter part of *Against the Gentiles* 2, he devotes six dense chapters to refuting Averroistic and Avicennistic errors about possible and agent intellects.[54] Exegetical arguments are mixed with dialectical ones throughout, and the last chapter is a line-by-line reading of Aristotle's *On the Soul* 3.5.[55] The same mixture of dialectic and

---

[52]   Pierre Mandonnet, *Siger de Brabant et l'Averroisme latin au XIIIme siècle* (rev. ed., Louvain: Institut supérieur, 1911), 1:39; compare Weisheipl, *Friar Thomas*, pp. 280–285. The view that the commentaries of Albert and Thomas were motivated or commanded by the desire to combat Averroism can be found in I. F. Bernardus de Rubeis, *Dissertationes criticae et apologeticae* (Venice, 1750), diss. 30, cap. 7, as in Leonine *Opera omnia* 1:cccxxiv–cccxxv.

[53]   Simon Tugwell, *Albert and Thomas: Selected Writings* (New York: Paulist Press, 1988), pp. 226–227.

[54]   *Contra gent.* 2.73–78.

[55]   *Contra gent.* 2.78. The procedure is different from that of the Aristotle commentaries. Here, Thomas quotes the whole Aristotelian lemmatum, interpolating glosses or explanations (nos. 1,586, 1,592a, 1,593a, and 1,594a). He then provides a series of arguments drawn from the text to establish its meaning, often collating it with other passages or refuting probable misreadings (nos. 1,587–1,591, 1,592b–d, 1,593b–e, and 1,594b).

exegesis is found in *On the Unity of the Intellect* and *On the Eternity of the World*, both of them works written during Thomas's second period of Parisian teaching with the explicit intention of correcting misreadings of Aristotle.[56] Thomas would have engaged prevalent misreadings, then, more characteristically and perhaps more effectively by concentrating on controverted passages. Indeed, he cites his own free-standing arguments and exegeses about them at particularly controversial points in the Aristotelian expositions.[57] There was no call to write a set of literal commentaries on whole Aristotelian books in order to combat misreading.

A second account, proposed by Gauthier in view of the chronology, holds that Thomas wrote the Aristotle commentaries "in the margin" of the *Summa*, as preparation or supplement for it.[58] This view has the merit of explaining the chronological coincidence of the undertaking of the *Summa* and of the expositions: both were begun in Rome during the two academic years from 1266 to 1268. There are also close parallels between some parts of the Aristotle commentaries and parts of the *Summa*. The exposition of *On the Soul* clearly treats questions central to the account of human nature in *Summa* 1, for example, while the exposition of the *Ethics* speaks to the account of the elements of moral life in *Summa* 1–2. It is easy to imagine, then, that Thomas wrote the commentaries in order to explore issues important for the *Summa* or even to master Aristotelian texts useful for its grand construction. Gauthier's account might further explain why certain expositions were broken off in the middle – that is, at a point beyond which the Aristotelian text might no longer be so useful.

What remains unexplained on Gauthier's account is, again, the detail and extent of the expositions. It is difficult to imagine that Thomas would have had to go through the meticulous work of complete division and explication in order to garner what he needed for the *Summa*. Especially during years when he was immensely preoccupied by other composition – the *Summa* itself, disputed questions, polemical tracts, occasional works – it seems unlikely that he would have wasted time polishing preparatory notes.

---

[56] See Weisheipl, *Friar Thomas*, p. 385, nos. 55–56, with the corrections on pp. 483–484.

[57] For example, *Sent.De Anima* 3.1. Compare the self-reference on the question of survival of death, *Sent. Ethic.* 1.17.

[58] See Gauthier's remarks in the Leonine *Opera omnia*, 45:288★–289★. Gauthier also holds that the project of the expositions arose from Thomas's understanding of the obligations of wisdom (289★–294★). One objection against subordinating the writing of the expositions entirely to the writing of the *Summa* is that Thomas continued expounding certain Aristotelian texts long after he had passed the point of the *Summa* where they would have been immediately useful. Thus *Sent. De caelo* was written after 1271, by which time Thomas was presumably well out of *Summa theol.* 1.

There would be no point to Thomas's detailed pedagogy unless pedagogy were part of his point. I conclude that the expositions may indeed have been undertaken in conjunction with the project of the *Summa*, but they cannot be viewed solely as instrumental to the *Summa*.

There remains a third account, on which the writing of the expositions on Aristotle was somehow required by Thomas's understanding of his office as teacher of wisdom.[59] The account is promising if it can be specified. How might the expositions fit within the larger pedagogical project given expression by the *Summa*? As preliminary exercises in the reading of authoritative texts that are propaedeutic to theology. The expositions are works both of Dominican formation and of university instruction, just as the *Summa* is a work of mixed genre, indebted at least as much to the Dominican tradition of casuistry as to the university traditions of dogmatic theology. While the *Summa* undertakes an integral pedagogy suitable for beginners in "Christian religion," which is as much the religious life as the study of theology, the expositions offer exemplary studies of magisterial texts from outside Christian wisdom. It is a sign of the hierarchical supremacy of theology that these texts have become more and more important in the preparation for theology, within both Dominican houses of study and the universities.

Choosing to write expositions of Aristotle, Thomas chose not to write a companion *Summa of Philosophy*. Nor was he merely making public more or less polished versions of his classroom teaching. The manuscript evidence shows, for some cases at least, that he dictated the expositions to his team of assistants in his ordinary manner of composition.[60] Thomas was offering, instead and in middle place, carefully constructed readings of texts that were important as preparation for theology. This does not mean that the Aristotelian texts are identical with philosophy. On the contrary, it is imperative to construe Thomas's stance in the expositions cautiously, especially at such points where he might seem to distance himself from Aristotelian doctrine. Otherwise one risks confusing both the role of authority in philosophy and the necessarily limited place of any philosophical authority in Christian study.

From these various features of Thomas's expositions of Aristotle – their circumstances, voices, exclusions, silences – I draw the conclusion that I proposed before so outrageously. If we intend to ask about Thomas's inheritance of Aristotle, we should not start with the evidence of the expositions. The expositions will show what Thomas takes Aristotle to be saying. They will

[59] Compare Gauthier in the Leonine *Opera omnia*, 45:290★–294★.
[60] J. Cos, "Evidences of St Thomas' Dictating Activity in the Naples Manuscript of His *Scriptum in Metaphysicam* (Naples, BN VIII.F.16)," *Scriptorium* 38 (1984):231–253.

not tell you how he judges Aristotle in relation to alternate authorities, philosophical or theological. The actual inheritance of Aristotle must be studied topic by topic, passage by passage, in works written for Thomas's own voice.

I can illustrate that kind of reading here by looking at how Thomas rereads a single Aristotelian work, the *Nicomachean Ethics*, in two different projects. Thomas belongs to the first generation of readers who were able to make use of the exegetical aids provided alongside Robert Grosseteste's Latin version of the *Nicomachean Ethics*, which became available in 1246–1247.[61] The "Lincoln translation" (so called after Grosseteste's diocese) was a revision of an earlier version, now largely lost, done with the aid of at least two Greek texts.[62] Its supplements comprised a Latin corpus of Greek commentators and a set of notes (*notulae*) by Grosseteste himself.[63] When Grosseteste's anthology began to circulate, Thomas was only 20 or 21, newly arrived in Paris and under the tutelage of Albert the Great.[64] In Paris, or earlier in Italy, Thomas probably learned something of the older translations of the *Ethics* and of the styles of commentary on it current in faculties of the Arts.[65] Whatever the extent of this early acquaintance, Thomas would soon share in one of the first systematic studies of the *Ethics* to make use of Grosseteste's work. After Thomas moved with Albert to Cologne in 1248, Albert turned from his commentaries on Pseudo-Dionysius to expound the *Nicomachean Ethics* in Grosseteste's translation, already somewhat corrupted, and with the aid of his supplements, already somewhat curtailed. Thomas was set to edit Albert's public explication (*lectura*) of the *Ethics*, though his exact editorial role remains uncertain.[66]

Albert's explication would have given even an ordinary student a thor-

[61] D. A. Callus, "The Date of Grosseteste's Translation and Commentaries on Pseudo-Dionysius and the *Nicomachean Ethics*," *Recherches de théologie ancienne et médiévale* 14 (1947): 200–209; confirmed by René-Antoine Gauthier in the introduction to his edition of the *Ethics*, *Aristoteles latinus*, 26:cci.

[62] René Antoine Gauthier in *L'Éthique à Nicomaque*, eds. Gauthier and Jean Yves Jolif, 2nd edn. (Louvain: Publications universitaires, and Paris: Béatrice-Nauwelaerts, 1970), 1/1:121. Compare his introduction to the *Tabula libri Ethicorum*, in the Leonine *Opera omnia*, 48:B33.

[63] Gauthier, *Éthique à Nicomaque*, 1/1:121–122; and Mercken, *Greek Commentaries on the Nicomachean Ethics*, 1:30*–66*.

[64] Weisheipl, *Friar Thomas*, pp. 36–38; Tugwell, *Albert and Thomas*, p. 208.

[65] Gauthier thinks that Thomas first learned the *Ethics* as a student of Arts at Paris; see Leonine *Opera omnia*, 47:246* and 48:xvi–xvii. His evidence shows no more than that Thomas has some acquaintance with the *Ethica vetus* and a few details in the Arts commentaries. The materials for constructing Thomas's biography are not continuous enough to support Gauthier's argument that Thomas could only have learned these at Paris.

[66] See the remarks by Wilhelm Kübel in Albert the Great, *Super Ethica*, as in Cologne *Opera omnia* 14/1:v–vi.

ough and laudably philological familiarity with the Aristotelian text. Thomas was no ordinary student. The impression made on him was remarkably deep. Thomas seems to remember details of the reading well enough after 20 years to cite it from memory.[67] Still Thomas's major works provide the more striking evidence of Albert's instruction. In the *Scriptum* on the *Sentences*, *Against the Gentiles*, and the *Summa of Theology*, four Aristotelian texts account for more than 80 percent of Thomas's citations to Aristotle. These are *Physics*, *On the Soul*, *Metaphysics*, and *Nicomachean Ethics*. In *Against the Gentiles*, *On the Soul* is the most frequently cited text, in large part because of the extended treatments of the human soul in Book 2. In both the *Scriptum* and the *Summa*, it is the *Ethics* that is cited most often – and by a wide margin. Citations to the *Ethics* make up exactly half of all the citations to Aristotle in the *Summa*. To say this in another way: the *Ethics* is cited in the *Summa* four times for every one citation of the next most frequent text, the *Metaphysics*. The figures for the *Scriptum* would be comparable. Thomas's early and thorough acquaintance with the *Ethics* is put to special use throughout his authorship.

It would be odd, however, for a reader of Thomas's gifts to construe so important a book once, at age 25, and then learn nothing more from it or about it. I note this without any desire to authorize the making of psychological fables or the postulation of Hegelian "developments." There are some small signs of changed readings – points on which Thomas moves further away from Albert, say. Still the more interesting changes in Thomas's reading of the *Ethics* reconfigure his relation to the whole Aristotelian text. Watching Thomas read and reread Aristotle, we learn something of how he understands relations to the texts of authoritative teachers.

The *Ethics* in the *Scriptum* on the *Sentences*

In the version generally received, each of the four books of Thomas's *Scriptum* on the *Sentences* draws on the whole of *Nicomachean Ethics*.[68] They do not do so equally or uniformly. The subject-matter of the first book overlaps least with the *Ethics*, so it is not surprising that it contains the fewest citations. The second book of the *Scriptum* contains four times as many, the

---

[67]   See Gauthier in the Leonine *Opera omnia*, 47/1:254★–256★.
[68]   I must leave aside the complicated questions about subsequent redactions of the text of the *Scriptum*. Hence, I take the Mandonnet and Moos text, less the passages omitted by the Parma edition, as substantially reproducing the text of the *Scriptum* at the time of its first public circulation.

third book eight times. What may be surprising is that the fourth book, in which the densely theological subject matter would seem not to require any lessons from pagan ethics, contains many more citations than the second book and almost as many as the third. The explanation for this is connected to the explanation for the lack of uniformity in citation. Thomas's uses of the *Ethics* are clustered around certain specific topics. In each of Books 3 and 4, for example, more than half of the citations are contained in ten percent of the distinctions. A single distinction of the third book contains 125 citations or 13 percent of the total for the whole of the *Scriptum*.[69]

The clustering of citations will appear more striking when citations are sorted by their specific importance to the construction of the argument. A citation to Aristotle in an objection (*argumentum*) is often less telling than a citation in a *sed contra* or the *corpus* of an article, but a citation in the *corpus* will often lie to one side of the point at issue. The citation may support a general maxim, explain a peripheral matter, or provide the other term for an analogy. A statistical summary of citations may raise questions about Thomas's deployment of Aristotle, but by itself it will not settle them because it cannot sort the citations by function. Let me sample instead some types of uses, with a few examples for each taken only from *Scriptum* 1. I can then turn to the types most important for understanding Thomas's reading of Aristotle and to more substantive texts in later books. I stress these are neither "ideal types" nor elements in a scheme of classification meant to cover all of Thomas's works. They are illustrations of the range of functions that citations to Aristotle are called to perform while Thomas writes.

(1) A first type of citation is a learned allusion – an overflowing of erudition. Thomas's writing is mostly free of such gestures, but there are exceptions. For example, in glossing the Lombard's prologue, Thomas cites both the *Poetics* and the *Metaphysics* to argue that a fable (*fabula*) is made up of wonders – this in reference to 2 Timothy 4.[70] The single such use of the *Ethics* in *Scriptum* 1 might be a reference to Aristotle's remark that small things cannot be beautiful.[71] The citation is incorporated into a Dionysian and Augustinian justification of Hilary's appropriation of qualities to the Persons of the Trinity. It looks to be more excessive association than argument.[72]

---

[69] *Scriptum Sent.* 3.33.
[70] *Scriptum Sent.* 1. prol. *divisio textus.*
[71] *Scriptum Sent.* 1.31.2.1 *solutio.*
[72] Valkenberg warns rightly about treating any citation as merely "ornamental." He shows as well the limits of any rigid classification of *auctoritates*. See Wilhelmus G. B. M. Valkenberg, *Words of the Living God: Place and Function of Holy Scripture in the Theology of St Thomas Aquinas* (Leuven: Peeters, 2000), pp. 44–48. My own typology is, I hope, sufficiently tentative and *ad hoc* to escape his justified criticisms.

(2) A second kind of citation is specious so far as it depends on a super-ficial misreading of some fragment from Aristotle. This type of citation occurs most often in objections or "doubts" (*dubia*) about the Lombard's letter. The first example comes in the first distinction of *Scriptum* 1. An argument there is buttressed by what Thomas takes to be a misconstrual of Aristotle's remarks on prudence in *Ethics* 6.[73] The Aristotelian remarks are being used to construct an analogy with the Augustinian notion of "use" (*uti*). Thomas does not reject the analogy, but he does correct a misunder-standing of the relation of prudence to the will according to Aristotle.[74] A similarly disputative example, not involving analogy, misuses Aristotle's defi-nition of counsel (*consilium*).[75]

(3) A third sort of citation to the *Ethics* establishes a general point in no way specific to ethical matter or to Aristotle. An early example in the *Scrip-tum* comes when *Ethics* 1 is invoked, after Boethius, to establish that each kind of science should proceed according to the consideration of its matter.[76] Other examples would be citations in support of assertions that God delights and that God cannot undo the past.[77] In such citations, Aristo-tle serves as a convenient but not indispensable authority. He offers a clear or memorable formulation of what could be supported from many other authors.

(4) Citations of a fourth type are more specifically Aristotelian, but they support a peripheral point. There is a good example in the first article of *Scriptum* 1, within the dispute over whether human minds need instruction beyond "physical bodies of learning."[78] While arguing that such a teaching is necessary, Thomas mentions that the incomplete contemplation of God attainable through creatures is said by Aristotle to be the source of contem-plative happiness – that is, Thomas explains, the happiness of the wayfarer.[79] The doctrine is specifically (though not exclusively) Aristotelian, but it is not integral to the argument here.

(5) A fifth group of citations supplies a general maxim or rule that can be used in a wide variety of ethical contexts. These are among the most frequent and most interesting of the substantive uses of Aristotle, since they contribute to the vocabularies and schemata within which Thomas

---

[73] *Scriptum Sent.* 1.1.1.2 *arg.* 2.
[74] *Scriptum Sent.* 1.1.1.2 *ad* 2.
[75] *Scriptum Sent.* 1.5 *expositio textus.*
[76] *Scriptum Sent.* 1. *prol.* 1.5 *solutio.*
[77] Respectively, *Scriptum Sent.* 1.8 *expositio secundae textus* and 1.39.1.1 *arg.* 1.
[78] *Scriptum Sent.* 1. *prol.* 1.1 *titulus.*
[79] *Scriptum Sent.* 1. *prol.* 1.1 *solutio.*

articulates his teaching on almost any point. A good example from *Scriptum* 1 is the use of the *Ethics* to support the distinction between operation (*operatio*) and motion (*motus*).[80]

(6) The sixth and final kind of citation, by far the most important, is both specifically Aristotelian and essential to Thomas's ethical purposes. Examples are the *Scriptum*'s second and third citations of the *Ethics*. Here Aristotle's Book 6 is used to establish the number of speculative habits and the character of wisdom. Both assertions are integral to the determination of the article, which concerns theology as speculative and practical.[81] Both invoke typically Aristotelian arguments. Thomas will also use Aristotle in this way when arguing that delight follows upon habit and that a good act requires three things: will or choice, a proper end, and firmness in performance.[82]

The list of six types of citations is not complete, but it should establish the main point. Thomas's citations of Aristotle's *Ethics* range from ornamental and specious to pertinent and important. The impression that "Aristotle is everywhere" whenever Thomas turns to ethics has to be corrected by noticing that Aristotle is not everywhere the same. Only the fifth and sixth types of citation, the generally or specifically constructive uses, are immediately pertinent to assessing Thomas's reading of the *Ethics*. They show his incorporation of Aristotelian terminology and argument into the analysis of inherited theological materials. They also mark an interesting departure from the immediately preceding *Sentences*-commentaries of Albert and Bonaventure, in both the boldness and explicitness of their reliance on the Aristotelian *Ethics*.

Important constructive uses of the *Ethics* are found in those sections of *Scriptum* 2, 3, and 4 that treat the Lombard's scattered remarks on moral matters – though not only of them. Thomas relies on Aristotle's notions of justice while discussing the adoration of the humanity of Christ.[83] Aristotle's teaching on friendship appears in every discussion of charity, as his definitions of fortitude figure in articles on the Holy Spirit's gifts.[84] Many more citations fall where one would expect them, in discussions of sin, grace, free choice and will, the virtues, repentance, contemplation, and happiness.[85]

---

[80] *Scriptum Sent.* 1.4.1.1 *solutio*, 1.7.1.1 *ad* 3, 1.37.4.1. Notice that the three passages cite two different texts in the *Ethics*, 5.4–6 and 10.3, in support of the same maxim.

[81] *Scriptum Sent.* 1. *prol.* 1.3.3 *solutio*. Compare the equally integral citations in 1.1.1 *solutio* and *ad* 1.

[82] Respectively, *Scriptum Sent.* 1.17.1.4 *solutio* and 1.46 *expositio textus*.

[83] *Scriptum Sent.* 3.9.1.

[84] Respectively, *Scriptum Sent.* 2.27–29 for the main treatment, but see also 1.17 and 3.34.

[85] *Scriptum Sent.* 2.22, 2.39, 2.42, 2.44 (sin); 2.24, 2.27 (grace); 2.25, 2.38–39, 2.44 (will); 3.23, 3.33, 3.36, 4.14 (virtues); 4.14–17 (repentance); 3.35 (contemplation); and 4.49 (happiness).

From this range, I would like to take only a single example, out of *Scriptum* 3.33. This is the distinction that contains, just by itself, some 125 explicit citations to the *Ethics*. The reason for this is that Thomas here interjects within the Lombard's sequence of topics an examination of moral virtue.[86]

The Lombard enumerates the cardinal virtues and provides a few definitions for them, but his main concern is with their survival into the afterlife. Thomas uses the enumeration as an occasion for offering a fuller doctrine of the moral virtues, including the cardinal virtues and their parts. In doing so, he goes considerably further than either Albert or Bonaventure do when explicating this passage. Albert's commentary on the *Sentences*, which would have been finished before the circulation of Grosseteste's anthology, offers four articles on the number, name, differences, and survival of the cardinal virtues.[87] The *Nicomachean Ethics* is cited only six times in two of these articles.[88] Only one of these citations could be regarded as programmatic; it concerns the order of treatment of virtues in the *Ethics*.[89] Bonaventure undertakes a more extended discussion of the Lombard's passage, including questions on the unity, locus, sufficiency, origin, and permanence of the cardinal virtues.[90] He also alludes to the *Ethics* somewhat more frequently, though many of the allusions are implicit or anonymous.[91] Bonaventure's manner of citation is also noteworthy. Though his commentary would have been finished at Paris well after the material from Grosseteste became available, he continues to cite the *Ethics* in the old manner.[92] By contrast to his immediate predecessors, Thomas introduces three Questions with 13 Articles on the moral virtues in common, then the cardinal virtues, then the parts of the cardinal virtues.[93] It is by far the longest distinction in *Scriptum* 3.[94]

Even in this lengthy discussion, which refers to Aristotle's *Ethics* on most pages, it is not easy to distinguish the functions of the citations. Many of

---

[86] This is not the first discussion of virtue as such in the *Sentences*-commentary. That has already come at *Scriptum Sent.* 2.27.1–6.

[87] Albert, *Super libros Sententiarum* 3.33.1–4 (Borgnet *Opera omnia* 28:606–615); on the dating, Tugwell, *Albert and Thomas*, p. 11.

[88] Albert, *Super libros Sententiarum* 3.33.1 *arg.* 7–8 and *ad* 7–9 (Borgnet *Opera omnia* 28:606, 608), 3.33.3 *arg.* 5 and *ad* 5 (28:610–611).

[89] Albert, *Super libros Sententiarum* 3.33.3 *ad* 5 (Borgnet *Opera omnia* 28:611).

[90] Bonaventure, *Super libros Sententiarum* 3.33.1.1–6 (Quaracchi 3:712–731).

[91] For example, Bonaventure, *Super libros Sententiarum* 3.33.1.2 objs. 3–5 and *ad* 5 (Quaracchi 3:713–714), 3.33.1.3 *sed contra* 3 (3:716), 3.33.1.5 *sed contra* 4 (3:722), 3.33.1.5 *dubium* 3 (3:729).

[92] For example, Bonaventure, *Super libros Sententiarum* 3.33.1.3 *sed contra* 1: "according to what the Philosopher says at the end of the New Ethics" (Quaracchi 3:716).

[93] *Scriptum Sent.* 3.33.1–3.

[94] The next longest are dd.3 and 34, which are each about two-thirds the length of d.33.

them are convenient tags in the construction of the dialectic. Almost half figure in objections, and some of them pass back and forth between objections, determinations, and answers to objections.[95] In a few places, an authoritative text from Aristotle is deemed sufficient, by itself, to constitute a *sed contra*, but Aristotle's texts are hardly given unique authority.[96] The last question of this distinction lines up divisions of the cardinal virtues from Aristotle, Cicero, Macrobius, and anonymous Greek philosophers, whom Thomas knows through Grosseteste – that is, through Albert.[97] Aristotelian terminology receives no privilege within the series. In other passages, indeed, Thomas remarks on the limited scope of Aristotle's inquiry. The Philosopher speaks, he says, of the acquired virtues that complete human life in the earthly city.[98] Just above, Thomas has invoked Macrobius's three-step transposition of the virtues of the active life onto the contemplative.[99] Aristotle's ethical texts are something like a local account bounded not just by the Gospel, but by neo-Platonic moral hierarchies. Aristotle helps much, but in comparison even with other philosophy he can help just so far.

Thomas's complex appropriation of Aristotle appears not only when he is juxtaposing sources. Aristotle figures importantly in the construction of certain doctrines, but not of others. He is the main authority for arguing that the virtues are found in the mean, as he is when describing the matters of the various cardinal virtues.[100] Aristotle is *not* an important authority for establishing the number and names of the cardinal virtues, their locus, or their relation to prudence.[101] Moreover, and decisively, Thomas qualifies Aristotelian doctrine about virtues at every turn with theological teaching. Experience establishes the Aristotelian tenet that virtues are acquired by practice, but we also need infused moral virtues to be ordered to our highest end, and these differ in species from the acquired.[102] All the kinds of virtues lie in the mean, except for the theological – that is, the most important.[103] Acquired moral virtues, being the virtues of the earthly city, do not remain in heaven; infused virtues do.[104] Reason appropriately rules over the

---

[95] For example, *Ethics* 2.2 (1004b4) is used in *Scriptum Sent.* 3.33.1.2.2 *solutio* and 3.33.2.2.2 *arg.* 3. *Ethics* 5.7 (1123b30) is used in 3.33.2.1.4 *arg.* 2 and 3.33.3.3.4 *solutio*. *Ethics* 6.14 (1138al) is used in 3.33.3.1.1 *ad* 2 and 3.33.2.4 *solutio*, and 3.33.2.5 *arg.* 6.

[96] *Scriptum Sent.* 3.33.1.3.1 *sed contra* 1, 3.33.2.2.2 *sed contra* 1, 3.33.2.2.3 *sed contra* 1.

[97] *Scriptum Sent.* 3.33.3.1–4.

[98] *Scriptum Sent.* 3.33.1.4 *ad* 5.

[99] *Scriptum Sent.* 3.33.1.4 *ad* 2.

[100] Respectively, *Scriptum Sent.* 3.33.1.3.1–3 and 3.33.2.2.1–3.

[101] Respectively, *Scriptum Sent.* 3.33.2.1.1–4, 3.33.2.4.1–4, 3.33.2.5.

[102] *Scriptum Sent.* 3.33.1.2.3–4.

[103] *Scriptum Sent.* 3.33.1.3.4 *solutio*.

[104] *Scriptum Sent.* 3.33.1.4 *solutio*.

acquired moral virtues, but the highest infused virtue, namely charity, resides in the will and commands reason.[105] At all these points, the Aristotelian doctrine is subordinated to other teaching in order to be corrected by it.

Three conclusions can be gathered from the citations to Aristotle's *Ethics* in Thomas's *Scriptum*. First, there is irreducible variety in Thomas's manner of using citations. Second, the Aristotelian citations are juxtaposed with other authorities of all kinds. Third, Thomas subsumes the variously deployed and unevenly distributed Aristotelian authorities within a framework that is not theirs.

The *Ethics* and *Summa of Theology* 2

Certain large similarities can easily be asserted between the second part of the *Summa* and the *Ethics*. Both begin with a hortatory or protreptic discussion of happiness, proceed then to examine the principles of human action, and consider next some particular virtues, in order to end with reflection on particular states of life. But a reader of the two texts could just as easily be struck by large differences. It is obvious that certain Christian doctrines make their appearance in *Summa* 2, among them the Old and New Law, grace, and the theological virtues of faith, hope, and charity. More pervasively and more subtly, Thomas changes the specificity and confidence of Aristotelian moral teaching. Where Aristotle begins by emphasizing the limitations of moral teaching and raising difficulties about happiness, Thomas offers a rapid ascent to a divine good. Where Aristotle offers a few remarks on the terms for ascribing and mitigating responsibility, Thomas gives a detailed analysis of nine interlocking acts of knowing and willing. Most profoundly, Thomas engages the structure of Aristotle's *Ethics* as a pedagogical analogy for the construction of a Christian moral teaching.

In his exposition, Thomas describes three very unequal parts of the *Nicomachean Ethics*. After a procedural introduction, he says, Aristotle "investigates happiness" in the first part, which is most of the first book. At the end of that book, Aristotle turns to what Thomas counts as the second part of the trichotomy, the main matter of the *Ethics*: the discussion of virtue. Aristotle begins with the moral virtues. In the second book and part of the third, he defines moral virtue in general and certain principles of moral action. In the balance of the third book and the fourth, Aristotle treats virtues concerned

---

[105] *Scriptum Sent.* 3.33.2.4.2 *ad* 3.

with interior passions, chiefly fortitude and temperance. In the fifth book, the subject is the virtue of external actions, namely justice. Aristotle's sixth book considers the intellectual virtues. The seventh, eighth, and ninth books describe things that follow on virtues or accompany them, namely continence and friendship. Aristotle's tenth book, which is the (short) third member of Thomas's original trichotomy, completes the treatment of happiness, individually and in the city.[106]

Compare Thomas's own order in the second part of the *Summa*. First, Thomas separates the definitions of virtue and the other principles or elements much more strictly from the treatment of particular virtues. Thomas insists, second, on the sufficiency of the four cardinal virtues as a comprehensive organization for all moral virtue. They are the organizing principles, and friendship or continence must be subordinated to them pedagogically. In the *Summa*, friendship becomes a quasi-potential part of justice,[107] while continence appears as a potential part of temperance.[108] Third, Thomas suppresses Aristotle's separate treatment of the intellectual virtues. Prudence is combined with the similarly named cardinal virtue. Art is excluded as not pertaining to moral matters. Wisdom, understanding, and knowledge are treated with their related gifts of the Spirit under the appropriate theological virtue.[109] Fourth, Thomas inserts into the investigation of principles a long treatment of the passions, which he thinks Aristotle had relegated to the *Rhetoric*.[110] Fifth, Aristotle's discussion of law is moved from the end of the tenth book, where it forms a bridge to the *Politics*, back to a point just before the consideration of particular virtues. It becomes part of the preliminary review of virtue and choice. Under Thomas's reorganization, then, the *Ethics* would proceed as follows: investigation of happiness; definitions of virtue, choice, passions, and law; the four cardinal virtues; and the personal attainment of happiness, especially in contemplation.

Thomas regards his revision of the order of the *Ethics* as an improvement in clarity and comprehensiveness even for the philosophical order of teaching. Of course the guide that enables Thomas to proceed so much more confidently and clearly through the uncertainties of moral life also requires that he regard a clarified and augmented philosophical ethics as inadequate

---

[106] Thomas's understanding of the order of the *Ethics* is drawn from his remarks in *Sent. Ethic.* 1.1, 1.3, 1.4, 1.19, 2.1, 3.14, 7.1, and 10.1.

[107] *Summa theol.* 2–2.114. Of course, many of the matters that Aristotle discusses in the books on friendship appear in Thomas under the acts of the theological virtue of charity. See, for example, *Summa theol.* 2–2.28–33.

[108] *Summa theol.* 2–2.155.

[109] Thomas explains this in *Summa theol.* 2–2. prol.

[110] *Sent. Ethic.* 4.17; compare 2.9.

·to moral life. At the center of the revised Aristotelian pattern, Thomas must insert two things: an eminent external principle for teaching good action – a principle much more powerful than the law of cities; and an eminent set of new virtues – virtues much more important for happiness than the cardinal virtues. The principle is grace, and the new virtues are infusions of faith, hope, and charity.

Thomas's Affiliations with the Aristotle of the *Ethics*

By way of concluding, I can restate the lesson in terminology with which I began. When we want to describe Thomas's affiliations with Aristotle, nothing is to be gained by talking about Thomas's "Aristotelianism." Aristotelianism as a descriptive category owes much more to the prejudices of Enlightenment historiography than to the medieval texts in hand. The model of "critical" historiography, made famous by Jakob Brucker, proceeds by identifying the irreducible philosophic content within a position. This model ought to be clearly distinguished from ancient and medieval doxographies by school. Thomas speaks frequently of "sects (*sectae*)" of philosophers, and he knows well the various doxographies in Aristotle and commentators on him. Sects are historical communities constituted by relations of students to teachers, by common practices of ways-of-life, by the tradition of certain texts. Schools are not "-isms." And so we betray Thomas's own understanding of the history of philosophy if we describe his relation to Aristotle as a relation to an "-ism." We betray it more ironically when we begin to speak of "Thomism."

An equally misleading description conceives Thomas as defending a set of Aristotelian doctrines or tenets by means of stipulated arguments. Thomas was famously willing to defend certain Aristotelian positions and to do so with some Aristotelian weapons. The defenses follow from his readings in Aristotle; they do not precede them as a declaration of allegiance. To subscribe to a fixed set of tenets beforehand would undo dialectic. It would render impossible the very procedures through which Thomas engages Aristotle. Thomas holds as a principle of disputative exegesis that salient points ought to be read back into the vocabularies and other contexts from which they emerge, but that does not mean that he thinks of an author's teaching as a bulky register of claims to which you subscribe entirely or not at all. Thomas feels free sometimes to revise particular teachings from Aristotle – if need be, quite profoundly – and always to sharpen them for application in a particular dialectic. They are not so much solid units to be transported whole as sources or occasions for invention.

Would we get at Thomas's relation to Aristotle more adequately by describing it as Thomas adopting or adapting Aristotelian vocabularies? Thomas learns from Aristotle a powerful and supple set of interlocking terminologies through which to talk about so many parts of the world. Thomas takes over large portions of these terminologies, as he takes over Aristotle's concern for the ranges of meaning in philosophic argument, for deduction from deep grammar, and so on. Still we have to add immediately that Thomas does this with other writers as well. There is a plurality of philosophic vocabularies in Thomas and they are constellated differently around different topics. Thomas treats the Aristotelian vocabularies as one voice in a variable hierarchy of traditions of philosophic speech. It may be the privileged voice in some cases, but it is never the only one, nor the only one to be privileged. Its juxtaposition with other voices, other vocabularies, modifies it in various ways. Thomas reads the *Ethics* in part to appropriate and modify Aristotelian discourses, but the appropriations and modifications are made in view of a hierarchy that extends beyond them.

A more attractive description interprets Thomas's successive readings of the *Ethics* as his appropriating larger and larger sets of heuristic schemata from Aristotle. By "heuristic schemata" I mean those marvelously useful patterns of distinction in which Aristotle is so rich: act/potency, form/matter, mean/extreme, intellectual/moral. Thomas's successive readings of the *Ethics* are so many ways of deploying and combining these schemata. He begins, first, with discrete schemata on small points together with those schemata needed in wide, analogous application at a goodly level of abstraction. Next Thomas takes a whole set of schemata, connected to one another by the progress of the Aristotelian *Ethics* read straight through. Then, finally, he puts these schemata together with others from diverse authors when composing the *Summa*. This description is correct and admirable, not least because it invites us to understand in more detail how Thomas analogizes Aristotle's schemata. Still it does not capture the central feature of Thomas's successive readings – namely, the progressive engagement with the structure of the *Ethics*.

There is one further step. The least misleading description narrates Thomas's progressive engagement with Aristotle's *textual pedagogy*. Many lasting texts in ethics propose exemplary pedagogies. They set forth – promise, prophesy, conduct – a pattern of education for readers' souls. Aristotle's *Ethics* is exemplary in just this way. It served ethical pedagogy most importantly by tracing a pedagogy of its own along which a reader can be brought to convictions about how to live. The whole of the *Ethics* provokes for Thomas a larger question about pedagogy in morals – and with it a question of whether there ought not to be a more encompassing textual pattern than Aristotle's for the formation of souls. The most serious response to the pedagogy of the *Ethics* is to propose a pedagogy in which the *Ethics* itself is preserved as a preliminary teaching.

Many neo-Thomisms reject this last description for assigning Aristotle too small a role. I attribute the rejection not to piety towards a particular Greek philosopher, but to a desire for a Thomistic philosophy, and especially a Thomistic ethics, independent of revelation. The desire was avowed in *Aeterni patris*, but it can be found for several centuries before that encyclical in some "Thomistic" attempts to resist, coopt, or outdo modern epistemologies. Many neo-Thomisms have dreamed of an apodictic and autonomous philosophy more beholden to Cartesian or neo-Kantian curricula than to Thomas – or, for that matter, to Aristotle. (The Aristotle in neo-Thomisms little resembles other Aristotles, and he speaks Latin much more fluently than Greek.) Since no significant part of Thomas's corpus fits within post-Cartesian philosophy except for the expositions of Aristotle, and since only Aristotle among Thomas's philosophic authorities figures prominently in modern canons, the Aristotelian expositions must then be designated Thomas's contribution to philosophy.

This project ends by claiming that Thomas is an original philosopher because he adheres so closely to Aristotle. Something so baffling must be explained by a fundamental mistake: it is the unhappy result of forcing modern notions of a discrete, secular philosophy onto a medieval corpus written from quite other notions.[111] The baffling claim also betrays a recognizably modern notion of *religious* authority. Neo-Thomist accounts of a Thomas who secures the autonomy of philosophy just by repeating Aristotle unwittingly disclose the churchly authority underneath too many philosophical neo-Thomisms. Since the nineteenth century, Neo-Thomism has named, among other things, the desire to safeguard reason by retrieving old texts at papal behest – and, a bit later, under the surveillance of the bureaucracy of anti-Modernism. In such a climate, claims for the autonomy of Thomistic philosophy or the philosophic genius of Thomas must sound

---

[111] If we wanted to apply "philosophy" to Thomas's corpus with something like a median modern sense, we would, as John Milbank argues, end up having to concede its inseparability from theology. See the second chapter in Milbank and Catherine Pickstock, *Truth in Aquinas* (London and New York: Routledge, 2001). Milbank argues that the paired contrasts reason/faith and philosophical theology/*sacra doctrina* are at most "distinct [but unbounded] phases within a single gnoseological extension exhibiting the same qualities throughout" (p. 21). Reason occurs in varying intensities wherever there is faith, as philosophical theology must be present whenever *sacra doctrina* is being expounded. The remark is true to Aquinas's use of philosophical reasons, but not to his use of the terms "philosophia" or "philosophus." My own argument has tried to follow him in the use of those terms.

like echoes of other campaigns. Thomas's "Aristotelianism" means Thomas's availability for recent ecclesiastical projects of intellectual security. "Aristotle" means reason, and "Thomas" means the church making use of reason. The first thing lost in that allegory are the texts through which a mendicant theologian writes out his ongoing dialectical engagement with a longtime student of Plato.

Neo-Thomism's relation to Thomas should be contrasted with Thomas's relation to Aristotle. Thomas is certainly more candid about retrieving Aristotle into a new hierarchy of sciences. He never pretends to be producing a copy of Aristotle's philosophic project. He never identifies himself as a "Peripatetic," much less a proponent of "neo-Aristotelianism" (the very form of the term would have puzzled him). For Thomas, Aristotle is not a unique or perennial authority. Aristotle is a pagan author whose texts can be brought into helpful constellation with other authorities. Thomas does not regard Aristotle as a block of doctrine to be carried in whole. He treats Aristotle instead as the teacher behind a set of pedagogical texts. The unity of the teaching is just the dialectical congruence that thoughtful reading can perform. For all of these reasons, Thomas is not tempted to misleading imitation of Aristotle. Because he does not construct Aristotle as a perennial authority to be put on whole, he is not tempted to make Aristotle into a mask of authority through which to speak his own projects. If only Thomas had been so fortunate in all his readers.

Chapter Five

The Protreptic of
Against the Gentiles

Thomas pays respect to his authorities by transforming them without pretending to reproduce them. He does not swear allegiance to their reified doctrines. He constellates them with other authorities around sequences of topics that strain to trace out new pedagogical patterns. Across the span of his writing, Thomas experimented with at least five major patterns: Peter Lombard's *Sentences*, the writings of Boethius, those of Pseudo-Dionysius, the so-called *Summa against the Gentiles*, and the *Summa of Theology*.[1] The first and the last of these are more or less radical variations on the verbal professions called creeds. The others are patterns for interrogating not so much doctrine as the languages in which it can be taught. All of Thomas's experimental structures have been liable to misreading, but perhaps no structure has been misread so aggressively as the one mislabeled *Against the Gentiles*.

How is a serious reader meant to be moved by the structure of this experiment in persuasion? Who is addressed by the work? In view of which ends? Taking up these questions, I begin to show what it means for Thomas to transfigure authorities into pedagogies.

---

[1]   In this and similar passages, I omit the *Compendium of Theology*, in part because of its brevity (at least as we receive it), in part because it returns to much older structures, especially Augustine's *Enchiridion*. The notion that Thomas's various works should be read as part of a more or less unified project became fixed for me in the course of studying Michel Corbin's *Le chemin de la théologie chez Thomas d'Aquin* (Paris: Beauchesne, 1974). If I cannot agree with Corbin's Hegelian narrative of development, I remain completely persuaded by the project of his title.

Circumstances

Circumstantial evidence about *Against the Gentiles* invites a fallacy of authorial intention.[2] Those who commit it classify the work as a missionary manual and include it in histories of missionary activity. In fact, the surviving evidence in no way decides the intention or even the title of the work known both as *Against the Gentiles* and *On the Truth of the Catholic Faith.*

In a narration of the deeds of James I of Aragon, as part of a reminiscence of Raymond of Peñafort, the Dominican chronicler Peter Marsilius recounts a story about the composition of *Against the Gentiles.*[3] Peter's text was finished on April 2, 1313; the frame for the story of Raymond is a narrative about Christmas, 1274; and the story itself lies even further back – more than 40 years before the date of writing. At that time, Peter says, Raymond asked Thomas to compose a work "against the errors of unbelievers (*contra infidelium errores*)" as an aid in conversion. "That master did what the humble rogation of such a father required; and he composed a *summa* called 'against the Gentiles,' which is believed not to have any equal for such material (*pro illa materia*)."[4] There have been some textual questions about this passage, but none is unanswerable.[5] Let the text stand as received, but then read it carefully. The story is introduced to illustrate Raymond's zeal for conversions and to show his influence within the order. Since the story is not repeated in the contemporary lives of Raymond or in any of the canonization proceedings for Thomas, it is presumed that Peter was relying on a local legend from the Dominican house in Barcelona, where he had worked with Raymond years before. We are presented with the only extant attestation for a bit of local hagiography. It has been argued that Peter would not have invented this story because there were many among his readers who would have had first-hand

---

[2]   The arguments that follow assume the generally accepted chronology for Thomas's writings, as in Weisheipl, *Friar Thomas*, and Torrell, *Initiation*. I reject the elaborate reasonings by Pierre Marc that would advance the time of composition to the second Parisian regency. For a specific but abbreviated rejoinder to Marc, see the review by Clemens Vansteenkiste in *Angelicum* 45 (1968): 353–355, and fuller criticism in his unsigned review for *Rassegna di letteratura tomistica* 2 (1970): 51–56, entry no. 67. The proposal to redate the *Contra gentiles* to the second Parisian regency was not new; it had already been considered and rejected in Pietro Castagnoli, "La data di composizione della *Summa c. Gentiles* di S. Tommaso," *Divus Thomas* [Piacenza] 31 (1928): 489–492, especially pp. 491–492. Marc's redating did not win general assent; consider the summary chart for works published ten years after Marc in *Rassegna di letteratura tomistica* 14 (1981): 49. One favorable vote can be had in Thomas Murphy, "The Date and Purpose of the Contra Gentiles," *Heythrop Journal* 10 (1969): 405–415.

[3]   The text is discussed and quoted extensively in Marc, 1:72–77 and 612–613.

[4]   Barcelona, Bibl. centr. MS 1018, fol. 179r, as quoted in Marc, 1:73.

[5]   The issues are summarized in Marc, 1:74–76.

knowledge of the events mentioned.[6] This argument is weakened by remembering that flattering inventions are less likely to be contested than scurrilous ones and by comparing this tale with the sorts of things being told, less than six years later, in the canonization proceedings for Thomas.

If we were to assume that the story is a luckily preserved fact rather than a pious invention, difficulties would multiply. The first difficulty is simply to know what Peter means and, particularly, what he intends by the phrase "such material (*illa materia*)." What is the "matter" or material of *Against the Gentiles*? To speak more practically, where exactly does it fit into the well organized Dominican missionary effort? Peter's story might be saying at least three different things: *Against the Gentiles* is a book to be given to potential converts, or it is a manual for field-training missionaries, or it represents a reference work that refutes all errors of unbelievers compendiously. Of these three readings of *materia*, only the third has any plausibility – and then not much. Still let me take them in order.

Against the Gentiles cannot have been directed to potential converts. From the first line and then on every page thereafter, Thomas speaks as one Christian to another. His rhetorical address is evident in the use of Scriptural and magisterial quotations, in a presumption of acquaintance with Christian letters, and even in the voice of the first person plural. Thomas argues in the prologue that the mysteries of Christian faith ought not to be presented argumentatively before non-believers for fear of making them think that faith depends only on probable arguments.[7] Precisely these arguments appear in the plan of the fourth Book (as Thomas himself promises, 1.9 [no. 56]). How could Thomas have intended, then, that his book be placed into the hands of non-believers, without giving them offense and exposing Christian faith to scandal?

It is no more likely that *Against the Gentiles* was intended to train Dominican missionaries in the field. There are external and internal reasons. Externally, *Against the Gentiles* is an unsatisfactory missionary manual by Dominican standards of the thirteenth century. The life of Raymond himself offers counter-examples. Raymond not only founded schools for Oriental studies within the Dominican order, as Peter narrates, but also figured promi-

---

[6]   See Robert I. Burns, "Christian-Islamic Confrontation in the West: The Thirteenth-Century Dream of Conversion," *American Historical Review* 76 (1971): 1,386–1,434, at p. 1,410; Alvaro Huerga, "Hipótesis sobre la génesis de la 'Summa contra gentiles' y del 'Pugio fidei,'" *Angelicum* 51 (1974): 533–557, especially pp. 551–552 and 556.

[7]   References to the *Contra gentiles* will be made parenthetically to the Pera, Marc, Caramello edition. The citations will list book, chapter, and unique section numbers. This edition reproduces the text of Leonine *Opera omnia* vols. 13–15.

nently in public debates with non-Christians. In 1263, for example, Raymond helped to set the rules for a debate between the Dominican Paul "the Christian" and Rabbi Moses ben Nachman of Gerona.[8] This Paul had converted from Judaism and his strategy was to argue from a detailed knowledge of rabbinical writings that the messiah had already come, that he was prophesied to be both divine and human, and that his advent had destroyed Jewish laws and ceremonies.[9] The strategy of refutation from within had been adopted by Dominicans in campaigns of Jewish conversion through the 1250s and 1260s in Spain and France.[10] They dealt similarly with Cathars and allied heretics.[11]

Equally expert devices and emphases figure in Dominican preaching to Islam. Here a central figure was another Raymond, Raymond Martí (Martinus, Martini).[12] As early as 1250, Martí appears in Tunis as founder of an Arabic school. In 1267, he published the *Muzzle of the Jews* (*Capistrum Judaeorum*), a detailed attack on Judaism much like the internal criticism practiced by Paul "the Christian." In 1278, Martí presented the *Dagger of the Faith* (*Pugio Fidei*), an attack on Islam and Judaism. The work has figured prominently in the history of *Against the Gentiles* because it borrows directly from Thomas.[13]

---

[8]   Robert Chazan, "The Barcelona 'Disputation' of 1263: Christian Missionizing and Jewish Response," *Speculum* 52 (1977): 824–842, especially p. 826.

[9]   Chazan, "Barcelona 'Disputation,'" p. 826.

[10]   See Chazan, "Confrontation in the Synagogue at Narbonne . . .," *Harvard Theological Review* 67 (1974): 437–457.

[11]   See François Sanjek, "Raynerius Sacconi O.P., *Summa de Catharis*," *Archivum Fratrum Praedicatorum* 44 (1974): 31–60; compare Thomas Kaeppeli, "Une Somme contre les hérétiques de s. Pierre Martyr (?)," *Archivum Fratrum Praedicatorum* 17 (1947): 295–335. In the prologues edited by Kaeppeli, it is interesting to note the remarks on recourse to *rationes naturales* in controversy with heretics (pp. 301–302); compare *Contra gent.* 1.2 (no. 11b).

[12]   See generally André Berthier, "Un maître orientaliste du XIIIe siècle . . .," *Archivum Fratrum Praedicatorum* 6 (1936): 267–311, especially pp. 295–312 on Raymond's "method."

[13]   These resemblances led Miguel Asín y Palacio to argue that Thomas had plagiarized portions of the *Pugio*; see his "El Averroismo teológico de Santo Tomás de Aquino," in *Homenaje a don Francisco Codera . . .*, ed. Eduardo Saavedra (Zaragoza: M. Escar, 1904), 271–331, especially pp. 320–323. The charge was refuted almost at once by Luis G. Getino on the basis of chronology; see Getino, *La "Summa contra gentes" y el Pugio fidei . . .* (Vergara: El Santísimo Rosario, 1905), pp. 8–19 generally, with replies to objections on pp. 19–27. The question of borrowings between Aquinas and Martí reappeared with Marc's redating of the *Contra gentiles*. Marc asserts a dependence of *Contra gent.* 1.6 on Martí's *Capistrum Judaeorum*; see Marc, 1:65–72, and Burns, p. 1,409, who adopts the thesis of redating apparently on the basis of Murphy's summary article. There is also the thesis of prior exchange between Aquinas and Martí in José María Casciaro, *El diálogo teológico de Santo Tomás con musulmanes y judios, el tema de la profecía y la revelación* (Madrid: CSIC/"Francisco Suarez," 1969), p. 44; J. I. Saranyana, "La creación 'ab aeterno': Controversia de Santo Tomás y Raimundo Martí con San Bonaventura," *Scripta Theologica* [Pamplona] 5 (1973): 147–155. These hypotheses become necessary only if one rejects the simpler explanation that Martí borrowed from Thomas in his *Capistrum* just as he would do later and at length in the *Pugio*.

Far from confirming Thomas's missionary intention, however, the borrowings show how little Thomas could be used in direct missionary activity. Martí turns to Thomas almost exclusively in *Dagger of the Faith* 1. That first book, only ten percent of the whole, is intended to combat the errors "of the naturalists and the philosophers."[14] Martí uses Thomas against errors arising from the reading of Aristotle and the Peripatetics. Thomas supplies most of Martí's argument on the eternity of the world, God's knowledge of singulars, and the resurrection of the dead.[15] When it comes to a detailed consideration of the claims and counter-claims of competing canons, or to the intricacies of Islamic and Jewish theology, borrowings from Thomas almost disappear. According to the judgment of one expert missionary, Thomas's *Against the Gentiles* helps in philosophical preliminaries, but not in missionary work properly speaking.

External comparisons are confirmed internally by scattered remarks in *Against the Gentiles* about Islamic religion. In the "prologue" to the work (1.1–9), there are two pertinent passages. The first pleads Thomas's excuses for not being able to contest particular errors. He is not familiar with them, he says, nor can he proceed against all adversaries on the basis of common Scriptural authorities (1.2, nos. 10–11a). Thomas mentions the "Mohammedans and pagans" as not sharing any Scriptural authority with Christians. The second passage contrasts the sober motives for accepting Christian revelation with improper persuasions to various errors. Thomas describes the inducements offered by Mohammed, namely "carnal pleasures" and easy living, which he promised in colorful fables, without the supporting evidence of miracles or previous prophecy, to a credulous and isolated people (1.6, no. 41). The description is backed by no particular knowledge of Islam. Indeed Thomas's source is not contemporary Dominican research, but the century-old *Summula* of Peter the Venerable.[16] Some readers have seen here a "singular discretion" on Thomas's part as he reduces Koranic religion to the preaching of violence, perhaps in order to justify the Christians' crusades.[17] It

---

[14] Raymundus Martinus, *Pugio Fidei adversus mauros et judaeos*, ed. Joseph de Voisin (Leipzig, 1587; rptd. Farnborough: Gregg, 1967), pp. 192–253.

[15] Marc provides an exhaustive summary of the textual relations in 1:62–65.

[16] The *Summula* is edited in Migne *PL* 189:651–658; for the parallels to Thomas, see especially cols. 653D-655C, and compare Peter's Letter 4.17 to Bernard (*PL* 189:321–345). For the composition of Peter's anthology of Islamic writings, see Marie-Thérèse d'Alverny, "Deux traductions latines du coran au moyen âge," *Archives d'histoire doctrinale et littéraire au moyen âge* 16 (1947–1948): 69–131, especially pp. 69–71, 74–79.

[17] Simone Van Riet, "*La Somme contre les Gentils* et la polémique islamo-chretienne," in *Aquinas and Problems of His Time*, ed. G. Verbeke and R. Verhelst (Louvain: Publications Universitaires, 1974), 150–160, especially p. 158.

is simpler to suppose, as Thomas has admitted, that he knew little about Islamic belief, or, indeed, about the course of Islamic civilization.[18] How could he write a paradigmatic missioner's manual for an order that prided itself on expert acquaintance with the languages and beliefs of its adversaries? It was not only the ideal of the order. We have from Thomas himself a letter *On the Reasons of Faith against the Saracens, Greeks, and Armenians*.[19] Written just after completion of *Against the Gentiles*, it repeats charges against the infidels only as claims made by a correspondent. Thomas reminds him that no one ought to attempt a demonstration of the truths of the faith.[20]

Against the Gentiles is not a manual for training missionaries – and so we are left with the third possibility, that it was intended to provide a reference book of philosophical arguments against the conceptual errors instanced in unbelievers, to be read by Christians living in intellectual contact with them. Here again the story of Raymond's request must be reinterpreted, always assuming its credibility. Perhaps Thomas received such a request and wrote what he could, within the limits of his knowledge: a foundational work that would undergird any detailed missionary attack. Perhaps he already had a work of comprehensive pedagogy in hand that he adapted for Raymond's sake, adding topical references in the prologue and elsewhere.[21] Of course, a fundamental work structured according to the needs of Christian pedagogy is not easily classed as missionary, except in that sense in which every Christian reader is constantly being called to conversion. Any number of works, including the *Summa of Theology*, have been used as foundations for missionary activity. Such uses have not drawn them into the class of missionary manuals.

Circumstantial arguments about the work's intention have run aground. We must turn from them to the work itself in order to appreciate its experiment in persuasion.

The Prologue

On opening *Against the Gentiles*, the careful exegete would want first to consider the meaning of its title. Unfortunately, here too there is un-

---

[18] See the conclusions of Louis Gardet, "La connaissance que Thomas d'Aquin put avoir du monde islamique," in *Aquinas and Problems*, 139–149, esp. p. 140.

[19] See Weisheipl, *Friar Thomas*, p. 389, no. 63, and p. 394, no. 72.

[20] *De rat. fidei* 1 (Leonine *Opera omnia* 40:B57, esp. ll. 25, 27, 41, 49) and 2 (40:B58, ll. 1–22).

[21] The autograph of the text lacks the folios that would show Thomas's rewriting of the first nine chapters. Such traces of the first redaction as are preserved in the "pA" manuscript tradition provide only a few variants for chapters 1–4, none of which are substantive. See the critical apparatus in the Leonine *Opera omnia* 13:3–23, and the summary remarks, p. xvi.

certainty, as is not unusual with medieval academic works. The title *Book* or *Summa against the Gentiles* appears in early lists from the Parisian booksellers ("stationers"), in the writings of Thomas's early exponents, and in catalogues of Thomas's works.[22] In the early copies of the work, however, there stands the title *Book of the Truth of the Catholic Faith against the Errors of Unbelievers* or variants of it.[23] Either title is easily derived from the text of the second chapter, where Thomas says "we propose as our intention to show, in whatever little way we can, the truth offered by the catholic faith (*veritatem quam fides catholica profitetur*), eliminating contrary errors" (1.2, no. 9). He then goes on to speak of the "errors of the Gentiles (*errores gentilium*)" (1.2, no. 10). Whether the book is a *summa* is not decided by the text (as it sometimes is elsewhere). The title "*summa*," even if authentic, would prove too equivocal for fixing rhetorical purpose. In the thirteenth century, "*summa*" covers a number of very different works, beginning with the simplest of collections. The decision among the various titles must be set aside, then, except insofar as the catalogue title raises a question about the meaning of "Gentiles."

M. M. Gorce argued more than 70 years ago that the Gentiles of Thomas's title referred immediately to the Parisian exponents of a radical Aristotle.[24] His evidence for the claim came from a Parisian document of 1277, which speaks of the "Gentiles" of the Arts faculty, and from the correspondences between heterodox views condemned in 1270 or 1277 and positions mentioned by Thomas. Gorce's arguments are unconvincing. He could not establish any direct connection between the coinage in the document and Thomas's use of the term, nor could he show that the correspondence of views is anything but the effect of a common philosophical problematic.

---

[22] For catalogues from around 1292 to 1375 with the title "*Contra gentiles*" or some variant, see Anton Michelitsch, *Thomas-schriften* 1 (Graz and Vienna: Styria, 1913), pp. 101 (no. 46), 102 (82/251), 104 (127/295), 105 (131/299), 107 (175/1372), 109 (245/192), 110 (254/200), 111 (285/232), 112 (311/1559), 115 (75), 127 (14), 134 (4), 137, 140 (30), 143 (6), 145 (4), 149 (4), 156 (3). The title "*Liber de veritate catholice fidei*" appears in some of the later catalogues: see Michelitsch, pp. 104 (117/286), 106 (165/1,083), 110 (268/214). Henry of Hereford, whose catalogue is dated 1,292–1,294, gives the conflated title *Summa contra gentiles de veritate catholice fidei*; see Michelitsch, p. 125 (76). For a Parisian stationers' list of 1286, see Denifle and Chatelain, *Chartularium Universitatis Parisiensis* 1 (Paris: Frs. Delalain, 1889), no. 530, pp. 644–649, especially p. 646 ("Summa fratris Thome contra Gentiles").

[23] See the summary in Leonine *Opera omnia*, 13:xii.

[24] M. M. Gorce, "La lutte 'contre Gentiles' à Paris," in *Mélanges Mandonnet* . . . (Paris: J. Vrin, 1930), 1:223–243, particularly pp. 228–233; see also his retrospective remarks on the work in *Bulletin Thomiste*, t. 3/an. 7 (1930), nos. 1,203–1,206, pp. [179]–[187]. Gorce's argument was attacked on its characterization of a persistent "Latin Averroism" by David Salman, "Sur la lutte *contra Gentiles* de S. Thomas," *Divus Thomas* [Piacenza] 40 (1937): 488–509.

Gorce does raise the issue, however, about what Thomas might mean by speaking of Gentiles in the prologue itself.

Elsewhere in *Against the Gentiles*, positions ascribed to the Gentiles are those of ancient Greek philosophy. Gentiles were misled by the "first natural philosophers" into holding a view that the heavens are animated by divinities (1.20, nos. 189–193). They relied on this error to defend their idolatry (1.27, no. 258). Gentiles also claimed some kind of eternity for the cosmos and, thus, a circular time (2.38, no. 1,150; 4.82, no. 4,171). When Thomas says in the prologue that Christendom's "ancient teachers (*antiqui doctores*)" could attack errors in detail because they had been Gentiles or were in conversation with them, he is thinking of such writers as Augustine, Ambrose, and Jerome – men who lived in or among the philosophic schools of late antiquity.

The same usage is found in others of Thomas's works and in "reports" or (edited) transcripts of his teaching. Thomas speaks of the Gentiles as exponents of pre-Christian learning. He writes that "the Greeks" is used metonymically for all Gentiles, since all received worldly wisdom from the Greeks.[25] He singles out the Platonists among the Gentiles because they posited a providence, though he holds that Gentiles typically recognized the existence of God.[26] Most interestingly, Thomas is reported as speaking about "Gentiles" in the present tense. He distinguishes them both from the (Byzantine) schismatics and from the (Islamic) infidels: "in the North (*in Aquilonari*) there are still many Gentiles (*gentiles*), and in the East many schismatics and infidels (*schismatici et infideles*)."[27] The reference must be to unevangelized tribes or groups, though here too Thomas may be speaking more from dated hearsay than from current fact. To summarize: "Gentiles" means for Thomas, historically, pre- or extra-Christian humankind and, metaphorically, the human mind under the tutelage of nature. The highest moment of tutelage is Greek philosophy. How do we understand an argument made by Thomas "against the Gentiles"? It is an argument that corrects the natural errors of mind especially as articulated by philosophers. Is this suggestion borne out in the work's prologue?

The prologue begins with an Aristotelian explication of a Scriptural verse in praise of wisdom (1.1). The explication connects this verse and other passages in Scripture with Aristotle's hortatory depiction of wisdom at the beginning of the *Metaphysics*. Thomas argues for wisdom's usefulness and

---

[25] *Expos. Pauli, I ad Cor.* 6.3; *ad Rom.* 1.5 and 1.6.

[26] *Sent. De cael.* 1.4.5, *Sent. Ethic.* 9.10.3, *Post. Psalmos* 21.23.

[27] *Post. Psalmos* 48.1. On the reliability and context of this text, see Weisheipl, *Friar Thomas*, pp. 368–369, no. 26, and Torrell, *Initiation*, pp. 376–378.

announces his intention to set it forth, despite difficulties (1.2). This is a standard topic in philosophical prologues. So is the claim that wisdom demands expression.[28] But how should wisdom be set forth? The next chapters answer this question in general (1.3–8), while the final introductory chapter draws out an implied table of contents (1.9). The whole prologue constitutes an extended teacher's preface or *accessus*, in which 1.2 gives the statement of intention while the remaining chapters describe the manner of proceeding in relation to the subject-matter. Understanding the matter requires a distinction between two types of truth in regard to God, a distinction that has provoked as much feuding as did the possibility of a missionary motivation.

The most recent round of the debate can be said to have begun as far back as 1924, when Guy de Broglie argued from the "general economy" of *Against the Gentiles*, as proposed in the prologue, to a formal distinction between philosophical and theological truths in it.[29] De Broglie's motive was not to comment on *Against the Gentiles* so much as to extract a polemical conclusion from it about the natural desire for God. Still De Broglie took Thomas as promising that the first three books of the work would deal only with "religious truths accessible to reason alone," thus constituting "a Christian philosophy that will have its own consistency."[30] De Broglie was answered instantly by Blanche, who argued that *Against the Gentiles* was an apologetic, theological work, which treated of everything under the formality of the revealed.[31] Blanche's brief comment was only the first of many.[32]

In the next year, Mulard, while rebutting De Broglie's main thesis at length, agreed with Blanche on the apologetic character of *Against the Gentiles* and added confirming evidence from its manner of citing Scripture.[33]

---

[28] See Ernst Robert Curtius, *European Literature and the Latin Middle Ages*, tr. Willard R. Trask (Princeton: Princeton University, 1953), pp. 83–85 and 87–88.

[29] Guy de Broglie, "De la place du surnaturel dans la philosophie de saint Thomas," *Recherches de science religieuse* 14 (1924):193–224 and 481–496, 15 (1925): 5–53. The most pertinent remarks fall in the first two installments.

[30] De Broglie, "De la place du surnaturel," p. 207; compare pp. 206–209, 482.

[31] M. Blanche, "Note" (appended to a report of a lecture by de Broglie), *Revue de Philosophie* 24 (1924):444–449.

[32] Indeed, there were really two debates, one concerning the natural possibility for beatitude (together with such related notions as "obediential potency"), the other concerning the distinction of two truths in the *Contra gentiles*. I will here notice only the second debate. For a bibliography of the first, see M. Matthys, "Quid ratio naturalis doceat de possibilitate visionis beatae secundum S. Thomam in Summa contra Gentiles," *Divus Thomas* [Piacenza] 39 (1936): 201–228, at p. 201, n. 2. Matthys himself provides a rigorous but falsely schematic reconstruction of the argument for the two truths (pp. 203–213).

[33] R. Mulard, "Désir naturel de connaitre et vision béatifique," *Revue des sciences philosophiques et théologiques* 14 (1925), nos. 195–196, pp. [192]–[195], though Mulard there adds nothing further with regard to the structure of the *Contra gentiles*.

Bouyges followed with a summary of the debate (after a heated two years) and the proposal that *Against the Gentiles* be regarded as a missionary apologetic structured by reference to the sensitivities of a non-Christian readership.[34] All specifically Christian matter is transposed into the fourth book, Bouyges wrote, while all matter common to Christians and non-Christians is arranged progressively in the first three books. For him, the distinction is not a formal division between two types of propositions characterized with regard to their demonstrability; it is an apologetic distinction between the "discussable and non-discussable" or between what is and is not "susceptible . . . of being established and defended, in different degrees, before non-Christian partisans of supposedly revealed religions."[35] Bouyges's hypothesis was substantially accepted in a general review of the debate published in 1930 by Balthasar and Simonet.[36] Since then, the tendency has been to argue for a wider audience and a larger intention.[37]

---

[34]   Maurice Bouyges, "Le plan du *Contra gentiles* de S. Thomas," *Archives de Philosophie* 3 (1925): 320–341 (or 176–197 in the separate pagination of this special volume).

[35]   Bouyges, "Le plan," p. 191 (of the separate pagination).

[36]   N. Balthasar and A. Simonet, "Le plan de la *Somme contre les Gentils* de saint Thomas d'Aquin," *Revue néo-scolastique de philosophie* 32 (1930): 183–214, especially pp. 185 (n. 1), 186–188, 203. Balthasar and Simonet consider as well the views of De Broglie, Blanche, and Mulard, adding those of M. Berten, "A propos de la *Summa Contra Gentiles*," *Criterion* [Barcelona] 4 (1928): 175–183. Compare the reviews by H.-M. Feret in *Bulletin Thomiste*, t.3/an.7, nos. 86–87, pp. [105]–[112].

[37]   From the 1950 edition of his *Introduction* on, Chenu holds that the *Contra gentiles* is a theological apologetic, but also a deeply historical work, engaged in the concrete reality of the confrontation between Christianity and Islam (see pp. 247–251 in 1974 reprint). Gauthier argues, to the contrary, that the intention of the work is the supra-historical "intention of wisdom"; see his "Introduction historique," pp. 87–99. In a persuasive essay, somewhat at odds with his introduction to the English translation of *Contra gent.*, Anton Pegis sees Thomas as transforming the Aristotelian project by ordering it to the Incarnation; see "Qu'est-ce que la *Summa contra Gentiles*," in *L'Homme devant Dieu: Mélanges . . . de Lubac* (Paris: Aubier, 1964), especially pp. 172, 181–182. Quintín Turiel argues that the work is intended to show educated believers the truth of what they hold by faith; see his "La intención de santo Tomás en la 'Summa contra Gentiles,'" *Studium* [Madrid] 14 (1974): 371–401. Among more recent works on *Contra gent.*, I can single out one for agreement and one for disagreement. I agree when Thomas Hibbs deftly traces the dialectical correction of philosophy by theology in his *Dialectic and Narrative in Aquinas: A Reinterpretation of the* Summa contra Gentiles (Notre Dame: University of Notre Dame Press, 1995). I must disagree when Norman Kretzmann argues a strictly philosophical reading in his *Metaphysics of Theism: Aquinas's Natural Theology in* Summa contra Gentiles *I* (Oxford: Clarendon Press, and New York: Oxford University Press, 1997) and *Metaphysics of Creation: Aquinas's Natural Theology in* Summa contra Gentiles *II* (Oxford: Clarendon Press, and New York: Oxford University Press, 1999). According to Kretzmann, *Contra gent.* 1–3 is "the fullest and most promising natural theology ever produced" (as in the latter volume, p. vii; compare p. 1., n. 1, "the paradigm of a fully developed natural theology"). Natural theology is understood in turn as the branch of *philosophy* that investigates "by means of analysis and argument, at least the existence and nature of God and, in this fuller

None of the positions taken on the two truths is entirely fair to *Against the Gentiles*, though Bouyges comes closest – not when he invokes the missionary character, but when he points to the rhetorical motivation of the division. Read in context, the famous division separates two possibilities for effective persuasion. The division is introduced, in 1.3, with an allusion to Aristotle's doctrine about the various ways disciplines produce conviction (no. 13). Since those who are wise teach truth so that it be learned and held, they must study the degree of conviction possible in any subject matter. The division is recalled again when Thomas says that there is a twofold mode of truth "in what we confess (*confitemur*) of God" (1.3, no. 14). The first truths "exceed every power of human reason"; the second truths "natural reason can also reach." These latter truths were "demonstratively proved" by the philosophers, "led by the light of natural reason" (1.3, no. 14). Note here that reason is said not to exhaust, but to touch these accessible truths. We must understand the demonstrative proofs of the philosophers not as Cartesian reductions, but as exemplary forms of rational instruction. To say that the philosophers proved the conclusions demonstratively is to say that they constructed fully rational pedagogies leading to them. Thomas stresses that some truths obviously exceed the power of human pedagogy because human beings do not now know God's essence and stand low in the hierarchy of created intelligences (1.3, nos. 16–17). They make daily mistakes even about sensible things (1.3, no. 18).

Thomas amplifies the warning in 1.4 when he concludes that truths of the second class are fittingly proposed for belief because of the weakness of human speculation. If even naturally accessible truths were left solely for philosophic demonstration, only a few would come to know God, and that after a long time and with much error mixed in (1.4, nos. 23–25). Thomas adapts these arguments from several sources, but especially from a longer list in Maimonides's *Guide of the Perplexed*.[38] Here he uses them to argue that the divine clemency acted therapeutically (*salubriter*) when it revealed naturally accessible truths to human pupils (1.4, no. 26). The converse argument is made in 1.5, where Thomas defends God for having revealed truths that exceed human reason altogether. He argues, first, that nothing will be

---

development, the relation of everything else – but especially of human nature and behavior – to God considered as reality's first principle" (p. 5).

[38] For a schematic analysis of the six texts in which Thomas treats this question, see P. Synave, "La révélation des vérités divines naturelles d'après saint Thomas d'Aquin," in *Mélanges Mandonnet* (Paris: J. Vrin, 1930), 1:327–370, particularly pp. 328–352. Synave concludes that the *Contra gentiles* marks Thomas's mature reformulation of Maimonides's five reasons (pp. 350–351).

desired or sought unless it is known. His examples are the promises of the Christian religion and the moral persuasion of ancient philosophy. The philosophers had to persuade their hearers to leave sensual pleasures for better ones by showing them that there were goods more powerful than the sensory; higher pleasures come with the exercise of active or contemplative virtues. Thomas gives no specific illustration, and there is none to be found in Maimonides's discussion of preparatory disciplines.[39] Thomas summarizes the project of "Gentile" persuasion to philosophic life, the pursuit of participation in the divine. As if to emphasize the Greek origin, Thomas takes three authorities from Aristotle – and then confirms them with two from Scripture.

The concern for justified persuasion leads to a distinction between sober and frivolous conviction (1.6, nos. 36–41), to analogies between divine and human teaching (1.7, no. 43), and to remarks on how useful and delightful it is to pursue what exceeds present capacity (1.8, no. 49). Persuasion stands forth most clearly in the final chapter of the prologue, where Thomas draws a conclusion for his own composition from the two modes of truth. Truths that the labor of reason can reach should be set forth by demonstrative reasons, "through which the adversary can be convinced" (1.9, no. 52). Higher truths cannot be reached by demonstrative reasons. The teacher ought not to try to "convince the adversary" by their means, but only to address or resolve difficulties (1.9, no. 52). Indeed, the only way of "convincing the adversary" in such cases is by the authority of Scripture, divinely confirmed through miracles (1.9, no. 53). For higher truths, the writer should provide verisimilitudes in order to exercise and comfort the faithful, not "to convince adversaries" (1.9, no. 54).[40] Thomas will write first about the truths that faith proffers and reason also investigates, using authorities from both philosophers and saints, "so that these truths might be confirmed and the adversary convinced" (1.9 no. 55). He writes only then about higher truths, in order to "resolve the reasonings of the adversaries" and to

---

[39] Maimonides, *Dux seu director dubitantium aut perplexorum*, ed. Giustiani (Paris, 1520; rptd. Frankfurt: Minerva, 1964), 1.33, fols. 13r–v. On the peculiarities of this Latin version, which reproduces that used by Thomas, see Wolfgang Kluxen, "Literargeschichtliches zum lateinischen Moses Maimonides," *Recherches de théologie ancienne et médiévale* 21 (1954): 32–50, especially pp. 32–35; and Kluxen, "Die Geschichte des Maimonides im lateinischen Abendland . . .," in *Judentum im Mittelalter*, ed. Paul Wilpert (Berlin: de W. Gruyter, 1966), 146–166, especially pp. 156–157.

[40] "Verisimilitudes" reminds the reader that another topic runs underneath this section of the *Contra gentiles*: the use of *rationes convenientiae*, of reasonings from appropriateness or aesthetic fittingness. On these, see now Gilbert Narcisse, *Les raisons de Dieu: Argument de convenance et ésthétique théologique selon saint Thomas d'Aquin et Hans Urs von Balthasar* (Fribourg: Éds. Universitaires, 1997), especially pp. 127–132.

declare the truth of the faith by probable arguments and Scriptural authority (1.9, no. 56).

I have here reproduced Thomas's language, even at the risk of illustrating faulty repetition, in order to show that the phrase "to convince an adversary (or adversaries)" recurs five times in three short paragraphs. Thomas proposes the structure of *Against the Gentiles* in terms of a rhetorical or pedagogical efficacy.[41] Who is to be persuaded and about what? The audience is not the "adversary," not the prospective convert. Thomas wants to show rather how an adversary could be convinced. To whom will he show this? He will show it to believers who are concerned with the persuasion of unbelievers – that is, to all thinking believers whatever. The means by which he shows it to believers – this is a second order of persuasion, a higher rhetoric, by which he teaches those who would persuade. Thomas means to write an anthology of exemplary arguments divided by a distinction in persuasion. This is the conclusion of the prologue and, I think, of the debate over the two truths.

In order to teach believers about what can and cannot be demonstrated, Thomas undertakes a persuasive clarification of the truth of faith. While it teaches believers how to persuade, *Against the Gentiles* also persuades believers to become habituated in the whole of Christian wisdom. Where do we place a work with this kind of rhetorical purpose?

Genre

Genre analysis inevitably risks essentialism. The essences may be deep patterns of representation offered to readers or tidy models for composition offered to writers, but they are essences all the same. The more like an essence genre becomes, the less useful it is as a category for readers and writers. Elaborately defined genres, for example, are invariably subject to

---

[41] R.-A. Gauthier has cautioned that "*convincere*" in these paragraphs means, not persuasion, but the refutation of error. See his remarks in the Leonine edition of *Sent. De anima* (Leonine 45:289*–293*). Gauthier seems to understand persuasion as a sub-rational activity opposed to critique or counter-demonstration. He also pictures it happening in mid-air, outside of particular human minds. By contrast, I take teaching truths to particular human beings as the paradigmatic activity of (fully rational) persuasion. But the debate continues: for two recently on the side of a logical construal of Thomas's project of persuasion, see Rudi A. te Velde, "Natural Reason in the *Summa contra Gentiles*," *Medieval Philosophy and Theology* 4 (1994):42–70, and (in much less detail) Rolf Schönberger, *Thomas von Aquins "Summa contra gentiles"* (Darmstadt: Wissenschaftliche Buchgesellschaft, 2001), notably at pp. 20–21; for one on the side of rational persuasion as concrete pedagogy, Matthew Levering, "Wisdom and the Viability of Thomistic Trinitarian Theology," *The Thomist* 64 (2000):593–618, at pp. 604–613.

innovation, admixture, variation, and rejection of the definition.[42] For that reason, among others, ancient rhetoricians often condemn attempts to systematize genre – as Plato's Socrates silences the rhetorical manualists with irony (*Phaedrus* 271c) and Cicero's Crassus shrugs off their advice as unhelpful for real composition (*De oratore* 1.32.145–146). Their points should be made more sharply for prose didactic works, which were never properly analyzed even by the manuals.

In didactic writing, a "genre" is a fluid cluster of vocabularies, tropes, argumentative logics, discursive structures, and rhetorical purposes. It becomes a useful category for analyzing philosophical or theological rhetoric only when it is conceived as something below a text's surface disposition. Too often "genre" is made to refer to a bewildering range of textual features and responses to them. It is more helpful to pick out in that confusion the features and responses that have to do with persuasive relations, the relations of teaching in view of which a work is properly considered didactic. In looking for other texts that might illuminate the structure of *Against the Gentiles*, I am not hoping to squeeze Thomas's writing into an antecedent kind. For me, asking about a work's genre is not a request to affix a taxonomic label. I want instead an increasingly specific appreciation of a particular text's pedagogical choices.

Thomas's prologue already suggests three generic antecedents in its use of sources. The first is the explicit authority of Aristotle's *Metaphysics*. The second is an implicit reliance on Maimonides's *Guide*. The third is the invocation of Hilary's *On the Trinity*.

At least since Jaeger, modern readers have recognized the connection between the opening of the *Metaphysics* and Aristotle's (lost) *Protreptikos* or exhortation to the study of philosophy.[43] They have thus known, though they have not always appreciated, that the opening of the *Metaphysics* is related to a long line of similarly motivated writings. Exhortations to philosophy were written for a millennium after Isocrates.[44] Extant or partially extant examples are whole Platonic dialogues or sections in them (such as the conversation between Socrates and Clinias in the *Euthydemus*), the (lost) *Protreptic* of Posidonius, Cicero's (lost) *Hortensius*, the 90th of Seneca's *Moral*

---

[42] Rosalie Colie has shown for Renaissance letters just how luxuriant the growth of types can be even in writers enamored of archaizing definitions. See *The Resources of Kind: Genre-Theory in the Renaissance*, ed. Barbara K. Lewalski (Berkeley: University of California Press, 1973).

[43] Werner Jaeger, *Aristotle* (2nd edn., Oxford: Clarendon, 1948), pp. 68–71.

[44] For a recent survey of protreptic in ancient philosophy, see Dirk M. Schenkeveld, "Philosophical Prose," in *Handbook of Classical Rhetoric in the Hellenistic Period (330 B.C. – A.D. 400)*, ed. Stanley E. Porter (Leiden: E. J. Brill, 1997), 195–264, at pp. 204–213.

Letters, Iamblichus's *Protreptic*, and the 24th oration of Themistius. For many of these texts, which share at best a family resemblance, exhortation to the study of philosophy presupposes that undertaking inquiry or moral reform requires persuasion, that this persuasion must be undertaken against competing claims, and that the character of the persuasion foreshadows the character of the inquiries and virtues practiced after it.

Of ancient works that might be called protreptics, Thomas knew only a small fraction. He inherited a number of books by Cicero, but not, of course, the *Hortensius*.[45] He might have gathered some sense of Cicero's protreptic from the remarks on wisdom in *On Duties*[46] or from those on philosophy in the *Tusculan Disputations*.[47] Seneca enjoyed a wide reputation for moral teaching among Latin readers in the twelfth century, but he figures in Thomas chiefly as an authority on how the wise may conquer passion.[48] It might seem more likely that Thomas would have learned of ancient philosophic protreptic through its description and imitation by early Christian writers. Unfortunately, Thomas speaks no judgment about Augustine's praise for Cicero's exhortation, and he does not notice the protreptic structure of early Augustinian works including *Against the Academicians*. He does not advert to the persuasive drama of Boethius's *Consolation*. Perhaps he passes over these allusions to protreptic because of his generally harsh judgment on teaching rhetoric.[49] Augustine mocks his professors of rhetoric, then outdoes them in performing the art. Thomas, who had never been a Gentile, begins already within the Christian practice of persuasion.

Thomas does understand the importance of beginning persuasion rightly. For example, he applies the Ciceronian model of the *exordium* to the opening of Aristotle's *On the Soul* and its remarks on delight in learning.[50] He makes no such explicitly rhetorical approach to the *Metaphysics*, but he

---

[45] Clemens Vansteenkiste, "Cicerone nell'opera di S. Tommaso," *Angelicum* 36 (1959): 343–382, especially pp. 378–379.

[46] For example, *De officiis*, 1.4.13, 1.6.18–19, 1.44. 1.155–156.

[47] For example, *Tusculanarum Quaestionum*, 1.4.7–8, 2.1.1–2.5.13, 3.1.1–3.3.7, 4.1.1–4.3.7, 5.1.1–5.5.11.

[48] See, for example, *Scriptum Sent.* 1.46.4 *arg.* 1, 2.33.2.2 *sed contra* 2, 3.15.2.2 *quaestiuncula* 1 *arg.* 2, and 3.35.2.1 *solutio* 2. There are other references on moral matters (such as the naturalness of death) and on miscellaneous bits of ancient culture. Seneca is cited only once in *De veritate* and then for a definition of "idea" (2.1 *sed contra* 1). He is never cited explicitly in the *Contra gentiles*. I leave aside the question, how far this decrease might signify a different judgment on Seneca and how far it is the result of Thomas's tendency to simplify his handling of *auctoritates* after the *Sentences*-commentary.

[49] There is an interesting exception in the *Contra impugn.* 3.5, where Thomas defends the utility of rhetoric in the setting forth of divine teaching.

[50] *Sent. De anima* 1.1.

does attend to its persuasive purposes. In his exposition of the *Metaphysics*, finished some ten years after *Against the Gentiles*, Thomas paraphrases at length Aristotle's remarks on the desirability of wisdom.[51] More summarily, Thomas says that the purpose of Aristotle's prologue is to show the dignity and end of metaphysics.[52] In works prior to *Against the Gentiles*, Thomas frequently appeals to these same chapters to secure lofty characterizations of wisdom.[53] Thomas sees that Aristotle begins the *Metaphysics* not just with a designation of the study, but with its praise.

Of course, Thomas cannot simply copy any ancient exhortation to philosophy. Philosophic protreptics often presume citizenship in a pagan polity and move from it to the call of philosophy, variously conceived. Thomas's protreptic presumes Christian baptism, membership in the Church, and calls not to initial conversion, but to progress in the practice of Christian wisdom. The protreptic of Christian wisdom is internal to faith, but it is needed for the duration of our pilgrim state. Thomas could find Christian transformations of persuasion to wisdom in many places. There are sapiential exhortations in a number of Latin academic works familiar to the Parisian schools. Consider Hugh of St Victor's *Didascalicon*, Gundissalinus's *On the Division of Philosophy*, and William of Auvergne's *On the Universe*.[54] Among works of mendicant authors prior to 1260, such prologues can be found in Robert Kilwardby's *On the Origin of Sciences* and in Bartholomaeus Anglicus, *On the Properties of Things*.[55] Thomas himself uses such a prologue based on the fourfold division of wisdom for his *Scriptum* on the *Sentences* of Peter Lombard; a similar topic is treated in his inaugural lecture as regent master of theology.[56] Still, these Latin antecedents are no more helpful than

---

[51] *Sent. Metaph.* 1.1, 1.2, 1.3.

[52] *Sent. Metaph.* 1.4.

[53] See, for example, *Super De Trin.* 2.2 *ad* l, 5.1 *ad* 2, 5.4 *sed contra* 3, 6.4 *arg.* 3.

[54] Hugh of St Victor, *Didascalicon* 1.1, ed. C. H. Buttimer (Washington: Catholic University, 1939), p. 4; Dominicus Gundissalinus, *De divisione philosophiae prol.*, ed. Ludwig Baur, BGPhM 4 (Munster: Aschendorff, 1903), pp. 1–19; William of Auvergne, *De universo* 1. *prol.* and *cap.* 1, as in *Opera omnia* (Paris, 1674; rptd. Frankfurt: Minerva, 1963), 1:593–594.

[55] Robert Kilwardby, *De ortu scientiarum* 1, ed. Albert Judy ([London:] British Academy, and Toronto: PIMS, 1976), pp. 9–10; Bartholomaeus Anglicus, *De proprietatibus rerum praef.*, as in *On the Properties of Souls and Bodies = De proprietatibus rerum libri III and IV*, ed. R. James Long (Toronto: PIMS, 1979). Examples of such prefaces after *Contra gent.* would include such diverse works as Gilbert of Tournai's *De modo addiscendi* 2, where it has a specifically pedagogical purpose, and the anonymous *Compendium philosophiae* edited by Michel de Douard (Paris: Broccard, 1936), pp. 121–122.

[56] *Scriptum Sent.* 1. *prol.*, *Princ.* Grabmann approaches the prologue to the *Summa theol.* by comparison with other prologues in the genre, especially that of Robert of Melun; see his *Geschichte der scholastischen Methode* (rptd. Graz: Akad. Druck- u. Verlaganstalt, 1957), 2:340–358, for the text from Robert and Grabmann's comments on it.

allusions to Aristotle's *Metaphysics* when it comes to specifying the structure of persuasion in *Against the Gentiles*. While Thomas may share with his theological predecessors' faith in a revealed wisdom, he construes differently the consequences for teaching that faith. How is his specific notion of persuasion to revealed wisdom connected to his specific compositional structure?

The second genre model behind Thomas's prologue is Maimonides's *Guide*, with which Thomas shares both acceptance of revelation and familiarity with the Aristotelian tradition of wisdom. Are there structural parallels here? The suggestion gains plausibility because Maimonides particularly influenced Latin academic circles through Albert and Albert's students, including Thomas.[57] How then did Thomas regard Maimonides's persuasive project in the *Guide*? Absent explicit comment, only a structural comparison can show whether Thomas is imitating Maimonides.

The *Guide* begins, in Thomas's Latin version, with a blessing on a nameless student and a dedicatory epistle addressed to him. The student is beloved because he so earnestly desires wisdom, though his prior training had not prepared him for its study.[58] Maimonides is writing the *Guide* to complete a hierarchy of learning that has again been interrupted. There follows an invocation compounded from Psalm 143:8 and two verses from Proverbs (8:4, 22:17). Maimonides begins his proemium proper with a plain statement of intention: the *Guide* will explain difficult locutions in the prophets. After stressing that he does not write for all, Maimonides says more fully: "the intention of this whole book is that the law be understood along the way of truth (*per viam veritatis*). For the intention of this book is to purge (*experge-facere*) the mind of the just man . . ." (fol. 2r.). Scripture shows forth its secrets briefly and through the veil of symbols. Any teacher wishing to expound its truth should explain Scriptural symbolism only with deliberate brevity and obscurity. Maimonides ends with specific instructions to the reader, including remarks on seven reasons for the semblance of self-contradiction in a book.

The prologue of *Against the Gentiles* may be said to agree with the opening of the *Guide* when it emphasizes wisdom, expresses desire to complete a hierarchy of knowledge, and subordinates philosophical study to Scripture. *Against the Gentiles* disagrees with the *Guide* crucially on private and public in spiritual teaching. There is no device of dedication to a single student in Thomas, though this was a common topic in earlier Latin prefaces; nor is

---

[57] See Kluxen, "Maimonides und die Hochscholastik," *Philosophisches Jahrbuch* 63 (1955): 151–165, especially pp. 157–165.
[58] Maimonides, *Dux*, fol. 2r.

there any long analysis of esoteric writing. On the contrary, Thomas begins with a Scriptural quotation that emphasizes the public and disputatious character of wisdom. (Thomas's opening citation is also taken from Proverbs 8, though not from Maimonides's verse.) Moreover, Thomas's notion about a double mode of manifesting truth replaces Maimonides's more elaborate and pessimistic hierarchy of minds in relation to divine radiance.[59] Maimonides writes obscurely for the just; Thomas writes publicly for a community of believers.

If Thomas's prelude at once echoes and reverses the project of the *Guide*, a comparison of structures will show even more ambivalence. It is possible to take the first 70 chapters of the *Guide*, to delete most of the short sections that gloss particular Scriptural locutions or passages, and then to match the remaining chapters with some plausibility against the topics of *Against the Gentiles* 1. Thomas's use of remotion to establish negative truths about God's simplicity corresponds to the reiterated emphasis in the *Guide* on God's incomparable incorporeality.[60] More particularly, Thomas's chapters on remotion (14), the metaphysics of divine simplicity (21–22), and divine bodilessness (20, 27) match chapters in *Guide* 1 exactly (respectively, 34 and 57, 56, 54 and 75). Again, Thomas's treatment of the divine names (30–36) corrects a similarly explicit treatment in *Guide* 1 (26, 51–52, 59, and 60–63 for the Scriptural particulars). The main tenets of divine knowledge, divine causality, and divine life are also established in the *Guide*'s first book (respectively 67, 68, and 45).

These correspondences, which can be explained in many other ways than as direct imitation, conceal great differences. The Scriptural hermeneutic of the *Guide* is lacking in Thomas as a compositional motive. Thomas is not concerned in *Against the Gentiles* to gloss the obscurities of Scripture, except incidentally (e.g., 1.42, no. 353b). *Against the Gentiles* does not follow the *Guide*'s order, either in sequence or division of topics. To take the obvious example: Thomas begins *Contra gentiles* 1 by reviewing demonstrations for the existence of God; Maimonides treats the demonstrations only at the beginning of the second book and then in the contexts of divine creation. Again, Maimonides tends to approach attributes of life before those of intellect and causality or will. Thomas's order is just the reverse. Thomas may be

---

[59] See Maimonides, *Dux prol.* fols. 2v–3r. Maimonides offers something like the doctrine of two modes of truth in *Dux*, 1.30, f. 11r. I return to the question of esoteric writing in Thomas below, in chapter 9.

[60] Of course, Maimonides is not the only source of the insistence against anthropomorphism. Thomas knows of it from many patristic sources, such as Augustine *De Trinitate* 1.1.1–3 and John Damascene *De fide orthodoxa* 1.

interested in Maimonides on the divine names, anthropomorphism, or specific details of the Islamic Aristotle, but he does not follow either Maimonides's structure or his general conclusions.

There is one peculiarity in the structure of the *Guide*, however, that points towards the central feature in the structure of *Against the Gentiles*. Maimonides ends with the following sequence of topics: providence, prophecy, the rationality of the Torah, and the implications of God's law for human life. So, too, *Against the Gentiles*, in all of its divisions, ends with depictions of the human good. The structure of *Against the Gentiles*, as of the *Guide*, is not so much a descending deduction as an ascending exhortation. The end of wisdom is an act, an exercise of life. Such wisdom is taught best not in a deduction to the last particular, but by tracing a route leading to the highest end. Thomas's chief rhetorical mode is not apodictic, but epideictic; not demonstrative, but hortatory. His work is a protreptic to the contemplation of God. It ascends to God through world and law in order to practice wisdom as vision. The protreptic of *Against the Gentiles* shares with ancient protreptics the use of persuasive devices as an introduction to the practice of contemplative virtues. It shares with Maimonides the structural suggestion that such virtues are completed beyond the simply natural by means of divine exhortation.

The third genre model for *Against the Gentiles* is *On the Trinity* by Hilary of Poitiers. Thomas invokes Hilary twice. In the first passage, Thomas quotes Hilary dedicating himself chiefly to knowledge and expression of God (1.2, no. 9). Towards the end of the introductory chapters, Hilary is invoked again to confirm the argument that it is both useful and pleasant for believers to reason about truths beyond reach of demonstration (1.8 no. 50). Joseph Wawrykow argues from these passages and others that Hilary's own *On the Trinity* guides the conception and construction of *Against the Gentiles*.[61] Thomas is more likely to be inspired in writing out the duty of wisdom by a patristic author than by Greek protreptic or by Maimonides. Thomas shares with Hilary not only creedal profession, but a tradition of elaborating Christian wisdom in the face of philosophical and heretical error.

Wawrykow's suggestion is a good one, but it raises again questions about Thomas's access to full texts of predecessor works. In both passages, Thomas turns to Hilary by a kind of word association. In the first, the word *officium* (office, duty) supplies an explicit link; in the second, it is the notion of

---

[61] Joseph Wawrykow, "The *Summa contra Gentiles* Reconsidered: On the Contribution of the *De Trinitate* of Hilary of Poitiers," *The Thomist* 58 (1994): 617–634.

presuming to comprehend the divine. Hilary appears, in other words, as the "author" of *sententiae* or excerpts already in circulation and already connected to certain topics, either literally (in an anthology) or virtually (by habit of memory). In thirteenth-century anthologies of patristic passages, the attempt to improve upon the sources by topical or indexical arrangement is balanced by the insistence on the importance of full citations and comparison with the original context.[62] As we have seen, and precisely on exegetical principle, Thomas prefers to know something of context whenever he deals with an authority. Still he is a medieval master, and he depends on quick access to an enormous range of usable text fragments. The suspicion that Hilary may be one of these is reinforced when the reader notices that *On the Trinity* is cited only one other time in the whole of *Against the Gentiles*, and then to support the notion that being is not an accident in God (1.22, no. 212). Is Hilary the inspiration for Thomas's structure or the remote source of a few loci useful for confirming discrete notions?

If Thomas had studied *On the Trinity* whole, he might have found it both interesting and unhelpful for his experiment in protreptic construction. Hilary declares his intentions and explains his structure in a prologue that adheres closely to Roman rhetorical models.[63] Hilary offers a symbolic autobiography that narrates his conversion from folly towards knowledge of God (1.1–14). God is disclosed progressively in creation and its philosophy, in the Old Law, and then decisively in the New. The stages of the narrative are fixed, formulaic, but the voice speaks as if in intimate autobiography.[64] Hilary tells of his own pedagogy through reflection on society and the discovery of a sequence of texts: Exodus 3:14, Wisdom 13:15, the opening of the Gospel according to John, and Paul in Colossians 2. There is no such autobiography in *Against the Gentiles*, because there was no such progressive discovery of Christianity in Thomas's life. The main conceit of Hilary's prologue is one that Thomas cannot use. Thomas notes that he lacks the familiarity with paganism possessed by some of the patristic writers. He means in part that he did not have their experience of conversion to Christianity.

After the prologue, Hilary turns from his curriculum of wisdom to the

---

[62] M. A. and R. H. Rouse, "Florilegia of Patristic Texts," in *Les genres littéraires dans les sources théologiques et philosophiques médiévales: Définition, critique, exploitation* . . . (Louvain-la-Neuve: Université catholique de Louvain, 1982), 170–176.

[63] Hilary of Poitiers, *De Trinitate* 1, ed. P. Smulders, Corpus Christianorum Series Latina 62 (Turnhout: Brepols, 1979). Smulders's edition of the first book is reprinted with a French translation and excellent notes by G. Pelland in *Hilaire de Poitiers: La Trinité*, ed. Michael Figura et al., vol. 1, Sources Chrétiennes no. 443 (Paris: Éds. du Cerf, 1999), 202–273.

[64] Contemporary readers are likely to recognize this narrative pattern from its later reworking in Augustine's *Confessions*, but Hilary could have learned it already in Lactantius.

upsurge of heresies that deny the Trinity (1.15–19). He certainly agrees with Thomas on the importance of refuting dangerous errors. He agrees as well in wanting to lay out a work on the Trinity that persuades the reader to undertake a fluent ascent (1.20). Of course, Hilary's book is only about the Trinity. Its exposition begins with divine generation – that is, at the point Thomas reaches only in *Against the Gentiles* 4.2. If Hilary (among others) could offer Thomas some confirming sayings, an admonition to refute error, and an ideal of compositional unity, he could not help at all with an experiment in a comprehensive curriculum for Christian wisdom.

Thomas experimented with a new kind of structure. The structure's intention – not to say, its success – can be read off many features in the finished work beyond the prologue.

Protreptic Structure

If *Against the Gentiles* is a protreptic, it ought to be possible to find in it the structures and devices of persuasion to an end.[65] The most obvious persuasive structure is the ascent to the human good in 3.1–63. The argument rises from a general assertion of teleological order (1–16), through the thesis that God is the end of all creatures and of intellectual substances particularly (17–26), to a comparison of contemplation with all other possible claimants to human happiness (27–47). Thomas ends the sequence by representing the contemplation of God in beatitude, which is both heaven and the fulfillment of philosophic longing for unfettered contemplation (48–63; compare 41–44).

The ascent combines features from classical and Christian protreptic. One feature is the *synkrisis* or comparison of wisdom with alternate goods (27–36). Thomas has already remarked that philosophers must lure their hearers away from other pleasures (1.5, no. 29c). So Thomas rules out claims that happiness consists in the exercise of political virtues or liberal arts – just as Greek philosophers had to keep their hearers from succumbing to the rival pedagogies of sophists or poets. Thomas offers, in second place, a

---

[65] This claim has already been made by Guy H. Allard, "Le 'Contra Gentiles' et le modèle rhétorique," *Laval Théologique et Philosophique* 30 (1974): 237–250. Allard compares the structure in Thomas with the Ciceronian paradigms for deliberative discourse. I differ from Allard both in regard to the importance of any particular rhetorical paradigm and in his emphasis on the political. But it may be that I rightly belong alongside Allard in any typology of views on the *Contra gent.*; see, for example, Helmut Hoping, *Weisheit als Wissen des Ursprungs: Philosophie und Theologie in der "Summa contra gentiles" des Thomas von Aquin* (Freiburg: Herder, 1997), pp. 45–48.

criticism of alternative descriptions of wisdom (41–44). This, too, is a kind of *synkrisis*, and it takes the place in Greek philosophy of the review of rival schools. Then Thomas adds, in third place, an evocation of the good to be attained in beatitude. He writes three lyrical chapters to show that the vision of God makes human beings eternal participants in divine life (61–62), even as it fulfills their every desire for knowledge, virtue, honor, fame, wealth, pleasure, immortality, and community (3.63, nos. 2,378–2,383). Thomas ends the peroration by juxtaposing Aristotelian and Scriptural praises of wisdom, so that the reader might see the one perfected in the other (3.63, no. 2,383).

Against the Gentiles 3 does not stop with that evocation – and it is important that it does not do so. Thomas turns with the briefest of connecting passages to a long consideration of providence. Teaching about providence is required to assure the reader that the distant end of contemplation, which so little resembles human life here, is within the power of the cosmic ruler. God the end is also God the "governor" or "ruler" of the means.[66] God's governance is not coercive. The second thesis of the treatment of providence is that human agents are free from the coercion of celestial bodies (84–87) and separate substances (88–89); they may follow God without fearing fortune or fate (91–92). At much greater length, Thomas analyzes divine rule over intellectual creatures (111–113) in order to show the necessity for God's teaching (114–129) and the usefulness of God's counsels (130–139). The teaching on providence culminates in the argument that humans need divine grace to attain the end that has been proposed (147–163). *Against the Gentiles* 3 ends with a chapter on election and reprobation that emphasizes human freedom under or within God's glory. The last line of the books is a doxology from *Romans* 11:35–36. It seals the teaching that the human goal cannot be reached without God's help.

The evidently hortatory structure of Book 3 finds echoes both earlier and later in *Against the Gentiles*. At the end of the prologue to the whole work, Thomas writes that the first thing to be demonstrated is God's existence, "without which every consideration of divine things is removed" (1.9, no. 58). The last demonstrative arguments conclude that there is some being "by whose providence the world is governed" (1.13, no. 115). The existence of God is not a fact only, but a force over human life. When he turns to God's perfection, Thomas must treat again of the divine names, in order

---

[66] Thomas says exactly this in his prologue to the exposition of Job, which is contemporary with *Contra gent.* 2–3; see Weisheipl, *Friar Thomas*, p. 368, no. 25, and Torrell, *Initiation*, p. 494. Thomas writes that the denial of providence is the destruction of all virtue and the fostering of vice; see *Expos. Iob prol.* (Leonine *Opera omnia* 26, ll. 41–48).

to secure resemblance between God and creatures (28–36). More specifically, he must show that his protreptic speaking about God is not "in vain"
(1.36, no. 301). It is appropriate to a protreptic that it should center on
God's understanding, willing, and living. God's understanding makes God
the final end for intellectual creatures; God's willing grounds providence;
God's life is the activity to which human beings are called. The last section
of Book 1 concerns the divine life (97–102); the last chapter argues that
God's beatitude exceeds every other beatitude (1.102). It rejects false happiness and adds a doxology: "To the one who is singularly blessed be honor
and glory unto ages of ages" (1.102, no. 850).

Against the Gentiles 2 aids the protreptic by establishing God's causality
over creation and humankind's indispensable place in the hierarchy of intelligences. The preface promises as much. Thomas supplies four arguments to
justify considering creatures within Christian wisdom: creatures imitate
divine wisdom and so produce wonder and reflection (2.2, no. 859). Studying them leads to fear of God and reverence (2.2, no. 860). It kindles divine
love (2.2, no. 861). Indeed, meditating on creatures produces a likeness of
divine wisdom (2.2, no. 862). Knowing creatures also helps destroy errors
that prevent contemplative ascent to God – by deifying matter, by exagger-
ating creatures, by exalting necessity, by debasing human teleology (2.3,
nos. 865–868). Each of these four reasons is directly connected to the protreptic. Each supposes that *Against the Gentiles* means to bring right order to
active pursuit of the divine. The considerations proposed hasten pursuit; the
errors rejected would prevent it. The protreptic purpose is confirmed in the
part's last section, which offers another doxology to the divine mind (2.101,
no. 1,860). In the parts leading up to the third, then, Thomas frequently
describes persuasion towards the highest good as a gracious gift from its possessor.

The order of *Against the Gentiles* 4 is often set out rather prosaically: the
Trinity (2–26), the Incarnation (27–55), the sacraments (56–78), and the final
resurrection together with the last judgment (79–97). Notice these structural
peculiarities. The Trinity is introduced under the rubric of "generation" in
God. Thomas shows how far God's life can be compared to that of other
living things (4.2, no. 3,354c; compare 4.26, no. 3,629, "in living things").
The passage ends by reiterating the likeness of human thought to the Trinitarian processions (4.26, nos. 3,631–3,632). The treatment of the Incarnation
ends with the question of its appropriateness or *convenientia* (4.53–55).[67] The
positive arguments assert that God's incarnation is the most effective help

---

[67] See the opposite order in *Summa theol.* 3, where the treatment of *convenientia* (q. 1) pre-
cedes the treatment of the manner of the Incarnation (qq. 2–19).

towards beatitude (beginning in 4.54, no. 3,923). The sacraments appear as applications and manifestations of Christ's role in human healing (4.56, no. 3,962). The final sacrament to be treated is matrimony, which extends through time the human search for the good (4.78, nos. 4,119, 3,124). The resurrection and the last judgment are concerned quite literally with the end of human life – indeed, of human history. Although such topics frequently appear at the end of comprehensive theological works, Thomas here not only designates human life after resurrection, he describes it (82–88). Some of his hypotheses may seem extraordinary, but they aim to convince the reader that human desire will be satisfied in the city of glory (see especially 4.86). The last chapter of the entire work begins with these words, "Thus when the last judgment has taken place, human nature will be constituted completely in its end" (4.97, no. 4,285). *Against the Gentiles* ends with the divine proclamation of eternal joy and exultation (4.97, no. 4,292).

It would be possible – indeed, necessary for a satisfying argument – to consider Thomas's rhetorical structure in greater detail and to show how far other reasons, such as traditional arrangement, might account for some of these features. Let me enunciate that large task and then suggest how a reader could begin to discover the protreptic character of *Against the Gentiles* at closer range, in its details – for example, in locutions that introduce authorities, in arrangements of multiple arguments for a single point, and in choices about which topics will be treated at length.

Thomas's phrases or locutions for introducing Scriptural authorities were mentioned by Mulard in the debate over De Broglie. Mulard's point was that they separated philosophical argument from theological authority.[68] The locutions are actually more complicated, at least before the fourth part, where they begin to sound more like rubrics for proof texts in doctrinal controversy. In the first three Books, the locutions clearly do not introduce Scriptural texts as syllogistic premises for philosophic demonstration. Their steady repetition of "also" shows that the citations they introduce are supplements to the arguments.[69] More interesting are the verbs: the authority of Scripture or of the faith is said to "confirm," "give testimony," "agree" or "harmonize," "profess," "confess," "commemorate," "attest," "show," "proffer," and "protest."[70] The

---

[68] Mulard, "Désir naturel," p. 8.

[69] See 1.14 (no. 119), 39 (323), 44 (380), 50 (428), 67 (566).

[70] In Book 1, for confirmation, see 14 (no. 199), 39 (323), 47 (402), 60 (505), 65 (539), 68 (574), 75 (646), 78 (666), 91 (764), 97 (815); for testimony, 15 (126), 43 (370), 55 (464), 57 (484), 66 (554); for agreement, 20 (188); for harmony, 58 (493), 70 (610); for profession, 22 (212); for confession, 44 (380), 72 (626); for teaching, 50 (428); for commemoration, 29 (271), 91 (765); for attestation, 49 (417); for showing, 67 (566); for proffering, 82 (698); and for protesting, 100 (835).

verbs suggest that citations add both evidence and emphasis. They add more evidence, because the Scripture already counts as true for the Christian reader. They supply emphasis, because the Scripture is supremely authoritative and beautifully moving. The most interesting locutions imply a causal connection: Scripture says something or faith holds something *because* of the reasons enunciated in the chapter.[71] Here the reader can see the protreptic connection between rational and authoritative persuasion. She has been led through a series of arguments; she has also been reminded that the same doctrine is found in the authorities of her faith. The complete persuasion to wisdom is accomplished when the reader grasps that the intelligibility of argument leads into the intelligibility of Scripture. The reasons of rational pedagogy pass over into the motives of Scripture.

A reader can see protreptic detail as well in the sequence of arguments. *Against the Gentiles* is remarkable for not conforming to the patterns of an academic dispute or commentary. In some sections, especially technical ones, Thomas falls back on the devices of the *quaestio*.[72] Much more rarely does he carry out a proper *lectio* (as in 2.61, 2.78). The typical chapter in *Against the Gentiles* has a short introduction or enunciation followed by a series of arguments that ends with confirming authorities or historical specifications or both. The multiple arguments are not interdependent. They can be grouped around certain basic premises, but they are better grasped as steps towards a cumulative persuasive effect. To show that the same conclusion can be derived from diverse premises makes it more plausible. Again, readers who are not convinced by one argument may be convinced by another. Thomas sometimes varies his starting points in the hope of casting a wider argumentative net. Finally, the last arguments in a chapter are sometimes more comprehensive or penetrating than the first.

A single passage can illustrate these persuasive structures. In 2.16, Thomas offers 12 arguments for creation *ex nihilo*, from no pre-existing matter. The first argument depends on a rule against regression in natural causes (no. 933); the second through the fifth invoke some principle of universality in effect and cause (nos. 934–937); the sixth through the ninth stress disanalogies or disproportions between matter and divine creation (nos. 938–941); the tenth

---

[71] "Et inde est quod . . ." (1.29, no. 271); "hinc est quod . . ." (1.37, no. 308; 40, no. 328; 41, no. 334; 56, no. 472; 61, no. 514; 99, no. 827); "propter quod dicitur . . ." (1.38, no. 315).
[72] See especially 1.10–11, 2.61/69, 2.74–75, 2.80–81, 2.88–89, 3.5–6, 3.8–9, 3.54, 3.68, 3.108–109, 3.131/134, 3.132/135, 3.136–137, 4.4.9, 4.10, 4.16/23, 4.25, 4.40/49, 4.51–52, 4.53–55, 4.62–68, 4.80–81. Note the preponderance of such sections in the fourth Book. This is due to the procedural limitation of answering objections against the mysteries of faith, as in 1.9, no. 56.

and eleventh argue from God as first being (nos. 942–943). One might also say that the principles are: no regression (no. 933), universality of causation (nos. 934–935), peculiarities in the causation of being (nos. 936–937), peculiarities in the reception of effects by matter (nos. 938–940), and asymmetrical relationships (nos. 941–943). On either account, there is a movement in the chapter from physical causality through its expansions and distensions to basic ontological relations. Note too that the arguments are designed to address readers of the *Physics*, the *Metaphysics* of both Aristotle and Avicenna, and the *Book of Causes*.

The third and last detail in which a reader can recognize protreptic structure is the selection of topics for fuller treatment. Principles of selection appear on the surface of Thomas's other works. In the *Scriptum* on the *Sentences*, selection is determined remotely by the Lombard's text and directly by the tradition of commentary on it. In the large *Summa*, by contrast, Thomas announces that the principle of selection is pedagogical concern for beginners. What is the equivalent principle of economy in *Against the Gentiles*? The missionary hypothesis would explain its selection of topics by pointing to the confrontation with Islam. Gorce would explain it as a reaction to the "Latin Averroists." In fact, the selection is motivated by the aim of persuasion to the practice of Christian wisdom. The topics that are treated extensively and technically bear directly on persuasion to the highest good.

Thomas evidently chooses to concentrate in *Against the Gentiles* 2 on refuting false views about the human intellect (for example, 2.59–62, 73–78). Thomas treats these views extensively not out of a technician's delight in detail, or from love of contention, but because human participation in the highest good depends on the individuality of intellects. A fashionable denial of individuality requires extensive correction if readers are not to be prevented in advance from accepting protreptic persuasion. The conclusion of the arguments against separation or unity of intellects serves as a premise in the first, syllogistic proof for human immortality (2.70, no. 1,598). A similar reading can be given to the technical analysis of the beatific vision (3.51–60). Coming at the end of the ascent to the highest good, these chapters carry great weight. They must show that God can be contemplated directly, but only by divine gift – otherwise the rest of Book 3 will be beside the point. If there is no direct contemplation, Thomas's protreptic has no end. If there is no need for grace, the protreptic is in no way Christian. Similar reasoning directs Thomas's technical emphasis on divine cognition of singulars (1.63–71), on human freedom from creaturely determination (3.84–88), and so on.

In three kinds of detail, then, *Against the Gentiles* shows protreptic motivation. It uses authorities, arranges arguments, and chooses technical disputes in order to persuade readers towards full Christian wisdom. This wisdom requires the exercise of Christian virtues, both acquired and infused. Persuasion to the practice of a virtue will be sterile unless it can offer some opportunity for enacting it. For Aristotle, famously, virtues, including intellectual ones, are acquired by practice. The best Aristotelian protreptic would not only exhort, but engage; it would speak about the virtues to be acquired while it provided exemplary occasions on which to imitate them. Here, too, Thomas succeeds in constructing *Against the Gentiles*. The work presents the virtues of Christian wisdom above all by requiring that its readers practice them – in following its structures, learning its locutions, discovering the order of its arguments, and understanding its technical digressions. Perhaps most helpfully, *Against the Gentiles* applies in hundreds of particular arguments drawn from dozens of predecessor texts the intelligible principles that are the seeds of speculative virtue. Its protreptic structure is not only an exordium to wisdom, but a school for its practice – not least in the proper handling of authorities.

Chapter Six

The *Summa of Theology* as Moral Formation

One of Leonard Boyle's most elegant arguments concerns the origin of the marginal texts in manuscript 95 of Lincoln College, Oxford.[1] He shows that the texts constitute a report of Thomas's second or Roman commentary on the *Sentences*. This commentary, composed by Thomas in Rome during 1265–1266, treats some topics from the Lombard's first book.[2] Thomas broke off writing it in order to invent the *Summa of Theology*. Still, the Roman *Lectura* survived: an early copy of it is mentioned by Ptolemy of Lucca. Since it was not included in the first catalogues of Thomas's works, it played no role in the history of Thomism. It has remained hidden for seven centuries.

We readers of Thomas, however grateful and delighted we are by its discovery, must now pose a candid question that cannot be solved by codices alone. Does this new text show itself to have been worth the wait? I can put the question most pointedly in this form. We had before the identification of the Lincoln College text a Thomist corpus of more than eight and a half million words, mostly unread. To hear that a few 10,000s more have now been identified might seem ambiguous news, as if it were announced that fragments of a 92nd novel by Balzac had just come to light. By Boyle's own account, the new text is not strikingly early or late. It does not take up subjects elsewhere neglected by its author, nor does it offer some secret or scandalous teaching. It is a middle text in every respect. What, then, can we learn from it? We can learn a great deal, and not only about Thomas's thoughts on the particular topics it treats. The opening section of the

---

[1] Leonard E. Boyle, "'Alia lectura fratris Thome,'" *Mediaeval Studies* 45 (1983): 418–429. Boyle's essay reconsiders and supplements the evidence adduced in H.-F. Dondaine, "'Alia lectura fratris Thomae'? (*Super I Sent.*)," *Mediaeval Studies* 42 (1980): 308–336.

[2] For the circumstances of its composition, see Boyle throughout, and Weisheipl, *Friar Thomas*, 216–217, with the addenda on 471.

Roman *Lectura* clarifies Thomas's authorship as a whole, but especially at its culmination in the *Summa of Theology*.

The Roman *Lectura* and the Invention of the *Summa*

What can be discovered about the origin of Thomas Aquinas's *Summa of Theology* suggests that it was a masterful improvisation in the face of very Dominican circumstances for the teaching of Christian theology. In June of 1259, at the age of 34 or 35, Thomas left Paris to attend the general chapter of Dominicans at Valenciennes, where he served as a member of a commission working on the promotion of studies within the order. In the months after that chapter meeting, and perhaps in response to it, Thomas returned to his ecclesiastical home, the "Roman" or Italian province of the Dominican order.[3] He had behind him a brilliant if occasionally controversial career as a student and regent master of theology in the University of Paris, but his work in Italy would be within the houses of his order and not at a university. Modern readers tend to forget this institutional setting. They picture Thomas teaching always in the streets of Paris, in the midst of the university and its turmoils. He spent more time as a licensed teacher outside the university, in houses of religious formation. After some five or six years of such service, in September of 1265, Thomas was assigned to open a house of studies for Dominicans in Rome – perhaps as a result of his own lobbying.[4] There was no university in the city and no previous academic establishment for the Dominicans. The new venture may have been the province's attempt to create a middle step between its conventual schools and the order's international houses of study (*studia*). The Roman school looks to have been the first attempt anywhere for an intermediate Dominican school of theology. It was centered on the theologian Thomas as *lector* or teacher. The way was open for his pedagogical invention. What he invented was a reform of Dominican theological education.

---

[3]   See the summary chronology in Torrell, *Initiation*, p. 480. The exact date of Thomas's departure from Paris and his exact whereabouts in the surrounding months are still uncertain (Torrell, pp. 145–148).

[4]   See Leonard E. Boyle, *Setting of the* Summa theologiae, pp. 9–12; Torrell, *Initiation*, pp. 207–211; M. Michèle Mulchahey, *"First the Bow is Bent in Study . . ."*: Dominican Education *before 1350* (Toronto: PIMS, 1998), pp. 278–306. The arguments against Boyle's thesis put by Jenkins seem to me to rely too much on contemporary evaluations of the work's scope or difficulty – as on an over-reading of the importance to it of Aristotelian paradigms of *scientia*. See John I. Jenkins, *Knowledge and Faith in Thomas Aquinas* (Cambridge: Cambridge University Press, 1997), especially pp. 79–97.

The prevailing theology curriculum in Dominican houses relied on Scripture and books of Scriptural history, of course, but also on collections of texts for sacramental doctrine, manuals of the moral life, and some reference works of canon law and the church Fathers. Thomas had other plans at Rome from the start. During his first year, he tried revising his earlier Parisian commentary on the *Sentences* of Peter Lombard. He began not with the fourth Book, often used by Dominicans for teaching on the sacraments, but with the first, with its doctrine on God as unity and trinity. After revising and supplementing parts of the first Book, Thomas set the project aside. He turned instead to what we call the *Summa*,[5] which begins much as the Lombard's *Sentences* does, but goes on to a more rigorously ordered consideration of the whole of theology. In short, the evidence we have from Thomas's writing at Rome suggests that his main effort was directed at expanding the pastoral and practical curriculum of Dominican houses by placing it within the frame of the whole of theology. The frame is the *Summa*. It is a frame meant to reform the Dominican tendency to separate moral manuals from theological or Scriptural treatises.

To view the *Summa* as Thomas's remedy for a defect of Dominican education in no way reduces it.[6] I have already argued that Thomas had a habit of conceiving occasions for writing in the widest terms. My two best examples come from the period immediately before his assignment to Rome. So if Thomas answered in Rome the needs of his Dominican students or the mandate of his provincial chapter, that does not mean that he gave them what they expected – or that the work he wrote has no wider usefulness.

There are other complications in my telling of the story. I have so far interchanged Thomas's writing with Thomas's teaching. They should be distinguished. The *Summa* was the centerpiece of Thomas's effort to counteract the neglect of studies often lamented by his provincial chapter, but the text we have of it is not the script or the record of what Thomas said in the Roman *studium*. It has been objected that if Thomas actually taught the first 40-odd questions of the *Summa*, he would have covered much of the same ground during his second year that he had already covered in

---

[5]   It is important to remember that this most familiar title may well not be Thomas's own. See the variety of early testimonies in Angelus Walz, "De genuino titulo *Summae theologiae*," *Angelicum* 18 (1941): 142–151. Nothing can be deduced about Thomas's work from speculations as to what a "*summa*" is supposed to be.

[6]   For a review of the historical evidence and an argument about its pertinence to the *Summa*, see Mark F. Johnson, "Aquinas's *Summa theologiae* as Pedagogy," in *Medieval Education*, eds. Ronald Begley and Joseph W. Koterski (Bronx, NY: Fordham University Press, 2005), pp. 133–142.

"reading" the first book of the *Sentences*.[7] But there are other issues here, more interesting ones. What exactly would it mean to say that Thomas "taught" a text like *Summa* 1 to his students in Rome, whether *in toto* or from q. 45 on? We cannot really imagine him conducting each article before the students as a separate *disputatio*. Thomas did conduct a number of disputes at Rome.[8] They look like his other disputed questions – and unlike the articles of the *Summa*, which are much simpler and more tightly sequenced. The *Summa's* articles form part of a structure promised in its main lines from the beginning – and not in the terms used to justify the stringing together of disputed questions.

If Thomas did not dispute the articles of *Summa* 1 at Rome, how might he have taught them? Do we imagine Thomas writing out sections and then reading them aloud? Or Thomas giving an oral summary that was copied down by his assistants and then redacted into finished form? Absent direct archival or anecdotal evidence, we can only reason from the texts. The articles of the *Summa* are unlike not only the questions Thomas disputed at Rome, but also both the notes of the Roman "reading" of the *Sentences* or the first redaction of the expositions of Paul and the expositions of Pseudo-Dionysius that may also have been written in Rome. To find a structural parallel to the *Summa*, we must go back a few years. The articles in the *Summa* most resemble those chapters of *Against the Gentiles* written as condensed disputes, except that the *Summa's* articles are more condensed still and more rigorously ordered. There is no evidence that Thomas taught *Against the Gentiles* verbatim to anyone. The resemblance suggests that he did not teach the *Summa* verbatim either. *Against the Gentiles* is, I have already argued, an ideal pattern of persuasion to Christian wisdom. The *Summa* is also an ideal pattern, though different in conception and end.

The *Summa* is not a transcript of Thomas's teaching nor is it a teacher's script for immediate classroom use. It is a single sequence of illustrative topics and typical arguments. It is not meant to "prep" the student for higher study, but to lead the student from the beginning of theology to its end along a single inquiry. The sequence is ideal in so far as it is exemplary – and in two senses. First, the *Summa* does not pretend to be comprehensive and, indeed, invites particular extensions or applications. Second, the *Summa's* ordering of texts, terms, and argument is non-exclusive in the way that Christian wisdom is. It offers itself with a kind of universality to all "beginners" in "Christian religion." Perhaps that is why Thomas chose not

---

[7]   Torrell, *Initiation*, pp. 233–234; compare Mulchahey, *"First the Bow,"* p. 294.

[8]   Mulchahey, *"First the Bow,"* p. 303, provides a summary of her own conjectures about the debates. Everyone would agree at least to the disputation of the 83 articles *De potentia*.

to be more explicitly Dominican in his prologue, his rhetoric, and his acknowledged sources.

The *Summa* is not so much the report of Thomas's classroom performance or his script for future teachers as it is the pattern for an ideal pedagogy, a pedagogy for middle learners in a vowed community of Christian pastors. When enriched by adaptation to a particular classroom, the pedagogy teaches the place of moral learning within theology in the only way anyone can (on Thomas's account of teaching). Learners are invited to study morals through a clarifying reminder of arguments about God as creator and governor; they are habituated into moral knowledge not only through practice with its disputative elements, but through dialectical narration of patterns for lived virtues and ways of life; and they are then shown, in the great disclosure at the turn from the second part to the third, that the power moving their inquiry back to God has been the power of their incarnate Lord. When Thomas began to write the program of the *Summa* at his Roman *studium*, and however exactly he adapted or amplified it in his own daily teaching, he invented it as a curricular ideal, not as a daily lesson plan. It is a strictly unified curricular ideal meant to guide moral teaching in various Dominican communities or other Christian schools. The teaching is to be a single, continuous solicitation to acquire and exercise the habit of theology in all of its parts.[9]

Reading the *Lectura* into the Corpus

Having located the *Lectura* with regard to the *Summa* and then contrasted them sharply, we can still learn something by comparing the *Lectura* with the opening of the *Summa* and other parallels in Thomas's corpus. Comparisons are needed at three levels: textual authorities and staple arguments, topical order, and pedagogical project. The interrelations of the texts are

[9]   Much debate on the structure of the *Summa* has been preoccupied by Chenu's suggestion about a neo-Platonic pattern of *exitus-reditus*, of outpouring from the divine and return to it. For a recent (and schematic) summary of positions around this suggestion, see Brian Johnstone, "The Debate on the Structure of the *Summa Theologiae*," in *Aquinas as Authority*, ed. Paul van Geest, Harm Goris, and Carlo Leget (Leuven: Peters, 2002), pp. 187–200. There are a number of problems with Chenu's suggestion, but the most important is that it eclipses the internal structure of *Summa theol.* 2, which is, I have been arguing, the major achievement in Thomas's writing. See, for example, the otherwise astute description of the *Summa*'s structure in Otto Hermann Pesch, *Thomas von Aquin: Grenze und Grösse mittelalterlicher Theologie – Eine Einführung* (Mainz: Matthias-Grünewald, 1988), pp. 387–400.

more complicated and more simultaneous than the separation of three levels would suggest, but there is no other way to lay out a reading discursively than by making artificial divisions.

The level of *textual authorities* and staple arguments is often one of the most revealing in Thomas. It registers not only remarkable persistences or surprising turns in the authorities used, but also the developing desire for selection and simplification. Unfortunately, the usual analysis of authorities cannot be carried out on this portion of the Roman *Lectura*. The text is not fully supplied with citations and many arguments or allusions are merely indicated, as if by gesture. Thomas would have polished the whole, particularly by filling in his footnotes, if he had prepared it for publication. You can see this by noticing points at which the Roman *Lectura* invokes a principle that is more fully cited in one of the parallel texts. So, for example, the *Lectura* offers an argument against sacred doctrine being a properly constituted body of knowledge: "Moreover, no science is of particulars, etc."[10] The reference is clearly to the argument in the Parisian *Scriptum*: "No science is of particulars, according to the Philosopher, *Posterior Analytics* 1. But in sacred Scripture particular deeds of particular men are described . . . Therefore it is not a science."[11] In its finished form, the *Lectura* would presumably have given us the argument and an authority. Even where the *Lectura* mentions an authority, it does so less explicitly than parallel texts: "Boethius" replaces "Boethius in the first book of *On the Trinity*," and so on.[12] On the other hand, maxims pass in and out of anonymity from one text to another. The Roman *Lectura* says: "As the Philosopher says, the subject of a science is that of which the passions and parts are sought."[13] In the exposition of Boethius, the same maxim is used in the same way, but without the citation.[14] It is thus impossible to carry out a comparison of authorities and arguments as if the Roman *Lectura* were a finished text or as if all authorities were explicit.

We can notice the persistence of arguments and terminologies from one Thomist text to the other. In the first two articles of the Roman *Lectura*, for example, every *argumentum* or *sed contra* has an exact precedent in the two

[10] *Lectura Sent. prol.* 1.2, as in Oxford, Lincoln College MS 95 fol. 4ra: "Preterea, nulla scientia est de particularibus etc." For subsequent references I will simply cite the apparent textual divisions and then the foliation of this MS.

[11] *Scriptum Sent.* 1. *prol.* 1.3.2 *arg.* 1 (Mandonnet and Moos 1: 11).

[12] For the Boethius, compare *Scriptum Sent. prol.* 1.4 *arg.* 1 *contra* and *Scriptum Sent. prol.* 3 *arg.* 4.

[13] *Scriptum Sent. prol.* 2 *arg.* 2 (fol. 4va): "Preterea, sicut dicit Philosophus, subiectum scientie est cuius queruntur passiones et partes."

[14] *Super De Trin.* 2.2 *arg.* 3.

earlier texts.[15] Many of them are not peculiar to Thomas; they can be found in the writings of his teachers and colleagues. Other textual continuities are peculiar to Thomas. The Roman *Lectura* mentions that a certain Simonides taught that we ought not to busy ourselves about divine things that are too high for us. The association of this doctrine with Simonides is Thomas's own addition to an Aristotelian text.[16] Again, the *Lectura*'s defense of the use of philosophical authorities in expounding Scripture seems almost a rearrangement of selected points from Thomas's commentary on Boethius.[17]

A second comparison occurs at the level of *topical order*, the sequence within which received topics are disposed and new topics invented. Precisely because of the strong continuities between Thomas's earlier texts and the *Lectura*, exact comparisons of topical orders can be made. They are quite revealing. If we look backward from the first question of the *Summa*, the Roman *Lectura* marks the point at which Thomas settled for himself the right order for raising issues about theological knowledge. He then used it in the *Summa* to organize all of the issues that had appeared in the previous treatments.

The orders adopted in the *Scriptum* and the commentary on *On the Trinity* are variously inappropriate. The *Scriptum* begins rightly by asking whether some study beyond philosophy is necessary, but it then moves to details of the doctrine of the Trinity before settling theology's character as knowledge. We ask whether it is one or many and whether it is practical or speculative before we know whether it is science.[18] The *Scriptum* further separates the question whether the needed teaching is (like) a science from the question what its subject might be.[19] Again, the *Scriptum* runs together under a single query about the mode of teaching such issues as the use of philosophical argument and the senses of Scripture.[20]

The commentary on Boethius does somewhat better. It takes as heading "the manifestation of divine cognition" in order to treat four issues: whether it is permitted to investigate divine things; whether there can be science about them; whether one can use philosophical reasonings in this science;

---

[15] Thus, *Lect. Sent. prol.* 1 *arg.* 1 = *Scriptum Sent. prol.* 1.3.2 *arg.* 2 and *Super De Trin.* 2.2 *arg.* 5; *Lect. Sent.* 1 *arg.* 2 = *Scriptum Sent. prol.* 1.3.2 *arg.* 1; *Lect. Sent. prol.* 1 *arg.* 3 = *Scriptum Sent. prol.* 1.1 *arg.* 1; *Lect. Sent. prol.* 1 *arg.* 4 = *Scriptum Sent. prol.* 1.2 *arg.* 1; *Lect. Sent. prol.* 1 *sc* = *De Trin.* 2.2 *sc* 1; *Lect. Sent. prol.* 2 *arg.* 1 = *Scriptum Sent. prol.* 1.2 *arg.* 1; *Lect. Sent. prol.* 2 *arg.* 2 = *De Trin.* 2.2 *arg.* 3; *Lect. Sent. prol.* 2 *arg.* 3 = *De Trin.* 2.3 *corp.*; *Lect. Sent. prol.* 2 *arg.* 4 = *Scriptum Sent. prol.* 1.4 *arg.* 1 *contra* and *De Trin.* 2.2 *arg.* 3; *Lect. Sent.* 2 *sc* = *De Trin.* 2.2 *corp.* and throughout.

[16] Dondaine, "'Alia lectura,'" p. 313.

[17] Dondaine, "'Alia lectura,'" p. 314.

[18] Recall the order of *Scriptum Sent. prol.* 1.2, *prol.* 1.3.1, and *prol.* 1.3.2.

[19] *Super Sent.* 1. *prol.* 1.3.2, 1. *prol.* 1.4.

[20] *Super Sent.* 1. *prol.* 1.5.

whether this science ought to speak esoterically.[21] Too much has still been left out – the unity of the science, its character as speculative or practical, its position in the hierarchies, its being most truly wisdom, and so on.

In the Roman *Lectura*, the mature order of topics emerges, combining the features of the two previous texts while opening the way to the *Summa*.[22] Thomas here divides the topics into four: the doctrine as science; the object of the science; the science as speculative and practical; the mode of the science. The last is then itself divided into four "little questions," which defend (in order) theology's narrative and poetic modes, the rational investigation of holy things, the use of philosophic authorities, and the use of theological authorities other than Scripture. In moving to the *Summa*, Thomas does little more than break up this pattern into coordinate articles and recall as separate certain sub-topics that had appeared in the earlier texts.

The third and last level of comparison considers *pedagogical projects*. A "pedagogical project" is the pattern of teaching that a whole text wants to enact for its readers.[23] The chief structural accomplishment of the *Summa* is to place a clarified and grounded theological account of human action at the center of an introduction to the whole of Christian teaching. This accomplishment is prepared in the opening of the Roman *Lectura*.

The prologue to the Parisian *Scriptum* unfolds a verse from Ecclesiasticus to reveal Christ as the fourfold wisdom of God. We especially attribute to the Word of God the works of manifesting the divine Persons, mediating creation, restoring it, and conserving all things in their last end. These four tasks of the divine wisdom are made to explain the division into four books of Peter Lombard's *Sentences*. The prologue to the Roman *Lectura* begins as well from a verse out of Ecclesiasticus, and ends rather more simply with a division of the *Sentences* into two pairs of books. In between, it rehearses a series of schemata, each of which insists on the double character of theology as contemplative and moral. Thomas begins the Roman *Lectura* by announcing that teaching is governed by a double intention, the demonstration of truth and the acquisition of blessedness. Every other science is typed to one half or another of this intention. Some seek only the cognition of truth, while others seek the means to blessedness. Only theology "completely contains and teaches" both the speculative and the practical.

---

[21] *Super Boethii De Trin.* 2.1–4.

[22] *Lect. Sent. prol.* 1–4.4

[23] When I insist, here and elsewhere, on taking the *Summa* whole or on the wholeness of its pedagogy, I am not claiming anything about its completeness or closure. On the contrary, I have also repeated in these pages my sense that the *Summa*'s pedagogy cannot and does not wish to be complete – except in the beatific vision. For the notion that a text's itinerary can be entire without being complete or closed, see Peter M. Candler, Jr, *The Grammar of Participation: Theological Reading as Manuduction* (dissertation, Cambridge University, 2002).

Abruptly the *Lectura*'s prologue changes direction. Since our happiness is found only in things above the human, Thomas argues that the speculative sciences are concerned with "sublime and elevated" truth. There are three degrees of elevation in speculative truth. The first corresponds to the "natural accounts [*or* reasonings, *rationes*] of particular things." The second answers to immaterial things that are knowable by accounts drawn from natural things. The highest degree, the third, belongs to theology, the science of Scripture. Theology speaks in the verse from Ecclesiasticus: "I dwell in the heights and my throne is in the column of cloud." The verse enunciates three features of theology: the height of its matter, the certainty of its cognition, and the perpetuity of its duration.

Thomas now bends back to his starting-point. Theology not only leads to the cognition of truth, but to complete blessedness. It does so in three ways: by considering the things that make us blessed, but also those that lead to what makes us blessed and those that serve blessedness instrumentally. These three relations to blessedness are projected into Christ himself. His divinity is the enjoyment of blessedness. His soul is the example of the virtues that lead to blessedness. His flesh is the instrument of blessedness because it offers remedies for obstacles. The triple nature of theology's concern with blessedness has now been led back to the threefold Christ.

Thomas does not stop. He adds a final schema, a final pattern of likeness through which theology appears as an image of Christ: Christ himself is the column of cloud that led the children of Israel in their exodus. He illumines and refreshes his children. More: Christ is the column because of his firmness and by his obscure divinity. So too theology is the column leading Israel out of Egypt. Its throne is fixed high above other sciences; it stands firm on God's eternal revelation; it consoles by pouring forth the spirit. The science of theology concerns itself both with the contemplation of truth and with showing the true way to blessedness. Peter Lombard's *Sentences* is then properly divided into two. The first part treats of God and creatures; the second, with Christ, the virtues, the sacraments, and blessedness.

Contemporary readers are accustomed to associate a breathless rehearsal of Scriptural patterns rather with Bonaventure than with Thomas. Perhaps we need to change our expectations. Thomas has coursed from a dichotomy of speculative and practical, through a trichotomy of intelligible objects, to a trichotomy of objects for the study of blessedness, which is reduced to the threefold Christ, who then becomes in two or three ways the cloud of Exodus, which cloud is also a figure for theology, which thus refuses the original dichotomy in order to teach contemplation of truth as the activity of blessedness. The whole succession of figures aims to show one thing: theology is the unique science that cannot be made either theoretical or practical. It must be both.

Thomas does not need to repeat the same typological introduction at the beginning of the *Summa* because the structure of the *Summa* enacts the unity of theoretical and practical. It is enough in the *Summa* to reduce the preliminary discussion of the issue to a single article, the shortest in the first Question, because the reader will see the issues resolved in reading the *Summa*, perhaps especially in grasping the order and position of its second Part. Those who need a more explicit introduction now have it, in the prologue to the Roman *Lectura*.

The second Part of the *Summa* is itself divided, as everyone knows, into a first half and a second. Everyone knows this, but few reflect on its implications. It is astonishing how many studies of moral topics in the *Summa* still run on for hundreds of pages without ever attending to its basic structure. When they do look to structure, they rarely look beyond the first Part. The character of moral teaching in the *Summa* is expressed in the structure of the second Part, which is by far the longest and most detailed. According to Thomas, the first half speaks more universally of the kinds and starting-points of human acts. The second half speaks more particularly of virtues and states of life.[24] The division is hardly simple. Its distinction between universal and particular, for instance, is relative, because moral science always remains universal in its terms and arguments. Again, the distinction between universal and particular is here curiously paired with a distinction between elements and compounds. The more universal consideration treats as if analytically the end, elements, and causes of human acting. The more particular consideration treats as if synthetically concrete actualizations in durable dispositions and choices about ways of life. Whatever the outcome of these reflections, the division between *Summa* 1–2 and 2–2 is the first and presumably the most fundamental difference that Thomas wishes to mark in moral science.[25] Any study of the structures in the *Summa* had best begin by treating the two parts separately.

---

[24] *Summa theol.* 1–2.6. *prol.*, 2–2. *prol.*

[25] Despite that, the distinction has not been well explained by modern commentators on the *Summa*. Sometimes it is collapsed into other distinctions, as that between *exitus* and *reditus*. See Th.-André Audet, "Approaches historiques de la *Summa theologiae*," in *Études d'histoire littéraire et doctrinale* (Montreal: Institut d'études médiévales, and Paris: J. Vrin, 1962), 7–29, at p. 15. Sometimes the two sections of the *secunda pars* are likened to the premises of a syllogism, their connection being somehow a deduction. See, for example, Martin Grabmann, *Einführung in die Summa theologiae des heiligen Thomas von Aquin*, 2d edn. (Freiburg: Herder, 1928), pp. 84–88; Francis Ruello, "Les intentions pédagogiques et la méthode de saint Thomas d'Aquin dans la *Somme théologique*," *Revue du moyen âge latin* 1 (1945): 188–190; Marie-Dominique Philippe, "La lecture de la *Somme théologique*," *Seminarium* 29 (1977): 898–915, at p. 904. Anti-syllogistic readings that emphasize the "journey" of the *Summa theol.* 2 can still falter at this point, explaining 2–2 as the application or out-flowing of 1–2 rather than as its integration or enactment. See, for a recent example, Thomas F. O'Meara, *Thomas Aquinas, Theologian* (Notre

Structural Innovations in *Summa* 1–2

For a reader accustomed to the textual arrangement of its predecessors, *Summa* 1–2 surprises in at least four ways: it divides the presentation of the soul's powers, it places beatitude unusually, it digresses at length on the passions, and it postpones the appearance of law and grace. Each of the four innovations marks a stubborn question about the order of moral teaching. Something must be said about each, and then about the effect of all.

1. Many moral works known to Thomas contain unified treatments of powers of the soul. Their patterns cannot be called Aristotelian, since Aristotle leaves unstated the relations between *On the Soul* and *Nicomachean Ethics. On the Soul* does not offer prolegomena to ethics. Aristotle did not intend that it should. Early on he faults his contemporaries for confining themselves to human souls.[26] Afterwards he conceives himself as moving within natural philosophy.

Thomas could not easily read *On the Soul*, however, without fixing its relation to moral science. This is due in part to the circumstances of the work's reception in antiquity and the medieval West. The circumstances include both general impulses to make the Aristotelian corpus coherent and particular modifications to *On the Soul*. So one finds the work's order under the five parts of Avicenna's *Book of the Soul*, where it is stretched to include a sustained dispute on optics and rewritten to accommodate treatments of visions and prophecy as highest acts of mind.[27] Less grandly, the Aristotelian pattern is adapted for such works as John Blund's *Treatise on the Soul* by replacing the original remarks on desire and motion with chapters on the soul's immortality, separate ontology, creation, and free choice.[28] The Aristotelian pattern can even be made to fit with the very different and more easily moralized schemata of Galenic medicine, as in Book 3 of *On the Properties of Things* by Bartholomæus Anglicus.[29]

Alongside traditions built around Aristotle's *On the Soul*, Thomas received

Dame: University of Notre Dame Press, 1997), pp. 109–110 in comparison with 120. Of course, even book-length studies of the *Summa*'s organization can excuse themselves from having to explain the plan or position of *Summa theol.* 2. See, for example, Ghislain Lafont, *Structures et méthode dans la Somme théologique de S. Thomas d'Aquin* (Paris: Desclée de Brouwer, 1961), p. 262.

[26] Aristotle, *On the Soul* 1.1 (402b3–5).

[27] Avicenna, *Liber de anima* 3 and 5.6, ed. S. Van Riet, Avicenna Latinus 4–5 (Louvain: Peeters and Éds. Orientalistes, and Leiden: E. J. Brill, 1968–1972).

[28] Johannes Blund (Blondus), *Tractatus de anima*, ed. D. A. Callus and R. W. Hunt, Auctores Britannici medii aevi 2 (London: British Academy, 1970).

[29] Bartholomew first goes through the Aristotelian order (3.7–13), then switches to the order of Constantine the African (3.14–24).

authoritative patterns for assimilating anthropology or psychology to the purposes of moral science. There is one pattern in Nemesius of Emesa's *On the Nature of Man*, known to Thomas as a work of Gregory of Nyssa.[30] Nemesius's purpose is not to summarize received opinions on soul so much as to use philosophical and medical doctrines in constructing an account that would justify human freedom under divine providence. He describes the soul on the way to conclusions about fortune, freedom, and providence. Although Nemesius includes Aristotelian material in his compilation, the purpose and order are certainly not Aristotelian.

A variation on Nemesius appears in another of Thomas's authorities, John of Damascus's *On the Orthodox Faith* 25–44. John's discussion of soul is evidently part of a grander scheme. It is preceded by a study of the whole visible world and followed by a much longer study of Christ. This order, taken just as stated, sounds much like the order of Thomas's *Summa*. Indeed John of Damascus is the only non-Scriptural authority to be quoted by Thomas in the prologues to the parts of the *Summa*.[31] But I want to notice now that John's chapters on the human creature rehearse – indeed, confirm – the Nemesian pattern for teaching about the soul, even while they reduce the amount of physical lore.

How surprising, then, that the consideration of the human soul in the *Summa* follows none of these patterns. No part of it is a treatise on the soul. Consider both its exclusions and its divisions, exclusions first. The *Summa* treats neither basic physiology nor sensation and the other "inner senses" that serve the mind. Thomas knew much more of these things than appears in the *Summa*, as we can read in the literal expositions of *On the Soul* and *On Sense and What Is Sensed* that he wrote around the same time. Thomas explains the exclusions as dictated by limitations on a theologian's interest. The theologian studies the human body only so far as it has bearing on the soul (1.75 prologue). Among the powers of the soul, the theologian attends to intellect and appetite; other powers are mentioned only on the way to intellect (as *praeambula*, 1.78 prologue, 1.84 prologue).

---

[30] The work was translated by Alfanus of Salerno in the eleventh century and again by Burgundio of Pisa in the twelfth. It suffered several confusions over authorship, including the transformation of "Nemesius" into "Remigius." There is a trace of the ascription to "Remigius" in Thomas's earliest treatment of the passions, *Scriptum Sent.* 3.15.2.1 *solutio* 2 (Mandonnet and Moos 3:485).

[31] *Summa theol.* 1–2. *prol.*: "Since, as Damascene says, ..." The other authorities are 1 Corinthians 3.1 (1. *prol.*) and Matthew 1.21 (1–2. *prol.*). For the importance of John Damascene and Nemesius of Emesa (whom we encountered as a medical authority in chapter 3), see Emil Dobler, *Zwei syrische Quellen der theologischen Summa des Thomas von Aquin: Nemesios von Emesa und Johannes von Damaskus. Ihr Einfluss auf die anthropologischen Grundlagen der Moraltheologie (S. Th. I–II, qq. 6–17; 22–48)* (Fribourg: Universitätsverlag, 2000).

Consider, next, Thomas's divisions of what is discussed. The most notable is the division of psychological topics between the first and second Parts. After a cursory treatment of the ground of the passions (*sensualitas*, 1.81), will, and free choice (1.83), Thomas excuses himself from discussing their acts in *Summa* 1 by invoking an ideal of moral knowledge or science, *scientia moralis*. "The acts of the appetitive part, however, belong to the considera-tion of moral science: so they will be treated in the second Part of this work, in which moral matter will be considered" (1.84.prologue). The *Summa's* division prevents any unified treatment of psychological and moral matters. The topics postponed from the first Part are not just treated elsewhere, they are treated differently. The speed of the first Part requires Thomas to strip its accounts bare. A reader learns nothing from its Questions on the human soul that she could not learn in more detail from Thomas's earlier works. This is not true for *Summa* 1–2. Its slow study of human willing or passion goes far beyond Thomas's earlier writings. A reader following the *Summa* in good order depends on the sections in the first Part only to fix preliminary schemata vividly so as to avoid many misunderstandings. Then the schemata are qualified, augmented, surrounded by the later teaching. Taking only the preliminary formulae can lead to gross misreading. The division between *Summa* 1 and 1–2 is not just a division within a sequence; it is a division of two teachings that differ sharply in pace and scope. The division cuts through every unified pattern of moral psychology.

2. The second innovation in *Summa* 1–2 is the placement of the treat-ment of beatitude or heavenly blessedness. It is not unusual for medieval moral treatments to begin with the good as such. Philip the Chancellor's *Summa on the Good* and Albert's work of the same name proceed in just that way. It is odd to combine an inquiry into the highest good with remarks on happiness. Philip's "showing" (*ostensio*) of the highest good is accomplished on hierarchical grounds, not by exhausting other candidates for human hap-piness.[32] Albert's initial treatment of the good includes a wider range of authorities, but is concerned chiefly to define the good and to consider some of its conceptual relations.[33]

Thomas offers a reason for his starting place: we can understand things ordered to an end only in view of that end (1–2.1 prologue). This is an Aris-totelian maxim, and the placement of the discussion recalls the opening of *Nicomachean Ethics*. The recollection can be misleading. Aristotle's diffident search for some archer's mark at which to aim human action is replaced in Thomas by a chain of arguments purporting to show that the highest

[32] Philip the Chancellor, *Summa de bono prol.* 4, ed. Nicolaus Wicki, Corpus philosophorum medii aevi 2 (Bern: Francke, 1985), 1:20–22.
[33] Albert the Great, *Summa de bono* 1.1.1–10, in Cologne *Opera omnia* 28:1–21.

human end lies only in the contemplation of God after this life. To Aristotle's outline sketch of the good, to his dialectical investigation of happiness, Thomas opposes a refutation of every false beatitude. In fact, the immediate structural precedent is not Aristotle, but Thomas's own *Contra gentiles* 3. Thomas elsewhere quotes to great effect Augustine's report of Porphyry's despair over philosophical disagreements about the good.[34] The confident discernment of the highest good, of human happiness, at the beginning of *Summa* 1–2 is, just by itself, a decisive criticism of ancient philosophy. It announces that we stand at the doorway to a theologian's treatment of "moral matter."

The revision of Aristotle accomplished by the beginning of *Summa* 1–2 introduces a string of revisions. Any survey will show how different Thomas's order in the second Part is from the order he reads in Aristotle's *Ethics*. Leaving aside entirely the insertion of Christian matter, I argued above that Thomas rearranges what philosophical elements he shares with Aristotle. The theologian's ideal of moral science does not merely add new topics to philosophy, it reorders the whole study.

3. The third structural innovation in *Summa* 1–2 is the large space given over to the passions. Many of the patristic and medieval works already mentioned classify the passions and point to them as trouble for rational conduct. Since Thomas has learned from Augustine, sometime after he commented on Peter Lombard,[35] about the importance of the passions in ancient moral theory, he expands his treatment into the 27 Questions that constitute one of the largest single blocks in the second Part.

At first glance, the expansion might seem to contradict theological selectivity. Aristotle had used anger as an example on the border between physics and moral philosophy, and many ancient discussions of the passions were to be found in medical works. Does Thomas's unprecedented concern with the passions digress from theology into natural philosophy? On the contrary, Thomas spends attention on the passions because he wants to win them over for theology. He means to show, with Augustine, that the passions must be discussed as elements of rational action. *City of God* gives Thomas the history of the conflict over the goodness of the passions between Stoics and Peripatetics. In it Augustine insists that what matters in the passions is human will, not physiology.[36]

---

[34] *Super De Trin*. 3.3. The whole passage depends explicitly on Augustine's *De civitate Dei*.

[35] I argue the case more fully in "Aquinas's Construction of a Moral Account for the Passions," *Freiburger Zeitschrift für Philosophie und Theologie* 33 (1986):71–97.

[36] See especially Augustine, *De civitate Dei* 14.6. Augustine goes so far as to criticize both Cicero and Virgil for naming grief with terms that carry overly strong physical connotations (14.7, just at the end).

Thomas elaborates Augustine's suggestions in detail. To assert that the passions fall under moral discourse is to assert that they are, in significant ways, subject to rational control. "Rational control" is neither mechanical nor mathematical. For Thomas, the chief thing for the moralist to know about passions is that they are open to rational persuasion. So he begins by explaining that they are morally good or morally bad only so far as they "lie under the rule (*imperium*) of reason and the will" (2–2.24.1). The political connotations of "rule" are important. In *Summa* 1, Thomas has argued that the defensive and desiring powers, the irascible and concupiscible, obey reason and the will (1.81.3). The relation of appetite to reason is not despotic, but political and regal (1.81.3 *ad* 2). In the present teaching on the passions, images of rule, obedience, and measure (*imperium, obedientia, regula*) can be found on every side. Political and regal governance is exercised in the city by means of education, habituation, and rational persuasion. So too within the soul. The enormous space given to the passions captures them for moral inquiry, but it also reminds the reader that the uncertainties of moral education are also to be found inside the soul. The limitations that Aristotle recognized in the teaching of ethics must now be repeated for an internal pedagogy. Since reason has to persuade the passions, reason's rule over them is subject to the limits on every moral persuasion.

4. The fourth and last structural innovation in *Summa* 1–2 is the delayed entry of grace and its pairing with law. In Peter Lombard, grace appears immediately after the discussion of free choice. He treats it both generally and as characteristic of the human state before the Fall.[37] He does not discuss the Old Law until the next book, where he places it as preface to the discussion of particular sins.[38] The Lombard's pattern is picked up in William of Auxerre's *Golden Summa*, except that a treatment of natural law is inserted between the theological and cardinal virtues.[39] For William, the Old Law and its sins still come near the end of the third Book.[40] In Philip the Chancellor, the entire discussion of human life takes place under the heading of grace.[41] By contrast, Albert the Great's *Summa on the Good* is concerned with the political virtues and so includes neither grace nor divine law.

Thomas justifies the joint and delayed appearance of law and grace when

---

[37]   Peter Lombard, *Sententiae* 2.26 and 2.28–29.

[38]   Peter Lombard, *Sententiae* 3.37–40.

[39]   William of Auxerre, *Summa aurea* 3.18, ed. Jean Ribaillier, Spicilegium Bonaventurianum 16–20 (Paris: CNRS, and Rome: Eds. Coll. S. Bonaventurae, 1980–1987).

[40]   William of Auxerre, *Summa aurea* 3.44–49.

[41]   Philip the Chancellor, *Summa de bono* "De bono gratiae in homine" (Wicki 2:489).

he describes them as exterior principles of human acts leading towards the good and given by God. God "instructs by law" and "helps by grace" (1–2.90 prologue). The reader is brought to law and grace from inside the human soul, from the prior study of the internal starting-points (*principia*) of human action. This approach does not denigrate God's assistance. It helps readers by starting with what is nearer to hand, with what they can control. *Summa* 1–2 is put under the teleology of the highest human end because only the end renders the rest intelligible. The sequence of articles is then dictated by approach to the end, beginning with the primary possibility of choice and ending with the uniquely efficacious gift of grace (1–2.6 prologue).

So far Thomas's explicit reasons. Delaying the discussion of grace and joining it to divine law also gives Thomas more room to describe the elements of moral science before he confronts paradoxes of direct divine intervention. The moral philosophy of the ancients has been declared disordered, more incomplete and insufficient than it knew. The declaration is made by a theologian, who himself must begin teaching from a theological view of the human end. The theologian concludes that this end, however much it is naturally desired, can only be attained with the aid of divine grace. The theologian's moral science is even less able to deliver grace, to compel the gift, than ancient philosophy was able to assure uninterrupted contemplation.

The tensions produced by the Questions on grace were hardly absent earlier. From the beginning of *Summa* 1–2, Thomas has insisted that happiness is not attainable without divine assistance. He makes the same point later and in other ways – saliently in the teaching on the necessity and preeminence of divinely infused virtues. But the Questions on divine law and grace emphasize that moral life depends on a free gift from God. Thomas must now show how any moral science whatever can be constructed in the face of such dependence. He shows it by writing a second half to the second Part.

Structural Innovations in *Summa* 2–2

If it was important to notice several structural innovations in the first half, it is important to concentrate in the second half only on the most obvious innovation: the disposition according to the three theological and four cardinal virtues. The innovation is bold for being so simple.

Organizations of the virtues and vices reach back through the desert monastic traditions and the church Fathers to pagan mythographers and philosophers.[42] The *Summa* presupposes no exact knowledge of the stages of transmission and elaboration. It is enough to know that by the twelfth century catalogues of virtues and vices were well established, but without a fixed order for their elements. The theological variations on the catalogues lengthen them by adding other elements in sequence – virtues, vices, gifts, and beatitudes one after another. The sequences grow longer still as later writers distinguish more carefully between theological and cardinal virtues, and as they continue to add new elements, such as the commandments. So William of Auxerre considers in turn virtues as such, theological virtues, cardinal virtues (with their annexes), gifts, beatitudes, properties and comparisons of virtues, and finally the commandments, with respective sins and cases.[43]

The cases are significant. Alongside the sequential treatments, there had developed before Thomas the moralist's and confessor's casebook (*summa de casibus*). An early example can be had in the sprawling *Summa of Sacraments and Counsels for the Soul* that goes under the name of Peter the Chanter.[44] The third part of this *Summa* is a *Book of Cases of Conscience* in 64 chapters. Some of the chapters do report particular cases calling for delicate moral judgments.[45] Other chapters deal with fundamentals – the virtues, merit, and sin as such.[46] The variety of the material is exceeded by its disorder, which worsens near the anthology's end.

By contrast, and with the benefit of intervening works, Raymond of Peñafort codifies the casuistic material by applying to it a schema of crimes. Crimes are committed either against God or one's neighbor, and they are fully direct, less direct, or indirect.[47] Raymond then establishes order within

---

[42]   Morton W. Bloomfield, *The Seven Deadly Sins* ([Lansing]: Michigan State College Press, 1952), pp. 43–87; Siegfried Wenzel, "The Seven Deadly Sins: Some Problems of Research," *Speculum* 43 (1968): 1–22, especially pp. 3–14.

[43]   William of Auxerre, *Summa aurea* 3.11, 3.12–16, 3.19–29, 3.30–34, 3.38–43, and 3.44–45, respectively.

[44]   According to the best arguments, it was finished by his colleagues and students shortly after his death in 1197. See the chronological hypotheses in the edition by Jean-Albert Dugauquier, Analecta mediaevalia Namurcensia 4, 7, 11, 16, 21 (Louvain: Éds. Nauwelaerts, and Lille: Libr. Giard, 1954–1967), 11:187–198.

[45]   See the medieval headings for 3.5, 3.29, 3.37, 3.44, 3.59, and 3.61 (Dugauquier 21:892–909).

[46]   See the medieval headings for 3.20, 3.58, 3.49, 3.60, and 3.63 respectively (Dugauquier 21:892–909).

[47]   In Raymond's *Summa de casibus*, direct crimes against God are simony (1.1–3), simple unbelief (1.4), heresy (1.5), schism (1.6), or the combination of these last two in apostasy (1.7). Less direct crimes against God are breaking vows (1.8), breaking oaths and other perjuries (1.9), mendacity or adulation (1.10), divination (1.11), and disrespect for solemn feasts (1.12). Indirect crimes against God are sacrilege (1.13), crimes against church sanctuary (1.14), refusal of tithes, first fruits, or oblations (1.15), and violations of the laws of burial.

each crime, usually by adopting some of a standard list of questions: what is it? Why is it called that? How many senses does the name have? How is it distinguished? What are its kinds? What are its punishments? What doubtful cases are there? Raymond's order is an achievement directly connected to his efforts at codifying canon law. The achievement has its price. The crimes here categorized do not even constitute a complete list of sins, much less a frame for a full account of the moral life. So the discussion of sinful cases still proceeds apart from compendious teaching on virtues and vices.

Something nearer a full moral account is given by William Peraldus in his *Summas of the Vices and Virtues*. The combined work is large, at least ten percent longer than Thomas's *Summa 2–2*. Peraldus reverts to a serial or sequential treatment, but with an extraordinary thoroughness that permits him to include cases. His *Summa of Vices* is organized around the seven capital sins, with pride allotted almost as many sections as the rest combined.[48] A host of lesser sins is attached to the seven. There is also a long appendix on sins of the tongue. In the *Summa of Virtues*, Peraldus adopts a familiar serial order: the virtues in common, theological virtues, cardinal virtues, gifts, and beatitudes. There is a regular sequence of sub-topics. Each cardinal virtue, for example, is given its several senses, then described, next commended, and finally divided into parts. Before or after the division, mention is made of helps and hindrances to the particular virtue.

William Peraldus's *Summas* were certainly on Thomas's mind, though not as models to be copied. Thomas begins *Summa 2–2* by announcing that he wants to avoid the needless repetition required by sequential treatment. It is more helpful – more teacherly, more persuasive – to gather in one place a virtue, its corresponding gifts, its opposed vices, and the entailed positive and negative commands. Thomas also insists that the table of the vices should be constructed by real differences rather than by accidental ones: "vices and sins are distinguished by species according to their matter and object, not according to other differences of the sins, such as 'of the heart,' 'of the mouth,' and 'of the deed,' or according to weakness, ignorance, and malice, and other such differences" (1–2 prologue).

The immediate references are to two distinctions passed down by Peter Lombard.[49] Both distinctions are used by Thomas himself in other texts,

---

[48]   The sections are allotted as follows: gluttony, 8; self-indulgence (*luxuria*), 36; avarice, 96; sloth (*acedia*), 49; pride, 138; envy, 4; and anger, 25.

[49]   The division according to "heart, mouth, and deed" from Jerome, *Super Ezechielem* 43.23–35, Corpus Christianorum Series Latina 75 (Turnhout: Brepols, 1964), p. 642, through Peter Lombard, *Sententiae* 2.42.4 (CSB 1:569). The division according to "weakness, ignorance, and malice" goes back to Isidore, *Sententiae* 2.17.3–4, Migne *PL* 83:620A–B, through Peter Lombard, *Sententiae* 2.22.4 (CSB 1:445).

even within the *Summa*, though he is always careful to point out that they are not classifications by genus or essential species.[50] Both triplets resemble the sorts of classifications in William Peraldus's *Summas* and other works like them. Thomas's criticism would surely apply to his addition of a special supplement on sins of the tongue. It must also count against his practice of distinguishing sins by their external occasions.[51] But the force of Thomas's criticism is felt most by the main principle of Peraldus's *Summa*, namely the order of the seven chief vices.

One of the best-calculated effects of Thomas's organization of *Summa* 2–2 is to push the seven capital vices to the margin.[52] They appear, each in turn, but without obvious connection or special importance.[53] This might seem odd, because Thomas himself uses the list of seven to arrange his disputed questions *On Evil*. Indeed, the two Articles in the *Summa* that introduce the seven vices are extremely close to the parallel in *On Evil*. A study of either text will show that Thomas makes very limited claims for a division of moral teaching by capital vices. Thomas insists that the seven are not the "roots" or "starting-points" of all sin. They are, according to *On Evil*, the ends that desire seeks "principally" or "for the most part."[54] They are, in the *Summa*, the vices out of which others arise "most frequently," but not exclusively.[55] For Thomas, then, a treatment of sins and vices organized around the Gregorian list of seven is fundamentally misleading.

Summa 2–2 innovates when it replaces the serial order with a more compendious, simultaneous order according to a list of virtues. The list itself is

---

[50]   For the use of the first triplet see, e.g., *Scriptum Sent.* 3.37.1.2 *sol.* 3, *De malo* 9.2 *sed contra* 3. For its qualification, see *Scriptum Sent.* 2.42.2 *sol.* 1, 4.16.1.1 *sol.* 3 *ad* 1, *Summa theol.* 1–2.72.7. For the use of the second triplet, see *De malo* 3.6–12, *Summa theol.* 1–2.76, 1–2.77.3, and 1–2.78, where the triplet is classed among the causes of sin.

[51]   See, for example, the multiplication of types of pride by types of ornament or, indeed, by sub-types, such as horse-trappings, buildings, books, singing, and so on, in William Peraldus *Summa*, fols. 293ra–299rb and 304ra–306vb, respectively.

[52]   Thomas's recasting of moral teaching did not stick, even within the Dominican Order. For instances of return to old classifications according to the seven capital sins, see Martin Grabmann, "De Summae divi Thomae Aquinatis theologicae studio."

[53]   In *Summa theol.* 2–2, see 35–36 for sloth and envy, 118 for avarice, 132 for vainglory, 148 for gluttony, 153 for self-indulgence, and 158 for anger. Thomas is well aware of the authority of Gregory the Great's list of seven capital sins. Indeed, he relies on it in arguing that each of the seven sins is a capital vice (35.4, 36.4, 118.7, 132.4, 148.5, 153.4, and 158.6). Moreover, Thomas explicitly defends Gregory's list as an appropriate classification of seven final causes for other sins (1–2.184.3–4). But he also explicitly denies that the classification of sin by final causes – or any causes – ought to count as an essential classification (1–2.72.3 *corp.* and *ad* 3).

[54]   *De malo* 8.1 *ad* 1, "principaliter"; 8.1 *ad* 6, "in pluribus" (195.402), and 8.1 *ad* 8, "in pluribus."

[55]   *Summa theol.* 1–2.84.4 *ad* 5.

traced back from accidental or causal classifications to an essential one. The result is not only greater clarity and compression, but also a theoretically justified form within which to arrange the sprawling matter of both moral catalogues and casebooks. *Summa* 2–2 hybridizes the theological genres it receives by a telling application of certain philosophical lessons about what counts in conceiving virtues.

If the innovations of the second half apply a theologian's interests and inspirations to the forms of ancient philosophy, its central innovation appears to do the reverse. It applies the conclusions of a philosophically astute moral analysis to what had been taught in the unruly theological forms of sentences or opinions, exhortations, exemplary tales, cases, and other pastoral genres. What follows for moral science from the mutual application of theological and philosophical principles or teaching structures? What kind of knowledge is the *Summa*'s moral formation?

Chapter Seven

What the *Summa of Theology* Teaches

To avoid gross misreading, readers of a didactic text must discern the character of its teaching. By "character" I mean especially the completeness, clarity, and certainty of the knowing that the text means to induce in its best readers. Discerning this character is particularly difficult for modern readers of Aquinas's texts. Whatever else our modernity might be, it is the residue of long debates over the completeness, clarity, and certainty of exemplary knowledge, that is, of "science." Thomas has always been counted a decisive figure in those debates. Sometimes he is depicted as the epitome of an anti-scientific Scholasticism, sometimes as the distant forerunner of modern science, sometimes as an alternative to both Scholasticism and science. Whatever he was, Thomas's variable roles in culturally constitutive debates about scientific knowing make it particularly easy to miss what his texts disclose about their own scientific characters.

The characters of Thomas's texts have been mistaken differently, but perhaps nowhere so painfully or so surprisingly as in his moral writings. The mistakes are painful because Thomas's moral teaching is central to his authorship. They are surprising because authors of quite different dispositions mistake Thomas's moral teaching in roughly the same way. The teaching has typically been confused with an Aristotelian, hyper-Aristotelian, or sub-Aristotelian science. One can see this on all sides in nineteenth-century exegesis. Liberatore, for example, supported his polemic against Kantian ethics by emphasizing how detailed and articulate were the demonstrations to be made from Thomas's notions of natural law.[1] Kleutgen defended Thomas's moral teaching against the Tübingen school in part by

---

[1] Matteo Liberatore, *Istituzioni di etica e diritto naturale* (Rome: Ufficio della Civiltà cattolica, 1865), especially pp. 250–266.

appeal to its scientific construction, imitated from Aristotle.[2] De Wulf summarized "Scholastic" moral teaching as a properly philosophic system combining theories of human ends and acts with deductions of obligations from natural law.[3] Surprisingly similar assertions can be found in contemporary scholarship. Nussbaum contrasts the rigidity of Thomas's ethical science unfavorably with Aristotle's own, more humane flexibility.[4] For Wieland, Thomas stands out among those who rediscovered the scientific character of Aristotelian practical science.[5]

To portray these readings fairly and to correct them convincingly would require much more than a chapter. A chapter may raise questions about any unexamined emphasis on the scientific character of Thomas's moral teaching. I begin with some peculiarities of the *Summa*'s use of "*scientia*" and "*ars*," the words usually translated as "science" and "art." The most significant of these uses will lead to the Questions on law in *Summa* 1–2. Much abused as they have been, those questions still provide decisive indications about the completeness, clarity, and certainty that Thomas allows to moral teaching.

"Science" and "Art" in the *Summa*

Thomas does speak of moral "science" in the *Summa*. The term is important, and I will return to it. Still I am convinced that mentions of "science" will mislead the modern reader almost entirely unless they are juxtaposed immediately with two other linguistic facts. The first is that Thomas does not propose a "moral theology." He does, of course, speak of a moral part of theology, and he famously analogizes theology to certain Aristotelian conceptions of science.[6] But there is no mention of a "moral theology" as an

---

[2]   Joseph Kleutgen, *Die Theologie der Vorzeit* (Munster: Theissing, 1853), 5:673–684. On Kleutgen's unhappy influence over the evolution of neo-Thomism, as well as of the conception of the history of neo-Thomism, see John Inglis, *Spheres of Philosophical Inquiry and the Historiography of Medieval Philosophy*, Brill's Studies in Intellectual History 81 (Leiden, Boston, Köln: Brill, 1998).

[3]   Maurice De Wulf, *Introduction à la Philosophie Néoscolastique* (Louvain: Institut Supérieure de Philosophie and Paris: Alcan, 1904), pp. 143–145.

[4]   Martha Craven Nussbaum, *Aristotle's* De Motu Animalium (Princeton: Princeton University Press, 1978), pp. 168–169.

[5]   Georg Wieland, "The Reception and Interpretation of Aristotle's Ethics," in *Cambridge History of Later Medieval Philosophy*, ed. Norman Kretzmann et al. (Cambridge: Cambridge University Press, 1982), 657–672, at pp. 661–662.

[6]   Compare the argument in Denis J. M. Bradley, *Aquinas the Twofold Human Good: Reason and Human Happiness in Aquinas's Moral Science* (Washington: Catholic University of America Press, 1997), especially pp. 3–24.

autonomous science. The second and equally striking linguistic fact is that "science" does not banish "art" from the *Summa*. On the contrary, art figures significantly in the *Summa* as an ideal of moral knowing.

Its appearances may surprise those who remember that Thomas explicitly excludes art from moral consideration: "art does not belong to moral science" (2–2 prologue). Art is concerned, Thomas explains, with things made, not with things done. He reiterates the distinction elsewhere in the *Summa*.[7] But these passages and the prologue itself are concerned with only one of the analogically linked senses of "art." Thomas recognizes explicitly that there are other senses, such as Augustine's, according to which virtue can be called an "art of living rightly" (1–2.58.2 *ad* 1). Even when expounding the letter of Aristotle, Thomas uses "art" interchangeably with "science."[8] He then follows Augustine in calling the Son the art of the Father.[9] Thomas will cite the precise Aristotelian definition only to assign art to the Holy Spirit as giver of gifts (1–2.68.4 *ad* 1). Analogies to art help elsewhere to explain sacramental causality (beginning in 1.43.6 *ad* 4).

Moral matter requires more rewriting of any strict definition for art. Thomas follows Aristotle's own lead in returning to analogies between art and virtue or art and prudence.[10] He introduces prudence thematically by working out its distinction from art, which turns out to be a kind of middle between the speculative intellectual virtues and prudence.[11] If art strictly defined is not part of moral matter because it is not a moral virtue, art understood analogously is an indispensable guide to teaching about elements of moral life. So, for example, an analogy to art is drawn on the way to the conclusion that moral virtue consists in a mean (1–2.64.1).

The reader of the *Summa* can confirm the importance of art not only in defining virtues, but in constructing law and justice. Law is, Thomas says, "a certain art for instructing and ordering human life" (1–2.104.4). Thomas

---

[7] For example, *Summa theol.* 1–2.34 *ad* 3, 57.5 *ad* 1, 68.4 *ad* 1 and *ad* 3. The definition of *ars* as "*recta ratio factibilium*" is based on Aristotle, *Nicomachean Ethics* 6.4 (1140a3–5); Thomas expounds it literally in his *Sent. Ethic.* 6.3.

[8] So, for example, in *Sent. Metaph.* 1.1, where Thomas distinguishes practical from theoretical art, which latter comprises the "logical sciences (*scientiae logicales*)."

[9] For example, in *Summa theol.* 1.39.8 and 3.59.1 *ad* 2 (with explicit reference to *De Trinitate* 6.10).

[10] For the analogy to any virtue, *Summa theol.* 1–2.9.1, 2–2.23.4 *ad* 2, 2–2.50.3; for the analogy to prudence outside the thematic discussion of 1–2.57–58, see 2–2.47.5, "art and prudence with regard to contingents (*ars et prudentia circa contingentia*)."

[11] *Summa theol.* 1–2.57.3–4. See the helpful remarks by Wolfgang Kluxen, *Philosophische Ethik bei Thomas von Aquin* (2nd edn., Hamburg: Meiner, 1980), pp. 26–35. The only qualification to be entered is that Kluxen follows the Aristotelian expositions too assiduously as guides to Thomas's thought about *ars*.

counts the analogy solid enough to argue from it: as art is divided into rules of practice, so ought laws to be divided. Again, as artifacts stand to art, so do just acts stand to their law (1.21.2, in an argument for God's justice). More technically, Thomas quotes from Celsus a definition of right (*jus*) as "art of the good and the fair" (2–2.77.1 obj. 1 and *ad* 1). These passages suggest that the art-like character of Thomas's moral teaching will best be seen by turning to his Questions on the analogous kinds of "law." To understand law will be to understand what Thomas thinks of one of the most art-like forms of moral intelligibility.

Certain cautions should be entered immediately before approaching these Questions. Much time has been wasted chewing over particular points in Thomas's remarks on natural law. The points are almost entirely traditional. Making them, Thomas rehearses commonplaces from familiar authorities. What is notable in his Questions on the law, what is new, is their structure. When disposing the Questions, Thomas clarifies the fundamental ordering among kinds of law, and so subordinates natural and human law to the divine. One can see this quickly by regarding the place of the Questions on law within *Summa* 1–2.

There is no "treatise" on law.[12] The *Summa* is not built out of treatises, but from clusters of Questions caught up into larger and larger dialectical rhythms. Within *Summa* 1–2, as we have seen, the reader begins with the end, with the goal towards which human life tends. The reader ends with law and grace, which Thomas counts as exterior principles of human acts leading towards the good and given by God. The entire structural unit moves forward in response to the pull of the highest human end. Its sequence of articles is dictated as a series of steps approaching the end, beginning with the primary possibility of choice and ending with the uniquely efficacious gift of grace (1–2.6).

God "instructs by law" and "helps by grace" (1–2.90 prologue). God teaches human creatures through law about how to reach the end that they most deeply desire. The central legal notion "*praeceptum*," which we English

---

[12] On the dangers of excerpting the Questions as a free-standing treatise, see recently, and among many others, Clifford J. Kossel, "Natural Law and Human Law (Ia, IIae, qq. 90–97)," in *The Ethics of Aquinas*, ed. Stephen J. Pope (Washington: Georgetown University Press, 2002), pp. 169–173, at p. 169; and, more emphatically, Servais Pinckaers, *The Sources of Christian Ethics* (Washington DC: Catholic University of America Press, 1995), pp. 171, 232. (Pinckaers also describes the "myopia" that leads readers to pluck out from the *Summa* just the Questions that pertain to their topic of the moment; see pp. 169–170.) The point about not isolating the first eight Questions on law is repeated so often by dedicated readers of Thomas that it might seem trivial, but a survey of translations or textbooks will show just how often the first few Questions on law are presented as a treatise – without grace.

blandly translate as "precept," should always be conceived with teacherly overtones. A "precept" of law is an act of moral teaching, a lesson issuing from counsel and judgment (2–2.47.8). Legal precepts prepare for the gift of grace as a more powerful means toward a pedagogical end. Natural law is nothing more than a dim and inarticulate anticipation of lessons to be taught more plainly and more forcefully in divine law and especially in the "law" of grace. We are told this, and we are shown it in the unrolling of Thomas's teaching.

Laws and Natural Law

Thomas is content when discussing the senses of "law" and "natural law" to rehearse familiar points from familiar authorities. Medieval readers learned about natural law not from vague intimations in the Latin Stoics, but from specific and detailed legal authorities. Both of the compilations of Roman law commissioned by Justinian begin with remarks on a law of nature and a law of peoples. The law of nature is the law written into all living creatures by which they seek their own survival and procreation (*Institutes* 1.2 prologue). The law of peoples comprises rationally discoverable rules for human society that are the common ground of all human law (*Institutes* 1.2.1). Each is called providential and immutable (*Institutes* 1.2.11).

The two laws are mixed by Isidore of Seville. For his *Etymologies*, natural law includes not only biological imperatives, but social ones as well – among them common property, equal liberty, and simple justice.[13] Texts from Isidore serve as the basis for Gratian's distinguishing types of law. Gratian begins with this note: "The law of nature, which is contained in the law and the Gospel, is that by which each is commanded to do to others what he wants to be done to himself, and is prohibited from inflicting on others what he does not want done to himself."[14] The law of nature is eminently contained in Scripture. Somewhat later, Gratian adds that natural law is first chronologically, since it begins with the creation of rational creatures, and that it does not vary over time.[15] Natural law comprises the common principles observed by all and binding on all, and it takes clear precedence over any human law.[16] Each of these points is familiar to readers of Thomas. There is more. Following upon Gratian, directly in the line of Dominican

---

[13]   Isidore, *Etymologiae* 5.4, ed. W. M. Lindsay (Oxford: Clarendon Press, 1911), l. 25 – l. 8 in the section.

[14]   Gratian, *Concordantia discordantium canonum* 1.1 [*prol.*] (Richter-Friedberg 1:1).

[15]   Gratian, *Concordantia* 1.5.1 [*prol.*] (Richter-Friedberg 1:7).

[16]   Gratian, *Concordantia* 1.8.1 and 1.9.1 [*prol.*] (Richter-Friedberg 1:12 and 1:16).

authors that leads to Thomas, there stands again Raymond of Peñafort. He inaugurates his *Summa of Law* by listing five meanings of "natural law": it is the power of reproduction, the desire for procreation and rearing of offspring, the common rational principles of equity, every precept of divine law, and finally the law common to all peoples.[17]

By the time Thomas reached Paris to study theology, these authoritative legal texts and others had been incorporated into theological teaching, even if their position had not been worked out. The *Summa* "of Alexander" contains a lengthy treatment of four kinds of law: eternal, natural, Mosaic, and evangelical.[18] There are about four times as many articles as in the corresponding Questions of Thomas's *Summa*. Moreover, this Franciscan *Summa* marshals a wider variety and greater quantity of authorities. By contrast, Thomas is laconic. He wants the reader to see through his selection of topics and pruning of authorities to the pedagogy that leads from law to grace. The pedagogy is a sign and consequence of the art-like character of moral teaching.

Thomas announces natural law as the rational counterpart of natural tendency to an end. It is "a participation in the rational creature of eternal law" by which the creature has "a natural inclination to the due act and end" (1–2.91.2). Where lower animals have mute tendencies, rational souls appropriate their teleological impulses rationally and recognize them as participations in God's creative wisdom. The "eternal law" from which natural law is participated is nothing other than God as providential maker and governor, as artisan (1–2.91.1 *ad* 3). Natural stands far below. It is, at best, an abstract and incomplete guide to action. Human law is needed as the completing specification of natural law, because human law offers particular conclusions drawn from the "common and indemonstrable principles" of natural law. There are corollaries. The natural human condition is to live under a political regime. Civil law is a natural supplement to natural law, which is no more than a limited and imperfect participation of the eternal law (1–2.91.3 *ad* 1).[19]

The positive content of the natural law, to the extent that it can be articulated, is described in the six Articles of *Summa* 1–2.94. Thomas quotes from Aristotle a traditional formulation of the first principle of practical

---

[17] Raymond of Peñafort, *Summa iuris* 1.1, ed. José Rius Serra (Barcelona: Universidad de Barcelona, Facultad de Derecho, 1945), 1:23.

[18] "Alexander of Hales," *Summa theologica* 3.2.1–4.

[19] On the historical and political character of human law in Thomas's moral thought, see Bénézet Bujo, *Moralautonomie und Normenfindung bei Thomas von Aquinas: unter Einbeziehung d. neutestamentl. Kommentare* (Paderborn, Munich, Vienna, and Zurich: F. Schöningh, 1979), pp. 287–306. Bujo provides a summary of natural law doctrine as it appears in Thomas's Scriptural commentaries on 232–283.

knowledge: "the good is what all desire" (94.2). The first precept of the law, then, is "the good is to be done and pursued, and evil is to be avoided" (94.2). The good, the end, is immediately stratified. A first stratum contains the good that human beings share with other natures. This is the good of existence; its precept is survival. Humans share the second stratum of good with animals. This is the good of life; its precept is generation and nurture. The third good belongs to human beings as rational. Its precepts enjoin living in society and knowing about God (94.2).[20] Thomas did not discover these strata. His three kinds of precepts are variations on the first three meanings of "natural law" catalogued by Raymond of Peñafort.

Thomas gives a few examples within each stratum. Generation comprises "education of children," and political life requires "that a human being avoid ignorance and not offend others, with whom he [or she] must share community" (94.2). Thomas does not perform anything like a transcendental deduction of the conditions for the fulfillment of each end. In the next Article, he argues that such a complete deduction of the natural virtues cannot be performed (94.3). He distinguishes between virtuous acts considered as virtuous and as particular acts. Natural law does include the inclination to act rationally, which is to act virtuously. It does not include a complete list of virtuous acts. Virtuous acts are discovered, rather, in the long political experience of the species (94.3). A full enumeration of entailments under the three branches of the first precept of natural law is not part of the law, but part of the history of human communities.[21]

Given the diversity of regimes, the contradictions in the history of conventions, what remains of the kernel of natural law? Is there a common content of practical participation in the law of God? Thomas's reply to such questions, in the fourth Article, requires that he deny any strict parallelism between practical and theoretical reasoning.[22] In speculative matters, the

[20] As Crowe says, this triplet "cuts across" the older distinction between primary and secondary precepts which had been adopted by Thomas in commenting on the *Sentences*. See Michael B. Crowe, *The Changing Profile of the Natural Law* (The Hague: M. Nijhoff, 1977), 179 and 174–184 generally. R. A. Armstrong finds the older distinction made most strongly within the *Summa* at 1–2.100, in connection with a discussion of the precepts of the Old Law. See his *Primary and Secondary Precepts in Thomistic Natural Law Teaching* (The Hague: M. Nijhoff, 1966), pp. 86–114.

[21] See especially on this point Pamela M. Hall, *Narrative and Natural Law: An Interpretation of Thomistic Ethics* (Notre Dame: University of Notre Dame Press, 1994); and, more recently, her "The Old Law and the New Law (Ia, IIae, qq. 98–108)," in *The Ethics of Aquinas*, ed. Pope, pp. 194–206.

[22] See Crowe, *Changing Profile*, 187–191, for similar arguments. The opposite view is represented by Gallus Manser, *Das Naturrecht in thomistischer Beleuchtung*, Thomistische Studien 2 (Fribourg: Paulusdruckerei, 1944), 51–61.

premises are knowable by all equally; the same conclusions are knowable, though not equally. Differences of knowledge with regard to the conclusions are explained by reference to the difficulty of demonstration in various cases. In practical matters, the first principles are known to all. The conclusions, however, are common neither in content nor in clarity of apprehension (94.3).

The more particular the case, the more difficult it is to arrive at consensus about a conclusion. Alternately, the more specific a norm or precept proposed in ethics or law, the more liable it is to justified exception. In many particular cases, the right course of action cannot be rigorously deduced. Matters become more uncertain when one considers the defects to which practical reasoning is liable, whether of passion, bad habit, or wicked political convention. Although Thomas urges that the most common principles are the same "among all both as regards rightness and as regards acquaintance" (94.4), he restricts "common principles" in his examples to such formulas as "one should act according to reason." The common natural law is so abstract that it provokes disagreement when expressed as precept, much more when applied to particular cases. Compare problems of articulation in the teaching of art.

The Old Law

The insufficiency of natural law is the starting point for Thomas's arguments on the need for a divine one. Because natural law participates in the eternal law only "according to the proportion of the capacity of human nature," God generously teaches a more articulate law, the divine law that is eminently contained in the Old and New Testaments (1–2.91.4 *ad* 1; compare 91.5 *ad* 3). The content of natural law only stands forth with the instruction of the Old Law. The natural law becomes practicable only with the gift of grace in the New.[23]

Thomas insists that the law of Moses is an essential moment in God's tutoring of the human race.[24] He finds the law completely in accord with

---

[23] Not a few readings of Thomas on law have emphasized these points. For a useful survey and commentary, see Fergus Kerr, *After Aquinas: Versions of Thomism* (Oxford: Blackwell, 2002), pp. 97–113.

[24] On the scope and continuity of divine pedagogy, see Matthew W. Levering, *Christ's Fulfillment of Torah and Temple: Salvation according to Thomas Aquinas* (Notre Dame: University of Notre Dame Press, 2002), pp. 15–30, though I would not agree with Levering that such remarks are a sufficient answer to the questions posed by Michael Wyschogrod.

reason. Its deficiencies are not irrationality so much as incompletion. Mosaic law falls short of the Gospel because it is partial, not because it is wicked. It gives rational instruction about the highest human end, but lacks the principle for reaching that end, which is the explicit invocation of full grace. Thomas affirms that there was grace in the time of the law. He teaches explicitly that many in Israel were saved. Still they were not saved by the Old Law, but by faith in a mediator, just as Christians are (1–2.98.2 *ad* 4).

Much of Thomas's labor in the Questions on the Old Law is spent in explaining how it constituted a rational pedagogy. Indeed, the *Summa*'s longest articles are those in which Thomas justifies the ritual and political legislation of the Hebrew Bible. He provides enormously detailed explications of Levitical worship and ancient Israel's political history. The third kind of Old Testament law, the moral precepts, Thomas understands as revelations of aspects of the law of nature (1–2.98.5). Mosaic law teaches precepts of natural law in two ways (1–2.99.2). First, it makes up for human reason's incapacity to derive particular practical conclusions from universal principles. Second, the Old Law supplies a number of subsidiary principles that human reason could not reliably deduce without mixing in many errors. Somewhat later, Thomas divides cases for moral decision into three groups (1–2.100.1). The first contains cases that are so clear that they can be approved or reproved after quick consideration by reference to first principles. The second group consists of cases that require much longer consideration by someone wise. The third group holds cases that can only be judged in light of divine instruction. These three groups correspond to three grades of precepts in the natural law. The first grade is practical principles knowable by everyone. Thomas's examples are: "Honor your father and mother," "Do not kill," "Do not steal." The second grade is precepts knowable only to the wise: "Rise up before the white head, and honor the person of the elderly" (Leviticus 19:32). The third grade comprises precepts that all human beings must learn directly from God: "Do not make a statue or any image [of God]," "Do not take the name of God in vain."

At each level, the examples are Scriptural. Thomas means by them to situate the three grades of moral precepts in relation to the commandments of the Decalogue (1–2.100.3). The ten commandments offer precepts of both the first grade and the third. They are united so far as they are taught directly by God. Some are taught by God through inwardly known first principles, others by the infusion of faith. The precepts of the second grade, those known only to the wise, are conclusions from the decalogue rather than principles of it. What Thomas earlier called "first [or primary] precepts" of natural law – the impulse to survival or to community – are deeper grounds behind the decalogue's explicit commands.

The division of precepts recalls another set of arguments in Thomas, arguments to justify God's revealing truths that are also philosophically demonstrable (1–2.99.2 *ad* 3). God reveals God's existence, even though it is demonstrable, because human reason is frail and preoccupied. God does not choose to leave so important a truth in the hands of metaphysicians. The same is true of the Old Law's moral precepts. God reveals basic moral truths because they are too important to be left to the contingencies of discovery or deliberation. The analogy between the revelation of metaphysical conclusions and of moral precepts is not an identity. There is an additional reason for the revelation of precepts. Human capacity for moral reasoning has been "darkened" by "the custom of sinning," "the abundance of sins" (1–2.99.2, 98.6). God reveals natural law precepts after human beings have experienced their own humiliating impotence, their failure to achieve human happiness by rational power (1–2.98.6). The natural law slips further and further into darkness until God speaks to Moses.[25]

The reader learns several things here about the character of Thomas's moral teaching. First, it is impossible for natural law to serve as an autonomous, scientific guide to human happiness. A number of precepts of natural law are not knowable, even to the wise, except by divine revelation. Second, Thomas cannot mean by "natural law" something that is known to the human creature in a "state of nature" if by that one means "absent divine intervention." On Thomas's account, the state of nature is, much like prime matter, a hypothetical construct. It is posited as a backdrop for explanation, not as an independent historical reality.[26] Human beings were created in grace, with the gift of what Thomas knows from the tradition as "original justice" (1.95.1). This grace was freely given by God to the human species at its creation. If human beings had not fallen through sin, each generation would have been born, by God's intention, into the renewed gift of a supernatural justice (1.100.1). They would thus have been born with a knowledge of the universal requirements of law, and they would have possessed this knowledge "much more fully" than we now do naturally (1.101.1 *ad* 3).

---

[25] John Bowlin suggests that the Questions on Old Law can illuminate the purpose of the whole series, which is to show in part how far Mosaic law is still binding on Christians. The reading is certainly preferable to ones that emphasize the autonomy and perspicuity of natural law, but it may still understate the pull of the final Questions on grace. See Bowlin, *Contingency and Fortune in Aquinas's Ethics* (Cambridge, UK: Cambridge University Press, 1999).

[26] Compare Isabelle Chareire, *Éthique et grace: Contribution à une anthropologie chrétienne* (Paris: Éds. du Cerf, 1998), p. 160, n. 1: "The Theologian poses a purely hypothetical state, which tradition calls pure nature, in which pre-lapsarian man would find himself if he possessed nothing other than his nature."

Human creatures chose sin. They fell, not into pure nature, but into nature deformed. They came to need the revelation of important parts of natural law – and more besides. From the beginning of his discussion of Mosaic law, Thomas urges that its revelation, while complete as doctrine, is not complete as pedagogy. The Old Law taught, but it could not provide. If the Law could reach so far as to teach the need for acts of love (*caritas*), it could not supply the grace by which alone it is possible to act in love (1–2.11.10 *corpus* and *ad* 3).

Thomas speaks this limitation of the moral precepts of the Old Law most pointedly in the last article that he devotes to them. The issue is "whether the moral precepts of the Old Law justified" those who observed them (1–2.101.12). Thomas answers with a double denial. Justice most properly speaking is a virtue infused by God. "This justice could not be caused by moral precepts, which are about human acts. And so moral precepts could not justify in the sense of causing justice" (1–2.101.2). Moreover, and granted that the moral precepts of Mosaic law taught proper actions, the sacraments of that law could not confer justifying grace, which is given only through the sacraments of the New Law as applications of Christ's passion.[27] The quest to complete natural law leads through the law of Moses to the law of Christ. So too the inquiry into the character of Thomas's moral teaching.

The New Law

The first thing that ought to strike a reader who turns to the Questions on the New Law is that they are so brief. Thomas devotes four times as many articles to the Old Law as the New (a ratio of 46:12). While many of the articles on the Old Law bristle with Scriptural quotations and their contested interpretations, articles on the New undertake disputative exegesis of details only once, when defending the Gospel as a sufficient guide to interior acts (1–2.108.3). Reasons for Thomas's brevity are not far to seek. One of them lies in the structural relations between the two halves of the moral Part of the

---

[27] *Summa theol.* 1–2.101.12. Note an important difference between the Leonine and Piana editions here. The Leonine omits the most interesting sentence: "If then 'justification' is understood as the execution of justice, then the moral precepts [of the old law] justified so far as they contained what is in itself just (*secundum se iustum*); but those sacraments of the old law did not confer grace as do the sacraments of the new law, which are said to justify on account of this." For the teaching that the sacraments of the Old Law did not confer grace "by themselves, that is by their own power (*per seipsa, idest propria virtute*)," but only as "professions (*protestationes*)" of the faith of Israel, see *Summa theol.* 3.62.6.

Summa. The detailed working out of Christian living is undertaken, not in the discussion of Gospel as moral law, but in the treatment of the virtues. A similar balance can be found in the theological works before Thomas.[28] The careful reader of the *Summa* will never forget that the general moral considerations of the first half are given their specificity and their full sense only in the more detailed analyses of the second.

A more important reason for Thomas's brevity is to be found in the very character of the New Law. It is not primarily written. The "whole power (*tota virtus*)" of the Gospel's law consists of "the grace of the Holy Spirit, which is given by faith in Christ. The new law is principally the grace of the Holy Spirit that is given by Christ to the faithful" (1–2.106.1). The precepts and counsels written down in the New Testament are dispositions to the reception of grace and guides to its right use. Without grace, the words of the Christian revelation are only another set of inefficacious regulations. The "ordinances for human feeling and human acts" contained in the "documents of faith" have no power as such to justify. The letter of the Gospel would also kill, unless faith healed inwardly (1–2.106.2).

Thomas is not here espousing some rude anti-nomianism. He knows, of course, that Christ's moral teaching has content. Some of the content is clarification of the Old Law; some, intensification of it; some, addition to it by way of counsel (1–2.107.2). Still the central "content" of the New Law remains a gift of grace, which grace issues in exterior acts by a kind of impulse (*ex instinctu*). If the Gospel prescribes actions, it does so either as suggesting dispositions to grace or as predicting consequences that will flow from it (1–2.108.1). Thomas reads most evangelical precepts as referring to what he calls the *usus gratiae*, the application or appropriation of grace by the human agent.

In this way, the New Law not only completes the natural, but restores its inward character. Neither the natural law nor the Gospel are primarily written. They are inward sharing of a direction towards the human end. In our present condition, the natural law participates in the human teleology darkly, uncertainly, inarticulately. The New Law, which is the grace given by Christ, participates in the teleology luminously and hopefully, but still inarticulately. Neither natural law nor New Law resides in a set of propositions. If precepts of natural law are written down, it must be as a means of helping someone understand what she truly desires and how she may begin to attain it. If the Gospel law is written down, it must be to help believers

---

[28] So in the *Summa* "of Alexander" the articles on the Old Law outweigh those on the New in the same ratio of 4:1, but the discussion of the New Law leads immediately into the discussion of grace and virtues. See "Alexander of Hales" *Summa theol.* 3.2.3, 3.2.4, and 3.3.

towards a fuller appropriation of the grace that will move them to act as they should.

I can say the same point historically. In the narrative of divine pedagogy, written law serves as a way of attaining unwritten law. Human beings end in unwritten law, in fully appropriated inward principles of action. That is one implication of the image from John Damascene with which Thomas opens the moral part of the *Summa*: the human creature is the image of God as "the principle of his [or her] own acts" (1–2 prologue). Having forfeited dominion over ourselves in sin, we must regain it by the instrumentality of written laws – human law and, especially, divine law. God reveals written law only in order to bring us to its unwritten origin and end.

Where now is the analogy of law from which this section of the *Summa* began? Thomas had concluded, famously, that law is "nothing other than an ordinance of reason for the common good promulgated by the one who has care of the community" (1–2.90.4). Sixteen Questions later, the most important law, the New Law, is described as an unwritten impulse to action which is "promulgated" by grace. The analogy's starting point in human experience has been inverted. The essence of law is expressed in the definition, but only when all of its terms have been reversed. Law is an "ordinance of reason," that is, an ordering from reason and for reason. It is for the "common good," that is, written into the nature of the creature by God, who has an artisan's care of all. Human laws are laws weakly and derivatively, by distant imitation of the eternal law expressed as creation and justification.

Inverting the definition of law brings into final prominence the relation of moral teaching to art. A human law is something made, the promulgated product of practical reasoning. Thomas compares it explicitly with the product of an art (1–2.90.1 *ad* 2). When the analogy of art is reversed, legislation and promulgation change. The eternal Law is promulgated by the Word, Who is the divine art. Eternal law's consequences for human actions are dimly participated by natural law, rendered somewhat clearer in various human laws, articulated comprehensively in the Old Law, and made attainable at last in the New. The divine art expresses itself as a providential pedagogy enacted in history. Still the revelation of divine law is also a making that constitutes the object of the theologian's study. Theology is the science of revelation, but especially of Scripture, the "sacred page." When Thomas writes of law in the *Summa*, then, he takes on multiple relations to various arts. He describes the natural law as a dim participation made possible by the divine art in creating. He explains and appropriates the human art of jurisprudence. He narrates and so rehearses the art of divine pedagogy in the history of Israel. He studies and very imperfectly imitates the Scriptural record of that pedagogy.[29] Whatever the role of science in the moral part of the *Summa*, the text is the description, explanation, narration, and imitation of a hierarchy of arts.

Ideals of Moral Science under the Limits of Art

After restoring art to its place through a more exact appreciation of law, it is possible for the modern reader to return to the notion of moral "science" without being entirely misled.

At several points in the *Summa*, Thomas invokes an ideal of "moral science" (*scientia moralis*) to settle some problem of textual order. He invokes it first in regard to the location of the discussion of divine providence (1.22 prologue). The sequence of topics in moral science serves as paradigm or analogue – the relation is not stated – for the sequence of Questions about God. Later, as I mentioned in the last chapter, Thomas invokes moral science to postpone the discussion of appetitive powers into the second Part (1.84 prologue). Finally, and most obviously, Thomas recalls the order of "moral consideration," and the character of "moral speech" (*sermo moralis*), to justify the largest structural features of the two halves of the second Part (1–2.6 prologue).

The ideal invoked in these passages is a pattern for distinguishing and disposing teaching on moral matters. At its fullest, the pattern would presumably settle a number of issues: What individuates a moral science among other sciences? What ought a distinctively philosophical or theological moral science to treat and in what order? Medieval Latin writers were familiar with set lists of questions to be asked about moral science or any other science.[30] Thomas uses one of these lists by way of introducing his literal exposition of the *Nicomachean Ethics*.[31] Unfortunately, many of the lists are

---

[29] The relation of theological writing to Scriptural interpretation or enactment is emphasized every time Thomas interchanges "holy teaching (*sacra doctrina*)" with "holy Scripture (*sacra scriptura*)" or "sacra pagina (*sacred page*)." Writing theology is a way of reading Scripture. See on this point Valkenberg, *Words of the Living God*, especially pp. 9–11.

[30] For samples of schematic analyses of ethics contemporary with Thomas, see Robert Kilwardby, *De ortu scientiarum* 36 (*de quo est, finis, definitio*), ed. Albert G. Judy, Auctores Britannici medii aevi 4 (London: British Academy, and Toronto: PIMS, 1976), p. 126, no. 357; Albert the Great, *Super Ethica: Commentum et quaestiones* prologue (*materia, finis, utilitas*), ed. Wilhelm Kübel, Cologne *Opera omnia* 14/1:1.1–55. Dominic Gundissalinus, who provides one of the most elaborate schemes for analyzing sciences, does not apply it to ethics, which he passes over in a few lines. See his *De divisione philosophiae* "De partibus practice philosophie," ed. Baur, p. 140.

[31] *Sent. Ethic.* 1.1, *de quo est, modum tractandi, qualis debeat esse auditor.*

mechanical, and even Thomas glosses over issues. We cannot use them to determine what an ideal of moral science would contain. Thomas's invocations of an ideal do show that it should decide the science's autonomy and disposition or order.[32] Both autonomy and disposition are pedagogical concerns. They arise within that tension between knowledge and its learners that Thomas confesses at the end of the *Summa*'s first prologue: "to pursue what pertains to holy teaching briefly and clearly, so far as the material permits" (1 prologue).

If the invocations of the ideal are too brief, and the prologues devoted to it elliptical or mechanical, where might one look to find depictions of it? The usual thing is to look in Thomas for explicit remarks about sciences or moral science. Explicit remarks can be useful, but they are not nearly so telling as the achieved organization of the texts in which moral science is offered. Thomas remarks on moral science rarely and then usually to repeat a commonplace. Outside his literal expositions of Aristotle, he has only a handful of things to say about it. He takes "moral sciences" generally as a name for the whole of practical knowledge. These sciences constitute one of the principal parts of philosophy.[33] Thomas does not assign any singular, technical meaning to the phrase "moral science" and so regularly alternates it with "moral philosophy," "moral teaching (*doctrina*)," "moral consideration," or simply "moral things (*moralia*)." Moral science and its alternates designate the study of voluntary human acts, of their sources and ends.[34] Any doctrine that denies voluntariness in human acting immediately abolishes moral science.[35] Because moral science deals with voluntary actions, with contingent particulars, it cannot have the certainty of mathematics or metaphysics.[36] Its lessons hold only for the most part.[37] Moral instruction aims at the practical end of judging what ought to be done in particular circumstances.[38] So its language is the language of the *exemplum*, the concrete and clarifying instance.[39] It is

---

[32] Under "autonomy" I include various issues in the individuation of the science – the source and character of its starting points, its relations with other sciences, its position in the order of study, and so on. Under "disposition" I include such issues as what is taught, in what order, and by what means of rational persuasion.

[33] *Scriptum Sent.* 1. *prol.* 1.2. *arg.* 1 and 3.23.2.4.2 *arg.* 2; *Super De Trin.* 5.1 *ad* 4; *Lect. Matt.* 2.3.

[34] *Scriptum Sent.* 3.34.1.1; *Summa theol.* 1.1.4 *sed contra*; *De virt. comm.* 2 *ad* 15. See also the early division of moral matter into *delectabilia, difficilia,* and *communicabilia* at *Scriptum Sent.* 3.34.3.2 *sol.* 1.

[35] *Contra gent.* 2.60 (no. 1,374) and 2.76 (no. 1,579); *De unitate int.* 3 and 4; *De malo* 6.

[36] *Scriptum Sent.* 2.24.2.2; *Super De Trin.* 6.1.1 *ad* 4, 6.1.2; *De malo* 3.6; *Summa theol.* 1.86.3 *sed contra*, 1–2.30.1.

[37] "In pluribus," *Scriptum Sent.* 4.14.1.2.1; *De malo* 8.1 *ad* 4.

[38] *Scriptum Sent.* 1. *prol.*1.1 *arg.* 2, 3.34.1.2, 3.35.1.3 *sol.* 2.

[39] *Princ.* 2, *Scriptum Sent.* 1. *prol.* 1.3.2; *Summa theol.* 1.1.2 *ad* 2.

also the language of exhortation.[40] Of course, to possess moral science is not yet to possess virtue. Someone instructed in moral science can say what a particular virtue requires without possessing it.[41]

These are, as I said, commonplaces of the moral traditions that Thomas inherits. The inheritance is not empty. The commonplace remarks make clear, for example, that "science" is an analogous term for Thomas. Moral science cannot be science in the same way that physics is. It cannot have the same demonstrative necessity, universality, certitude, or kind of end. To say this positively, Thomas's ideal of moral science requires that it be self-limiting in ways that physics is not. It must resist temptations to overstate its certainty or comprehensiveness. Thomas prefers the quieter, structural means of self-limitation. So he multiplies terminologies, juxtaposes rival accounts, and places every utterance – his own included – within an ongoing dialectic. If his textual devices for self-correction are less obvious than Socratic irony or Maimonidean self-contradiction, they must still be appreciated if Thomas is not to be misunderstood badly.

Whatever the internal delimitations of moral philosophy, the limits on it discovered by moral theology are more severe. If we want to see Thomas's judgment on the ideals of moral science known to him, we had best look beyond his borrowing of philosophical commonplaces to a summary description, however tentative, of his deliberate composition of the second Part of the *Summa*.

In the hybrid structure of the *Summa*, Thomas gives the ideal of a clarified and unified theological ordering for moral matter. There is no mention of "moral philosophy" in the *Summa*, much less the labeling of any part of it as philosophy, moral or otherwise. It is all formally theology. Thomas sometimes draws explicit contrasts between the theologian's procedure, which is his own, and the procedure of the philosopher. Thus the theologian considers fault (*peccatum*) principally as an offense against God, while the moral philosopher considers it as contrary to reason (1–2.71.6 *ad* 5).[42] Thomas elsewhere counts the word "ethics (*ethica*)," which does not appear in the *Summa*, a foreign term – not only Greek, but philosophical.[43] The *Summa* is

---

[40] Here the best evidence is from the Scriptural commentaries. See for example *Expos. Pauli: in Rom* 6.3, "moral exhortation (*moralis exhortatio*)"; *in Phil* 1.2, "moral admonition (*moralis monitio*)"; *in Heb* 13.1, "moral instruction (*moralis instructio*)," which requires commendation and exhortation.

[41] *Summa theol.* 1.1.6 *ad* 3 and 2–2.45.2, to which compare *Super De Trin.* 5.1 *ad* 3.

[42] Compare *Scriptum Sent.* 2.40.1.5: "not only according to the theologian, but even according to the moral philosopher."

[43] *Scriptum Sent.* 3.23.1.4 *sol.* 2, where the "*nos*" is not so much "we speakers of Latin" as "we Christians."

not a philosophical ethics; it is theology that has at its center a moral part. The difference between the theologian and the philosopher makes for exclusions and shifts of attention in the *Summa* that we have already seen. Others are required so far as the second Part is a component of an integral theology. The ideal theological order, unified and clarified, is strongly selective. That is the first of its self-limitations.

The second self-limitation can be seen not in order, but in content. Thomas presents through the *Summa* a set of patterns for the analysis of moral life. One staple of Dominican moral preaching was the sermon *ad status*, the sermon concerned with the perils and opportunities of a particular profession or social class. The closest Thomas comes to that kind of direct address is in the final Questions of *Summa* 2–2 on the choice of religious life. In those sections, as throughout the whole part, Thomas keeps considerable distance from the particular. He offers no more than schemata for pastoral applications or analyses yet to be done. A few particular issues are treated, of course. Thomas considers whether it is licit to baptize non-Christian children against the will of their parents (2–2.10.12), how one is to proceed in fraternal correction (2–2.33.7–8), and when one is to fast (2–2.147.5–7). Still the overwhelming majority of Questions in this "more particular" section of the *Summa* concern the classification, causality, order, and opposition of virtues or vices. It is more taxonomy than exhortation, more causal classification than spiritual direction. So Thomas's ideal of moral science is self-limiting in a second way: it recognizes the intrinsic universality of moral teaching and does not pretend to particularity.

Then, third, Thomas reminds his readers in the *Summa* of the limitation of any theological teaching about morals. A complete life of virtue requires the personal gift of divine grace. The gift brings more vivid awareness of one's place under God's direct providence. It thus threatens the whole enterprise of moral science. What is the point of teaching a Christian moral doctrine if the enactment of that doctrine depends utterly on God?[44] The *Summa* addresses the question with two explicit correctives to any over-estimation of the value of human teaching. One comes, prominently, at the end of the first Part (1.117.1). It is the opening Article in a set of three Questions "on human action" (1.117 prologue). Thomas argues that a human teacher can do no more than minister externally to the learner. The human teacher provides "helps and instruments," such as examples, analogies, disanalogies, or more proximate propositions. The human teacher proposes an order of learning, a

---

[44] Thomas knows one formulation of this puzzle in Augustine's anti-Manichean writings: *De correptione et gratia* 1.2.3–6.9 (Migne *PL* 44:917–921).

path for the learner's insight. That is all. The *Summa*'s other reminder about teaching comes at the end of the second Part. In the final Question on special graces and conditions of life, human teaching itself is analyzed as a divine gift. The freely given grace of the "word of wisdom" or "of knowledge" (*sermo sapientiae, scientiae*) enables a human teacher to serve as instrument for the Holy Spirit.[45]

These remarks on teaching are not casual asides. They are deliberate reminders of a third self-limitation in the ideal of *scientia moralis* that Thomas embodies in the *Summa*. The *Summa* is neither Scriptural exegesis nor pastoral care. It is intermediate between them – dependent on Scripture, intended for the formation of pastors. The *Summa* is intermediate between divinely inspired books that embrace every important genre of teaching and the specialized genres of spiritual guidance. It is at once a clarifying simplification of Scripture for the sake of preaching or confessing, and a clarifying generalization of pastoral experience brought back under the science of Scripture, which is to say, under the whole of theology. Nothing more ought to be asked of a theologian's moral teaching. The ideal of moral science must insist first and last that it serves the workings of divine grace in individual human souls.

In drawing this conclusion, I have spoken of the whole *Summa* – and quite deliberately. Thomas wrote the *Summa* for the sake of the second Part, that is, in order to situate the moral component of theology within a properly ordered account of the whole. Thomas undertook the writing at the end of a series of experiments in comprehensive theological composition. Reading through these experiments, we can argue over Thomas's motives for moving from one project to another. Yet the largest contrast between the *Summa* and the earlier works stands beyond argument: it is the contrast created by the second Part, by the large and ingeniously arranged teaching of moral art and science at the center of theology. Any account of the *Summa*'s purposes that fails to explain the unprecedented size and scope of the moral teaching is an inadequate account.

---

[45] *Summa theol.* 2–2.177.1. Compare the remarks on teaching for the sake of saving souls in 2–2.181.3, 187.1, and 188.4–5.

Chapter Eight

Philosophy in a *Summa of Theology*

Nothing occurs more spontaneously to the modern reader of the *Summa* than to ask about the relations in it between Thomas's philosophy and his theology. The query supposes that Thomas would admit to having two separate doctrines and that he would agree that a doctrine was his in any important sense. Thomas was by vocation, training, and self-understanding an ordained teacher of an inherited theology. He would have been scandalized to hear himself described as an innovator in fundamental matters and more scandalized still to hear himself – or any Christian – called a "philosopher," since this term often had a pejorative sense for thirteenth-century Latin authors. Still, contemporary readers do need to ask about Thomas's ample use of philosophical terms and texts or about his having been regarded by some of his contemporaries as too indebted to pagan thinkers. What is the appropriate formulation of that kind of question? How in particular might it be applied to the *Summa*?

An appropriate formulation must admit that any philosophy "in" the *Summa* must be approached through theology if it is to be approached within the book's structure.[1] It is notoriously difficult to separate out the

---

[1] Here I disagree with the premise of many attempts to extract from the *Summa* a "philosophical theology." See, for a recent example, Leo J. Elders, *The Philosophical Theology of St Thomas Aquinas* (Leiden: E. J. Brill, 1990). Elders defends his extraction of "philosophical elements" from the unity of *Summa theol.* 1 in this way: "Despite this overall theological order the *inner* arrangement of the treatises on God, on creation, on man, etc. appears to obey the requirements of ordering reason and is not immediately derived from revelation" (p. viii; compare 2–4). This claim seems to me to restrict the notion of revelation (or graced understanding), as it seems to forget that *Summa theol.* 1 was not written to stand alone – or for its own sake. Pasnau provides a more extended argument for why modern (analytic) philosophy may justly claim to study the *Summa* philosophically, but he admits (with admirable candor) that he disagrees with Aquinas on the nature of theology. He also acknowledges that he must

philosophical passages in this or others of Thomas's works. His writings are overwhelmingly on the topics and in the genres of the medieval faculties of theology. Thus the three largest portions of his corpus are, in ascending order, a required commentary on a theological source-book, a pedagogically motivated rethinking and extension of the topics in that source-book, and commentaries on Scripture.[2] In some texts Thomas seems not to write as a theologian, but these texts are at best ambiguous in their classification. The largest block of texts in which Thomas seems not to write as a theologian is literal expositions of Aristotle, whose purposes I considered above. Besides the expositions, the other seemingly "philosophical" works are either reca-pitulations of received doctrine (such as *On Kingship*) or polemical pieces (*On the Unity of the Intellect, On the Eternity of the World*) or letters (*On the Principles of Nature*).[3] *On Being and Essence* (as it is known), which has often been taken as a programmatic statement of Thomistic metaphysics, is a set of youthful variations on themes by Avicenna. In short, Thomas wrote no single work for the sake of setting forth a philosophy.

Thomas chose not to write philosophy. He did so partly because of other choices he had made – for example, to become a Dominican and a master of theology. Still those earlier choices might not have settled the issue. After all, Thomas's teacher Albert wrote at length in philosophical genres, and some of Albert's other students or disciples would do so as well. Thomas's decision to write as a theologian when he wrote in his own voice was chiefly the result of his view that no Christian should be satisfied to speak only as a philosopher.[4]

---

ignore other parts of the *Summa* that just might have some bearing on the Questions he means to study. See Robert Pasnau, *Thomas Aquinas on Human Nature: A Philosophical Study of Summa theologiae Ia 75–89* (Cambridge: Cambridge University Press, 2002), pp. 10–16. A similar view, indebted to Kretzmann's understanding of *Contra gent.*, can be found in Eleonore Stump, *Aquinas* (London: Routledge, 2003). For Stump, "*Summa theologiae* is the paradigm of philosophical theology." (p. 29).

2   I round off the word counts from the *Index Thomisticus* for *Scriptum Sent.* (1,498,000 words, 17.2% of the *corpus*), *Summa theol.* (1,573,000, 18.1%), and the Scriptural commen-taries (2,178,000 words, 25.1%). It will be seen that these three make up more than half of Aquinas's entire corpus.

3   I leave aside, of course, philosophical treatises falsely or uncertainly attributed to Aquinas, as well as gross retitlings of his works, such as the early modern custom of calling the *Contra gent.* a "*Summa philosophica*."

4   For a recent attempt to dodge this conclusion and reassert the claims of Thomistic phil-osophy, see Paul O'Grady, "Philosophical Theology and Analytical Philosophy in Aquinas," in *The Theology of Thomas Aquinas*, eds. Rik van Nieuwenhove and Joseph Wawrykow (Notre Dame: University of Notre Dame Press, 2005), 416–441, at pp. 420–423.

Philosophy and Theology

No one can doubt that Thomas admired pagan philosophers both for their zeal in inquiry and for their way of life. He praises the philosophic pursuit of contemplation, just as he holds up the philosopher's abandonment of earthly goods.[5] But Thomas also diagnoses the origin of philosophic contemplation as self-love, and so distinguishes it sharply from Christian contemplation.[6] The philosopher's asceticism is not the Christian's, since the Christian must renounce worldly goods for the sake of Christ.[7] The philosophers seek authority by dispute, while the Lord teaches believers to come peacefully under a divinely constituted authority.[8] Philosophers offer a dozen causes for the arrangement of the cosmos, but the believer knows that divine providence has arranged the world so that human beings might have a home.[9]

If these appear to be only scattered or incidental remarks, the reader should turn to Thomas's explicit judgments on the doctrines and the promises of the philosophers. He judges that their doctrines were severely constrained by the weakness of human reason. Before general audiences, Thomas is reported to have said that all the efforts of the philosophers were inadequate to understand the essence of a fly.[10] In academic writings, whenever Thomas argues for the appropriateness of God's revealing what might have been demonstrated, he insists on the weakness and fallibility of unaided human reason.[11] He notes the same failings in distinguishing philosophical and theological knowledge about God.[12] He judges philosophy's promises even more harshly. Pagan philosophy presented itself as love of the best knowledge of the highest things, that is, as a way toward happiness. Yet philosophy could not provide it. The ancient philosophers multiplied views on the human good but they could not achieve it.[13] Philosophers were

---

[5]   On philosophic poverty, see *Summa theol.* 1–2.186.3 *ad* 3, 188.7 *ad* 5. Compare *Contra impugn.* 2.5 and a passage from the sermon "Beatus gens, cuius est dominus . . . / Multis modis sancta mater ecclesia . . .." In *Expos. Post.* 2.8, Aquinas follows Aristotle in seeing philosophy as a remedy for the loss of material goods.

[6]   *Scriptum Sent.* 3.35.1.1.

[7]   *Catena aurea: in Matt.* 19.2.

[8]   Sermon "Beati qui habitant in domo . . . / Unam esse societatem Dei et . . ." 3.

[9]   *Post. Psalmos.* 23.1.

[10]   *Coll. Symb. Apost. prol.*

[11]   *Scriptum Sent.* 1. prol. 1, *Super De Trin.* 3.1; *De verit.* 14.10; *Contra gent.* 1.4–5; *Summa theol.* 1.1.1, where he summarizes his view by saying that philosophic truths about God were discovered "by a few, and over a long time, and with the admixture of many errors."

[12]   *Super De Trin.* 2.2, 5.4. See also the contrasts between the philosopher's wisdom and the Christian's in *Summa theol.* 2–2.19.7.

[13]   See, for example, *Super De Trin.* 3.3, 6.4; *Contra gent.* 3.48; *Comp. theol.* 1.104; *Summa theol.* 1–2.3.6.

unable to convince even their fellow citizens, because they could not offer a teaching about life that was firm, comprehensive, and useful.[14] No philosopher had enough wisdom to call men back from error; instead they led many into error.[15] The philosophers could not avoid sin, because they could not undergo the unique purification of the true worship of God, which begins in the philosophically unknowable coming of Christ.[16]

Thomas gathers these observations into a handful of contrasts. Frequently he draws a line between what the philosophers think or say and what "we" believers say.[17] He makes the contrast clear when he constructs a trichotomy of philosophy, the Law of the Old Testament, and the Gospel of the New. The light of philosophy was false; the light of the law was symbolic; the light of the Gospel is true.[18] Again, philosophy is "earthly" and "carnal" wisdom, "according to the natures of things and the desires of the flesh"; "we" Christians live rather by grace.[19] It cannot be a surprise, then, that Thomas glosses the Scriptural condemnation of secular pretension as applying specifically to philosophers, or that he groups philosophers with heretics as opponents to the faith.[20]

Nevertheless, Thomas uses philosophic texts and teachings. He urges their study on writers of theology. How can this be? He explains or justifies the appropriation by what he likens to a miraculous change in philosophical teaching: "those who use philosophical texts in holy teaching, by subjugating them to faith, do not mix water with wine, but turn water into wine."[21] "Subjugating" philosophy to theology means several things. First, the theologian takes truth from philosophers as from usurpers.[22] The ground of philosophic truth is the revealing God who is more fully and accurately described in theology. Theology serves, second, as a constant corrective to philosophy. As Thomas puts it in one of his sermons, "Faith can do more than philosophy in much; so that if philosophy is contrary to faith, it is not to be accepted."[23] Again, in a commentary on Paul, he turns aside to raise a

---

[14]   *Catena aurea: in Matt.* 13.3.

[15]   *Lect. Ioan.* 6.1.

[16]   *Expos. Pauli: in 2 Cor.* 7.1; *in Col.* 1.6.

[17]   For example, *Scriptum Sent.* 2.3.3.2; *Summa theol.* 2–2.19.7.

[18]   *Lect. Ioan.* 1.5. Compare the triplet "light of prophecy," "light of faith," and "light of reason" in *Expos. Isaiam* 6.1 and the contrast from Avicenna between the way of speaking "among the philosophers" and "in the Law" at *Scriptum Sent.* 2.14.1.3.

[19]   *Expos. Pauli: in 2 Cor.* 1.4 on 2 Cor. 1:12, where he is paraphrasing Paul.

[20]   On pretension, *Expos. Isaiam* 19; *Summa theol.* 1.12.13 *sed contra*, 32.1 *ad* 1; on heretics, *Scriptum Sent.* 2.14.1.3; *Summa theol.* 2–2.2.10 *ad* 3.

[21]   *Super De Trin.* 2.4 *ad* 5.

[22]   *Expos. Pauli: in 1 Cor.* 1.3, following Augustine.

[23]   Sermon "Attendite a falsis prophetis, qui . . . / Duo esse in verbis istis . . ." 2.

general objection: "Are the reasoning and the traditions of men always to be rejected?" He answers, "No, but rather when matter-bound reasoning proceeds according to them and not according to Christ."[24] To proceed "according to Christ" requires, third, that the impure motives of philosophy – vanity, contentiousness, arrogance – be transformed into the motives of the Christian believer. Philosophical inquiries ought always to serve a theological end. Applied to texts, this rule requires that philosophical argumentation start and go forward only from the believer's motive of the twofold love of God and neighbor.

If procedural admonitions are somehow helpful, they remain abstract. To see how Thomas enacts them one has to study moments when he changes philosophy into theology. I turn to the *Summa*'s definition of the virtues and to its analysis of sacramental efficacy as examples of how Thomas converts the water of philosophy into the wine of theology.[25]

Defining the Virtues

Readers familiar with Thomas's teaching on analogy and with his views of philosophical language will not be surprised that he treats "virtue" explicitly as an analogous term (1–2.61.1 *ad* 1). The analogical range of "virtue" is something more than the richness of any important philosophical term. Thomas is clearly aware not only that there are different authorities on the definition of virtue but also that the term itself, even on its best definition, must apply to a sundered range of cases. He must not only collate authoritative texts, he must show that the various cases covered by them are ordered around one primary case – or else "virtue" will be equivocal.

Thomas inherited a number of authoritative definitions of virtue, including quite distinct ones from Cicero and Aristotle's physical works.[26] The main contest is between two further definitions, the first from Aristotle's

---

[24] *Expos. Pauli: in Col.* 2.2.

[25] A decade after writing and publishing a first version of this argument, I discovered the extraordinary 1998 lecture by Victor Preller, "Water into Wine," now available in *Grammar and Grace: Reformulations of Aquinas and Wittgenstein*, eds. Jeffrey Stout and Robert MacSwain (London: SCM Press, 2004), pp. 253–267. In it, I find so much with which to agree, including this succinct summary of my abiding concerns: "I shall now simply put all my cards on the table and say that whenever Aquinas writes he writes as a theologian, for a theological purpose, making use of theological assumptions. He talks about philosophy as a theologian. He does not do philosophy" (p. 262).

[26] Cicero, *De inventione* 2.53.159, is quoted by Aquinas in 1–2.56.5. For some earlier uses, see Augustine, *De diversis quaestionibus 83* q. 31, ed. Almut Mutzenbecher, Corpus Christianorum Series Latina 44 (Turnhout: Brepols, 1975), 2–3, and Albert, *Lectura super Eth.* 1.15

Ethics and the second from Augustine by way of Peter Lombard's *Sentences*. The Aristotelian definition is the famous conclusion that virtue is a voluntary habit leading to action that lies in the mean, as specified by reason and a prudent person.[27] The *Summa* paraphrases this definition variously when discussing the virtues,[28] although not in 1–2.55 when it comes time to define them. The reason for the omission will appear in a moment. The competing definition comes from the Lombard's *Sentences*: "Virtue is a good quality of mind, by which one lives rightly and which no one uses badly, which God alone works in man."[29] It is, as Thomas knows, a conflation of Augustinian texts and especially of passages from *On Free Choice* 2, which supplies the middle clause of the Lombard's definition.[30] The definition from the *Sentences* is the only one that Thomas sets out explicitly to defend.[31]

The tension between the two definitions is palpable. Aristotle's definition has in view humanly acquired virtue, and it stresses how prudential judgment by the virtuous sets the mean. The definition that Peter Lombard composes out of Augustine is a definition of virtue infused by God. It is not immediately clear whether it speaks both of the (infused) theological virtues of faith, hope, and charity and of (infused) moral virtues. Thomas attempts to resolve the tension between these two definitions by constructing a more comprehensive analogy of the term "virtue," one ample enough to contain both Aristotle and Augustine. He succeeds in the attempt only by subordinating Aristotle to Augustine.

Thomas introduces virtue, in good dialectical fashion, with a remark on its least specific sense: "'virtue' names a certain completion of power" (*quandam potentiae perfectionem*, 1–2.55.1). This sense is divided next between natural powers, which are themselves called virtues as determined to specific ends, and "rational" powers, for which virtue names the habit or cumulative disposition that determines the power to act. This distinction is displaced by a

---

(Cologne *Opera omnia* 14/1:76.67–69). Aristotle *De caelo* 1.11 (281a15) is quoted by Aquinas in 1–2.55.1 *arg.* 1, and *Physics* 7.3 (246b23) in 1–2.55.2 *arg.* 3 and 56.1 *sed contra* 1.

[27]   Aristotle *Nicomachean Ethics* 2.6 (1106b36–1107a2).

[28]   *Summa theol.* 1–2.58.1 *arg.* 1, 58.2 *arg.* 4, 59.1, 64.1 *sed contra*, 64.2 *sed contra*, 64.3 *arg.* 2.

[29]   Peter Lombard *Sententiae* 2.27.1 no. 1 (CSB 1:480).

[30]   See *Summa theol.* 1–2.55.4 *sed contra*, and Augustine *De libero arbitrio* 2.18.50, ed. W. M. Green, Corpus Christianorum Series Latina 29 (Turnhout: Brepols, 1970), p. 271.

[31]   *Summa theol.* 1–2.55.4c: "Now the efficient cause of infused virtue, for which the definition is given . . ." John Inglis emphasizes the importance of the infused virtues in Thomas's predecessors and shows how fully it must be considered the starting point for Thomas's own accounts. See Inglis, "Aquinas's Replication of the Acquired Moral Virtues: Rethinking the Standard Philosophical Interpretation of Moral Virtue in Aquinas," *Journal of Religious Ethics* 27 (1999): 3–27.

second: virtues enable being or acting (1–2.55.2). In *Summa* 2, Thomas is concerned with peculiarly human virtues of acting and restricts the use of virtue accordingly. He can thus add yet another piece for a fuller definition, namely, that virtue is an "operative habit" (1–2.55.2). It is very easy to conclude that it must be a good operative habit, since the notion of completeness forms part of the moral notion of virtue. Then something puzzling happens. Thomas turns, in the last Article of the Question, to defend the definition of infused virtues taken from Augustine through Peter Lombard.

What is the point of jumping, as it seems, from a general notion of virtue inherited from Aristotle to a specific and theological definition provided by Lombard? If a full definition is needed to cap the dialectical development of Question 55, why not supply Aristotle's definition of moral virtue from the *Ethics*? The answer cannot be simply an appeal to Augustine's authority, because Thomas has a dozen ways of rereading Augustine or of fashioning revisionist contexts for him when he finds something imprudent or misleading in the Augustinian texts. The answer must rather be that the center of the analogy of virtue lies not in civic virtues as Aristotle understood them, but in virtues infused by God. The full definition must be given for the first and clearest member of the analogy. The clearest case is not acquired, but infused virtue.

Making the principal definition of virtue theological has any number of consequences. For example, Thomas must rework the notion of habit that he has constructed so carefully in Questions 49–54 using Aristotle and Aristotle's interpreters.[32] Another consequence is that he now understands even the pagan virtues as if from above. By way of concluding with the cardinal virtues, Thomas introduces a passage from Macrobius that quotes Plotinus. In it Plotinus multiplies the four cardinal virtues into four steps or stages corresponding to four states of the soul: the political, the purgative, the already purged, and the exemplary (61.5 *sed contra*). The passage appears several times in Albert's *Lectura* on the *Ethics* and is familiar to Thomas from many other texts as well.[33] He does not correct its teaching, but he follows his predecessors in giving it a thoroughly Christian reading.

---

[32] One sign of this is the explicit invocation of Aristotle in important *sed contra* arguments. Of the 19 *sed contras* that cite an authority in Questions 49–54, 15 cite Aristotle and not merely for an intermediate premise. Another sign is the concerted attention to the exegesis of Aristotle's texts, marked particularly by the reliance on Simplicius. Simplicius is cited eight times in these Questions (49.1, *ad* 3; 49.2c and *ad* 2; 50.1c and *ad* 3; 50.4, *ad* 1; 50.6; 52.1). At least three of these passages contain lines of direct quotation, and one of them (49.2) uses a long quotation from Simplicius as a starting point for Aquinas's reformulation of an important distinction.

[33] For Albert's use of it, see *Lectura* 2.3 (Cologne *Opera omnia* 14/1:100.27–30), 4.12 (272.71–73), 5.3 (320.36–39), and 7.11 (568.1–8).

The political stage of the virtues corresponds easily to the human being as naturally political, "according to the condition of his [or her] nature." The exemplary stage refers to the virtues as they are in God. Here Thomas simply follows Macrobius's reading of Plotinus. The two middle stages must then help the soul toward its end in God. The purging cardinal virtues are virtues of motion toward God. Prudence is reinterpreted as the virtue of despising worldly things in favor of contemplation. The virtues of the soul already purged are those exercised while possessing the highest end: they are the virtues of the blessed in heaven. At the third stage, prudence means seeing only the divine.

This allegorical reading of the four stages of virtue, by which each cardinal virtue is carried upward from the human realm to the divine, extends the analogy of the terms in an unexpected direction. In the first discussions of cardinal virtues, theological virtues had been held at bay. Now it becomes clear that the political cardinal virtues are most important for the present human condition, but not for the final one, which lies beyond human capacity (61.1 *ad* 2). The purging and already purged virtues are related directly to the last end. They are some of the few cardinal virtues that last into the state of glory (67.1). Indeed, they must be among the infused moral virtues rooted in charity (63.3).

Here is the crux: infused moral virtues differ in kind from acquired moral virtues precisely because they prepare human beings for citizenship in the heavenly city, not the earthly (63.4). If they are different in kind and take a different definition, how can they be called by the same name except equivocally? Similar questions arise at other points. The three theological virtues are ordered to an end different from that of the acquired virtues. They have God as their object, they are infused only by God, they are taught only by divine revelation (62.1). They differ in kind or species from the moral and intellectual virtues (62.2). The difference is not merely categorical; it has consequences for action. Theological virtues are more than supplements in aid of the cardinal. They both enable and require different actions. The theological virtues are not virtues lying in the mean, except accidentally, since their rule and measure is God (64.4). So they prescribe different standards even for subject matter also considered by the moral virtues. For example, infused moral virtues demand a degree of bodily asceticism not required (or encouraged) by acquired moral virtues (63.4).

The analogy of virtue stretches almost to breaking. Can it be held together by clarifying the hierarchy of cases that fall within it, by distinguishing proper and improper senses? Thomas does clarify the hierarchy when he discusses the connection and equality of the virtues. On the surface, these topics are familiar from ancient philosophy. He knows from a number of sources, such as Simplicius and Augustine, that the Stoics taught the unity of virtues and the equality of faults. More important for him is the connection between the acquired virtues and infused virtues, whether moral or theological. The ancient philosophical topics become occasions for trying to display the unity-and-difference in the analogy of virtue itself.

Four arguments are posed against the connection of acquired moral virtues. Thomas replies with four authorities in the *sed contra*, three from patristic authors and one from Cicero (65.1). His counter-argument depends less on these authorities than on a distinction between complete and incomplete virtue. Incomplete virtue is no more than an inclination to do some good thing, an inclination that can arise as much from natural endowment as from practice. Imperfect virtues are not connected to one another, whether they are understood as common components of good action or as related to specific cases or matters. The connection arises in the common structure of action, and it runs through prudence. Without prudence, a habit of repeated self-restraint when faced with one kind of temptation, say, will not become the virtue of self-restraint, because it will fail to cover similar temptations. The operations of moral virtues are ordered to one another in such a way that habit in one operation must require a habit in all (65.1 *ad* 3).

So far the consideration has proceeded in an apparently philosophical manner. The next Question asks whether this unified complex of moral virtues can exist without charity (65.2). Thomas's reply is nuanced. If "virtue" means something aimed towards a naturally attainable human end, it can be acquired by human effort. This virtue can exist without charity, as was the case among many pagans. Still, pagan virtues do not "completely and truly satisfy the notion (*ratio*) of virtue." The notion is satisfied only by virtues that lead to the highest human end, which is supernatural. Strictly speaking, there can be no virtue without charity. Moral virtues are infused by God, together with the prudence on which they depend, after the infusion of charity. "It follows then from what has been said that only the infused virtues are complete, and are called virtues simply, because they order the human being rightly to the last end simply speaking." Thomas holds that charity cannot be infused without the attendant moral virtues, of which it is the principle (65.3), or without the other two theological virtues, which make possible friendship with God (65.5).

For Thomas, then, no single inclination toward the good, standing by itself, can be called a virtue simply speaking. It is only an incomplete or anticipated virtue that needs to be taken up into the unity of the virtues centered on charity. Pagan virtues are only virtues in a certain respect (*secun-*

dum quid), as ordered to some particular good that is not the complete and final good of human life. Thomas approves a gloss on Romans: "Where acquaintance with the truth is lacking, virtue is false even when connected to good customs" (*in bonis moribus*, 65.2 *corpus*). Securing the analogy of virtue requires not only substituting a theological for a philosophical definition, but also judging human life otherwise than Aristotle did. Thomas has changed philosophical water into theological wine.

Analyzing Sacramental Efficacy

Thomas is often credited with the definitive formulation of sacraments as causes of grace. Part of the credit usually goes to his philosophical account of causality: he was able to explain the sacraments because he understood Aristotle so well. In other contexts, Thomas does indeed prove himself an attentive reader of Aristotle on causes. Of course, he often supplements the Aristotelian classifications of causes – for example, by borrowing from Avicenna and by insisting on the importance of exemplary causality, that is, causality by participative likeness. Thomas does not hold for one and only one proper cause behind a natural event, nor does he teach any strict doctrine of causal determinism in nature. He is careful not to reduce the complex discourse about causes to one or several tightly worded "principles." He is even more careful when theological analyses are required. Thomas's understanding of theologically important cases of causality leads him to reformulate causality in general.

Thomas is by no means the first Scholastic theologian to call the sacraments causes. Scholastic usage goes back at least a century before him. Peter Lombard distinguishes sacraments from other signs by pointing to their causal efficacy: "'Sacrament' is said properly of what is so much a sign of the grace of God and so much the form of invisible grace, that it produces the image of it and stands forth as a cause" (*ipsius imaginem gerat et causa exsistat*).[34] The Lombard's language is taken up explicitly by such older theologians as Guido of Orchelle and William of Auxerre,[35] not to mention such influential Franciscan masters as Bonaventure.[36] Assertions

---

[34] Peter Lombard *Sententiae* 4.1.4 no. 2 (CSB 2:233).

[35] See Guido de Orchellis, *Tractatus de sacramentis ex eius summa de sacramentis et officiis ecclesiae*, eds. D. and O. Van den Eynde (St Bonaventure, NY: Franciscan Institute, 1953), 3–5, especially 5.10–13; and Guillelmus Altissiodorensis, *Summa aurea*, ed. J. Ribaillier (Paris: CNRS, and Grottaferata: CSB, 1980–1983), 4:12.15–16.

[36] Bonaventura *Sententiae* 4.1.1.3–4 and *Breviloquium* 6.1.

of sacramental causal efficacy can also be found in many of Thomas's Dominican predecessors.[37]

If Thomas is not the first to speak of sacraments as causes, he does give new prominence to sacramental causality when he asserts it separately and straightforwardly. In the *Sentences*, for example, Peter Lombard's whole treatment of sacraments is part of the "teaching about signs" (*doctrina signorum*), and so its discussions of causality are inevitably subordinated to discussions of signification.[38] In Bonaventure, a lengthy review of controversies over sacramental causality ends on a note of skeptical reserve:

> I do not know which [opinion] is truer; since when we speak of things that are miracles, we ought not to adhere much to reason. We thus concede that the sacraments of the New Law are causes, that they produce effects and that they dispose things, according to the loose sense of "cause" . . . and it is safe to say this. Whether they have something more, I wish neither to affirm nor to deny.[39]

Even Albert is careful to describe sacramental causality as a kind of material disposition, and to deny that saving grace is somehow tied to the sacraments or that they "contain" grace in any ordinary sense.[40] Against this background, Thomas's steady assertions of causal efficacy in the sacraments are striking.[41]

The organization of the *Summa*, unlike that of the Lombard's *Sentences*, makes sacramental causality more prominent than signification. Thomas divides the common consideration of the sacraments into five topics: what they are, why they are needed, what their effects are, what their causes are, and how many of them there are (*Summa* 3.60 prologue). Each topic takes one Question, except for the topic of effects, which is divided between principal and secondary (3.62–63). The topic of sacramental efficacy is more highly articulated than the others from the start.

Thomas begins traditionally enough by defending the claim that sacra-

---

[37]   The pertinent texts are collected by H.-D. Simonin and G. Meersseman, *De sacramentorum efficientia apud theologos Ord. Prad.* (Rome: Pontifical Institute Angelicum, 1936), fasc. 1:122–126.

[38]   Peter Lombard, *Sent.* 4. *prol.* (CSB 2:231). The large structure of the *Sentences* depends upon Augustine's distinctions between things to be enjoyed and things to be used, and between things and signs.

[39]   Bonaventura *Sent.* 4.1. *unic.* 4 at end.

[40]   Albert, *Super libros Sententiarum* 4.1.B.5 (Borgnet *Opera omnia* 26:18).

[41]   Consider the following examples from texts before *Summa theol.*: Scriptum *Sent.* 4. 1.1.1.3 *ad* 5, "Now simply speaking a sacrament is what causes holiness"; *De verit.* 27.4, "it is necessary to hold that the sacraments of the New Law are in some way the cause of grace."

ments are a kind of sign. He defends it even against the objection that they cannot be signs because they are causes (3.60.1 *arg.* 1 and *ad* 1). He speaks here most broadly: "sacrament" refers to any sign of something holy that serves to sanctify those who perform or receive it appropriately (60.2). In this loose sense, "sacrament" refers not only to the rites of the Old Testament, such as the paschal lamb or priestly blessings, but also to the worship of God practiced before or beyond the special revelation recorded in Scripture.[42] When Thomas wants to specify Christian sacraments within the broad genus, he asserts their causal efficacy (62.1, 65.1 *ad* 6). To state this differently: Thomas speaks of sacraments as signs when he has in mind the whole range of human religious ritual. When he wants to restrict himself to the seven sacraments of the Christian church, he speaks of sacraments as causes.

What exactly does Thomas mean by calling them causes? He does not mean something that can be found immediately in Aristotle. At least, he does not point the reader toward Aristotle for help with the pertinent notion of cause. There are some 60 explicit citations in the two Questions on sacramental effects. Only five are to Aristotle, and he is the only pagan author mentioned.[43] Two of the remaining three citations assert only that a power is a cause and that there are powers in the soul.[44] The third asserts that political ministers are instruments – a maxim that Thomas applies, somewhat disingenuously, in order to bring priesthood under the account of instrumentality.[45] More interestingly, he appears to avoid citing Aristotle when he could. He cites Augustine for the common Aristotelian principle that a cause is higher or nobler than its effect (62.1 *arg.* 2). He cites no authority whatever for a Peripatetic maxim on teleology of nature (62.2 *sed contra*) or for the logical teaching about the categorical difference between figure and power (63.2 *arg.* 1).

The absence of Aristotle is confirmed by Thomas's elaboration of an account of sacramental causality. It begins by distinguishing between a cause and a conventional sign (62.1). The sacraments are asserted to be causes "in many of the authoritative pronouncements of the saints" (62.1). They are not principal causes as much as instrumental causes. A principal cause works in virtue of its own form, and so its effects are likened to that form. An

---

[42] For the Israelite cases, 60.2 *ad* 2, 60.6 *ad* 3; for the others, 60.5 *ad* 3, 61.4 *ad* 2, 65.1 *ad* 7.

[43] They are 62.2 *arg.* 3, *Metaphysics* 7.3 (1043b36); 62.3 *arg.* 1, *Physics* 4.14 (212a14); 63.2 *arg.* 4, *Metaphysics* 4.12 (1019a15); 63.2 *sed contra*, *Nicomachean Ethics* 2.5 (1105b20); and 63.2, *Politics* 1.2 (1253b30).

[44] *Metaphysics* 4.12 (paraphrased): "a power takes the account of a cause and principle"; *Nicomachean Ethics* 2.5 (quoted): "'Three things are in the soul: power, habit, and passion.'"

[45] *Politics* 1.2 (paraphrased): "now a minister possesses the manner of an instrument."

instrumental cause does its work in virtue of the motion of some principal cause, so that the effects of an instrument are not like its form, but instead like the form of the principal cause moving it. Any instrument has two actions, of its own form and of the moving cause (62.1 *ad* 2). The actions are connected: the moving cause achieves its effects through the instrument's proper action.

Thomas explicitly defends the image of the moving cause working "through" an instrument when he explains how the sacraments can be said to "contain" grace (63.3). He argues by exclusion. Grace is in the sacraments not according to the likeness of species, or according to some proper and permanent form, but rather "according to an instrumental power (*virtus instrumentalis*), which is flowing and incomplete in the being of nature" (63.3). The puzzling last phrase is not a lapse. Thomas repeats it when he says that the grace has a "flowing and incomplete being" (*esse fluens et incompletum*) (63.3 *ad* 3). To say that a sacrament is an instrumental cause obliges one to say that there is "some instrumental power" in the sacrament that is "proportioned to the instrument" (63.4). The power has an incomplete being that passes from one thing to another.

It is difficult enough to imagine this power in any case, but more difficult still for the Christian sacraments. In them, physical instruments connect an immaterial being, who is cause, to a partly immaterial being, who receives a spiritual effect. The same instrumental power is found in the diverse elements of a sacrament – in its verbal formulas, prescribed actions, and material elements. Finally, the instrumental efficacy of the sacraments depends on the efficacy of the humanity of Christ, itself an instrument of his divinity (62.5). Whereas the human instrument is conjoined to its principal cause, the sacramental instruments are separated from it. To understand sacramental causality requires conceiving instruments composed of many kinds of material things or motions that receive and contain their causal power from a remote being of a different order, in order to pass that power along to beings of yet another kind.

Much ingenuity has been spent in trying to explain that Thomas cannot possibly mean any of this literally, that he must mean something more philosophically familiar. Bernard Lonergan, for example, has argued elegantly and emphatically that Thomas's causality must be spoken of generally either as a "formal content" in the agent or as a relation of dependence in the effect; it cannot be something added to the cause.[46] Again, Lonergan holds that "a causally efficient influence" passing from agent to patient in

---

[46] Bernard J. F. Lonergan, *Grace and Freedom: Operative Grace in the Thought of St Thomas Aquinas*, ed. J. Patout Burns (New York: Herder and Herder, 1971), p. 69.

cases of efficient causation is "either a mere *modus significandi* [mode of sig-
nification] or else sheer imagination."[47] Others have applied Lonergan's
reading of Thomas on causality to Thomas on the sacraments. Thus
McShane argues that a sign can become an efficient cause of grace without
itself changing, without "doing" anything "in any popular sense of the word
'do.'"[48] Again, "action is predicated of the agent only by extrinsic denomi-
nation."[49] Unfortunately, these readings do justice neither to Thomas's
language nor to his choice of topics. We should not seek to explain away
important features of Thomas's texts so much as to see that he uses the
sacraments to extend ordinary notions of causality. It is not sheer imagination. It is the transmutation of philosophy into theology.[50]

A full account of instrumental causality would include passages in which
Thomas argues at length that creatures are instruments in relation to divine
action or applies the notion of instrument to the humanity of Christ.[51] In
them, a reader can see that Thomas's notion of instrumental causality far
exceeds an Aristotelian account. Thomas must elaborate an account of
instruments, which Aristotle mentions only casually in his main classifications of causes.[52] He goes beyond Aristotle as well by stressing the presence
in the instrument of a power capable of producing effects far beyond the
instrument's own nature.

The second revision of Aristotelian causality is underscored in the *Summa*
when Thomas turns to another kind of sacramental effect. Here the reader is
asked to understand that three unrepeatable sacraments – baptism, confirmation, priestly ordination – produce not only grace, but a permanent
"character" in the soul of the recipient (3.63). As Thomas's scholarly glosses
suggest, theological formulations defining such a "character" were rather
new in Latin. His most technical definition of it is an anonymous one to be
found no further back than his immediate predecessors (63.3 *sed contra*). He
uses the notion, however newly formulated, to extend instrumental causality.

The sacramentally bestowed, permanent "character" is a spiritual power

---

[47] Lonergan, Review of E. Iglesias, *De Deo in operatione naturae vel voluntatis operante*, *Theological Studies* 7 (1946):602–613, at p. 603.

[48] Philip McShane, "On the Causality of the Sacraments," *Theological Studies* 24 (1963):
423–436.

[49] McShane, "Causality of the Sacraments," p. 430.

[50] I do not mean to suggest that there are no difficulties in Thomas's account that need
further analysis. For a recent restatement of them, see Liam G. Walsh, in *The Theology of
Thomas Aquinas*, eds. Nieuwenhove and Wawrykow, 326–364, at pp. 344–347.

[51] For creatures generally, *Contra gent.* 3.70, *De potentia* 3.7, *Summa theol.* 1.105.5.

[52] Instruments are mentioned briefly as one kind of means in *Metaphysics* 5.2 (1013b3), but
not at all in the parallel passage in *Physics* 2.3.

(*potestas spiritualis*) that enables its possessor to participate appropriately in the worship of God (63.2, 63.4 *ad* 2). The power is instrumental so far as it creates "ministers" in the divine service. Becoming a minister is not simply acquiring an extrinsic attribution. It requires that something be put into the soul. This something, the "character," establishes a relation that is then signified as the minister's particular office in the service of God (63.2 *ad* 3). The relation remains in souls as a permanent intrinsic attribute – more permanent than normal habits of grace, which can be lost. The "character" is permanent because it participates in the permanency of its divine cause (63.5 *ad* 1), which is the universal priesthood of Christ (compare 63.3).

Standing back from its details, a reader can appreciate this teaching as a remarkable extension of the notion of causality. Complex events, involving words, gestures, and physical objects, can properly be said to be causes of permanent changes in the moral condition of those who participate in them. The changes enable participants to perform virtuous actions, such as the just worship of God, by which they are brought nearer their end. The recipient who performs these actions is brought closer to the vision of God, which is her highest end and profoundest desire. Thomas explicitly contrasts his account with any appeal to legal ordination or convention (62.1). He wants to assert a causal power in the sacramental instruments to produce effects that are permanent and decisively significant alterations of the powers of the soul.

The analysis of sacramental efficacy itself converts philosophy into theology. At the very least, Thomas has added another wing onto the account of causality by developing the instrumentality of events, just as he has required any full survey of causes to include sacraments. He reverses the analogy of "cause" as he did with "virtue." The richest kind of causality is the causality by which God brings rational creatures to share in divine life. We readers apprehend the causality concretely in the sacraments, which are central, rather than exceptional, for the fullest account of causes available to us.

Philosophy within Theology

Thomas likens the theologian's use of philosophy to the miraculous transformation of water into wine. In context, he is answering an Old Testament admonition read allegorically with a New Testament miracle read literally.[53] He makes a point about arguing from Scripture, but he also suggests that a

---

[53] See *Super De Trin.* 2.3 *arg.* 5 and *ad* 5, where the objector cites Isaiah 1.22 and Aquinas replies with an allusion to Jesus's miracle at the wedding feast in Cana (John 2:1–11).

miracle of grace gives a theologian confidence to illuminate what philosophers labored so hard to see so partially.

Thomas offers the image of substantial change seriously. Just as the water became wine, so the philosophical materials become something else when taken up by Christian theology. This image from John is stronger than the Pauline one with which Thomas juxtaposes it: "subjugating" philosophy to Christ. I suggested above that "subjugation" could refer to several rights that theologians might exercise over philosophy: to own philosophical truths, to correct philosophical errors, and to redirect philosophical motivation. The image of turning water into wine promises more. It urges theology to strengthen philosophical reflection and to improve philosophical discoveries.

We have seen as much in the two examples from the *Summa*. The theologian's definition of virtue is ampler and more properly ordered than the philosophers' definitions. The theologian's notion of causality both embraces more kinds of causes and deepens the accounts of causes already recognized. What the philosopher thought of as virtues and causes are now seen to be only particular and incomplete cases of each. The theologian's acceptance in faith of the discourses of revelation encourages a thorough revision of what philosophers thought they understood only too well.

Thomas prepares two responses for a contemporary reader's question about the relation of philosophy to theology in the *Summa*. The first response is that the question must be reformulated so that it asks about theology's transforming incorporation of philosophy. The second response is that a Christian theology done well ought to speak more and better about matters of concern to philosophy than philosophers themselves can. If a work of Christian theology cannot do this, Thomas would not count it theology written well.

Chapter Nine

Writing Secrets in a *Summa* of Theology

In the prologue to his *Summa*, Thomas promises to teach simply and clearly, as a teacher should when addressing novice readers. The promise has been applied to his whole corpus. Traditions of reception sometimes imagine him the most accessible of authors. They presume that his authorship is motivated entirely by a desire to make things clear.[1] So Thomas has been praised over the centuries for the simplicity of his style, the clarity of his organization, and the moderation of his views on controversial subjects.[2] He becomes both the angelic doctor and the common doctor – a translucent intelligence open to all, neither subtle nor seraphic.

Many features in the imaginary portrait are good likenesses. Thomas's Latin is generally unadorned and uncomplicated. His favorite stylistic devices are rhythmic rather than lexical or ornamental. His most remarkable achievements of composition are structures for sorting textual traditions. His views often fall somewhere between extremes known to us from the thirteenth century – though they were not so regularly in the middle as later Thomists have made out. Still these virtues of Thomas's teaching do not of themselves imply that his authorship intended to provide easy access for all. Nor does the imaginary portrait explain how Thomas could have kept faith with authoritative traditions, both theological and philosophical, that urge

---

[1]   For a recent specimen of this presumption, see Brian Davies, *The Thought of Thomas Aquinas* (Oxford: Clarendon Press, 1992), pp. 19–20.

[2]   See, for example, Erasmus's praise of Aquinas at the beginning of the *Methodus*, as in his *Opera omnia* 5 (Leiden, 1704; rptd. London: Gregg Press, 1962), col. 78E. Aidan Nichols praises the style more suitably for its flexibility and range: it can switch "from the most austere metaphysical analysis to some extravagant metaphor taken from a Greek Father or a Carolingian monk." See Aidan Nichols, *Discovering Aquinas: An Introduction to His Life, Work, and Influence* (Grand Rapids, MI: William B. Eerdmans, 2002), p. viii.

caution or concealment in teaching about the most important things. To say this differently: if the portrait were a good likeness, then Thomas flouted ancient and important precepts about teaching the divine. He must have flouted them, because he was not ignorant of them.

Thomas shows his familiarity with the traditions in many places. In his incomplete commentary, for example, Thomas explicates a part of Boethius's proemium to *On the Trinity*. Boethius announces that he will write to be understood only by his select recipient.

> Wherever I have cast my glance beyond you, it has met in part with sluggish indolence, in part with shrewd envy, so that anyone who throws these matters before such monsters of men, to be trampled underfoot rather than appreciated, would seem to bring dishonor to divine inquiries. Therefore I adopt a concise style, and what I have taken from the innermost studies of philosophy (*ex intimis sumpta philosophiae disciplinis*) I veil with the significations of new words, so that they may speak only to me and to you, if you should ever turn your eyes to them.[3]

Thomas comments on the letter of the passage in two ways. First, he explains each phrase in the manner of a continuous gloss. So he provides synonyms for Boethius's archaic locutions and explains that the "monsters of men" are so called because they carry a bestial heart inside a human body.[4] Then, second, Thomas supplements Boethius's text by supplying authoritative citations (to Matthew 7:6, to Horace) and by noting that the "innermost studies of philosophy" are those most distant from matter.[5] Thomas not only paraphrases Boethius, he seems to endorse and to amplify him.

Thomas does all of this in a work undertaken to present Boethius for a wider audience. His exposition of Boethius's proemium is built around two *accessus* patterns, two heuristic schemes used by exegetes to open up a text. In a typical Scholastic preface or *accessus*, as I have noted, the medieval exegete asked a number of questions about the work to be studied. These included questions about its intention, utility, order, authenticity, title, and position in the hierarchy of studies.[6] More succinctly, the exegete could give

---

[3]   Text as in *Super De Trin.*
[4]   *Super De Trin.* expositio proemii.
[5]   *Super De Trin.* expositio proemii, Matthew 7.6, Horace *De arte poetica* 25ff.
[6]   See Richard William Hunt, "The Introductions to the 'Artes' in the Twelfth Century," in *Studia mediaevalia in honorem . . . R. J. Martin* (Bruges: "De Tempel," [1948]), 85–112, especially "Type C," pp. 94–97. Greek antecedents to the medieval philosophic prefaces are considered in Edwin Quain, "The Medieval *accessus ad auctores*," *Traditio* 3 (1945): 215–264, especially pp. 243–256, with a summary chart on p. 250.

an account of the book's matter, intention, order, and mode.[7] Aquinas himself used exactly such abbreviated patterns to begin his commentaries on Isaiah, Jeremiah, and Lamentations.[8] A modified and expanded *accessus* opens expositions of Aristotle. Because he was adept at teaching, Thomas did not find it necessary to provide such schematic introductions to his own major works, though echoes of an *accessus* may be heard in them. The opening of the commentary on Boethius recalls, by its form, Thomas's other labors of philosophical and theological manifestation. His affirmation of the need for esoteric writing appears to be contradicted by the very genre in which he makes it. He admires brevity and obscurity in a work designed to expand the brief and to elucidate the obscure. How to make sense of this? How to reimagine Thomas's authorship so that there is room in it for a tension between the hidden and the manifest?

The questions are not trivial, and it is not easy to find satisfying answers for them. To ignore them altogether only repeats the difficulty without addressing it. We might begin by noticing that the passage from Thomas on Boethius adduces authorities from two different orders when it asserts the need for caution in teaching. The first order is that of the pagan philosophers and poets. Boethius speaks, as is his habit, from behind the mask of Greek philosophy, and so Thomas adds a reference to Horace. The second order is that of Christian revelation and its handing down. Boethius does allude implicitly to Matthew, after all – "to be trampled underfoot rather than appreciated" – and so Thomas supplies the explicit citation. These two orders of authority represent two sets of motives for esoteric teaching. Thomas regards the motives differently, so I will treat them in sequence, separately: pagan philosophical motives, Christian theological motives. I will then try to acquit Thomas of the charge of having failed to take these motives seriously enough in his own writings, which seem so clear, so simple, and so public. In the course of all three parts, I hope to gain some ground on the question, how far Thomas might appropriately be called an "esoteric" writer.

The term deserves a moment's reflection at the beginning. Etymologically, *exoteric* discourses are intended for public consumption, for those outside, and so must deploy devices of misdirection and mendacity when they come near secret teachings. *Esoteric* discourses, being addressed only to those already inside, can speak of secrets plainly. This distinction often presumes that esoteric discourse will be unwritten. Any discourse committed

---

[7]   See Robert of Melun's pattern as in Hunt, "Introductions," p. 96.

[8]   *Post. Isaiam prol., auctor, modus, materia; Super Ieremiam prol., auctor, materia, modus, utilitas; Super Threnos prol., auctor, modus, utilitas, materia.*

to writing is potentially public, and so an esoteric discourse put into writing becomes something more dangerous than a simple exoteric discourse. As esoteric, it must tell secrets; as written, hence public, it must keep them. "Esoteric writing" or "esotericism" in writing is shorthand for this challenge. The challenge varies, of course, with the secrets to be kept and the "public" to be kept out. The devices borrowed or invented by esoteric writers vary even more. If Thomas is an esoteric writer, it may be by means of very particular devices. The choices in his writing may differ strikingly from those in other medieval texts.[9]

Ancient Philosophical Motives for Esoteric Writing

Boethius begins by reminding Symmachus – his father-in-law, mentor, protector – that their shared inquiries could properly be spoken only between them.[10] Boethius pleads this as one excuse for the roughness of his writing. He has had little chance to polish it in conversation. He also reminds Symmachus of what a lettered patrician hardly needs explained: there are venerable customs of reserve in the most respected philosophic schools that they inherit together.

The customs would have needed more explaining to Aquinas, who knew only small portions of the library of ancient philosophy. So, for example, Thomas was largely ignorant of the texts of Platonic and neo-Platonic esotericism, not to speak of the mystagogical collages made from them in late antiquity. Of the practice of esotericism in Islamic authors such as Farabi, he seems to have known little or nothing. He does not even remark on the esoteric prologue to Maimonides's *Guide*, parts of which he borrowed. Despite the limits on his reading, however, Thomas did know some of the chief motives adduced in antiquity for philosophical esotericism. He refers to them in a number of places.

In his literal exposition of Aristotle's *On the Heavens*, Thomas explains at some length the difference between exoteric and esoteric genres.

. . . one should consider that there were two kinds of dogmas (*dogmata*) among the philosophers. There were some that were placed before the public

---

[9]   Ernest Fortin suggests, for example, that the techniques of esoteric writing were rediscovered by the generation after Thomas. See E. L. Fortin, *Dissidence et philosophie au moyen âge: Dante et ses antécédents*, Cahiers d'études médiévales 6 (Montreal: Bellarmin, and Paris: J. Vrin, 1981), p. 68.
[10]   As in Thomas Aquinas, *Super De Trin. expositio proemii*.

(*lit.*, the many) from the beginning according to the order of teaching; these were called *encyclia*. Others, more subtle, were proposed to already advanced listeners; these were called *syntagmatica*, that is, coordinate [teachings] (*coordinalia*), or *acroamatica*, that is, [teachings] for listening (*auditionalia*).[11]

Thomas refers to the same distinction when he explains the traditional subtitle of Aristotle's *Physics*: "This is the book of *Physics*, which is also called *Concerning Physics or Natural [Philosophy] that is Listened To*, since it was handed down to listeners in the manner of teaching (*per modum doctrinae*)."[12] Thomas correlates the two genres with two manners of teaching adopted to two different audiences, one open and one restricted.

Boethius announces that he will restrict his audience by coining new and obscure terms. While Thomas endorses the distinction of philosophic audiences, he is not happy to approve deliberate obscurity. He has learned that the earliest philosophers or proto-philosophers were "theologizing poets" who composed in meter.[13] His harsh view of the limits of poetry prevents him from regarding their writings as anything more than a prelude to philosophy.[14] Thomas has read further that some ancient commentators believed that Plato wrote so as to conceal his true teaching behind stories and enigmas.[15] These readers faulted Aristotle for attacking only the surface meaning, while others defended his interpretations. Thomas shrugs off the controversy as beside the point of his reading: what matters is to get through dialectically opposed opinions to the truth about things.

The only passages in which Thomas paraphrases advice about writing obscurely are passages in theological works. Thus, in the commentary on Boethius, Thomas does not dissent from the terminological innovations. Again, in the commentary on Pseudo-Dionysius's *Divine Names*, Thomas explains that the obscure style is not due to the author's ineptitude, but rather to his care that sacred truths should be concealed from unbelievers.[16]

---

[11]   *Sent. De caelo* 1.21. The terms "*coordinalia*" and "*auditionalia*" occur only here in Thomas's entire corpus. They derive from Moerbeke's translation of Simplicius's commentary on *De caelo*, which text Thomas has on his desk as he writes.

[12]   *Sent. Phys.* 1.1.

[13]   *Sent. De Anima* 1.12. The "poet theologians," including Orpheus, are elsewhere placed before philosophy or distinguished from it; see *Sent. Phys.* 2.2, *Sent. Metaph.* 12.6 and 12.12, *Sent. Meteora* 2.1.

[14]   On the contrast between poetry and philosophy, see *Sent. Metaph.* 1.3–4 generally and such specific remarks as occur in 1.15. For the somewhat different, but no weaker contrast between poetic and theological use of images, see *Scriptum Sent.* 1.1.5 *arg.* 3 and *ad* 3, *Summa theol.* 1.19 *arg.* 1 and *ad* 1.

[15]   *Sent. De caelo* 1.22, which reports the disagreement between Simplicius and Alexander.

[16]   *Super De div. nom. proem.*

Yet Thomas immediately corrects the Platonic error that leads to some of the oddest locutions in Pseudo-Dionysius. The point is evident: the Platonists were mistaken about being and about how to describe being. Pseudo-Dionysius has license as a Christian author to adopt the Platonists' style, because he is presumed not to share their errors.[17] Still Thomas does not excuse philosophers from writing clearly, especially if their lack of clarity is due to bad philosophy. While Thomas is perfectly willing to admit distinctions of audience in philosophic teaching, he is not ready to admit as corollary the philosophic use of dissimulation or obscurity.

For Thomas, the real issue in philosophical esotericism concerns pedagogical order. What is suitable for the public is what is suitable at the beginning, since they are presumed to be beginners. Different things can be taught to advanced students, to the listeners who have already been through a course of study. The connection between esotericism and curriculum is underlined whenever Thomas treats Aristotle's practice of teaching. One famous passage comes at the beginning of the *Nicomachean Ethics*, where Aristotle urges that neither the young nor the morally immature can study ethics well. Thomas explains that the young ought not to study ethics or any part of politics because they lack experience enough to judge the truth or falsity of what they hear.[18] Exposed to the words of ethics or politics, they would risk skepticism or credulity. Passion's followers and the incontinent ought not to study ethics because they cannot act on it. The overly passionate are addicted to particular things and do not rise to the universality of knowledge; the incontinent do not act on what they know.[19] Thomas leaves the risk here unstated, but it appears to be frustrating the natural end of learning. Those who can never reach the end of a study are at risk of hating it and all other learning.

Somewhat later in the exposition of *Nicomachean Ethics*, Thomas encounters the passage in which Aristotle explains why the young can become mathematicians, but not students of natural philosophy or of metaphysics. The reason is again a lack of experience. Thomas adds that the proper order of study is to move from what requires little experience to what requires much: logic, then mathematics, then natural philosophy, then moral matters, and then the things of wisdom, divine things.[20] Experience is not merely the passage of time. Moral matters require "experience and a soul free from passions"; wisdom requires a powerful capacity to escape from

---

[17] For another example, *De spir. creat.* 8 *ad* 9.
[18] *Sent. Ethic.* 1.3.
[19] *Sent. Ethic.* 1.3.
[20] *Sent. Ethic.* 6.7.

imagination. Thomas endorses the order of study even when he is not reading Aristotle. So, in the commentary on the *Book of Causes*, he repeats as the proper order an ascent from logic through mathematics to natural philosophy, then to ethics, and finally to metaphysics.[21] More tellingly, he approves the Aristotelian sequence when arguing through issues raised by Boethius's *On the Trinity*.[22]

Thomas treats the order of philosophic study apart from questions about the political conditions for philosophy. Nowhere can I find that Thomas considers an author's desire to escape persecution a motive for esoteric writing. The dangers to be forestalled by reserve in teaching are not dangers of civic reprisal against the teacher. They are dangers for those who might be hurt by learning philosophy badly. When Thomas adopts Maimonides's list of the failures that plague the actual pursuit of philosophy, there is no mention of violent regimes. The failures follow on weakness, slowness, and preoccupation.[23] Esotericism addresses the dangers posed by these failures when it enforces a pedagogical order. Pedagogical order is internal to philosophy, which is presumed to have sovereignty over its teaching.

Thomas does rehearse passages in which Aristotle says that even speculative studies are to be governed by civic rulers. He ends by emphasizing that no ruler can prescribe doctrine. The city may regulate the circumstances of teaching, never its truths. To take one example, from the exposition of the *Ethics*:

> Politics may order that some teach or learn geometry. For these acts, so far as they are voluntary, belong to the matter of morality and can be ordered to the end of human life. But the student of politics does not teach the geometer what to conclude about the triangle, since this does not fall under human will, nor can it be ordered to human life, but depends rather on the very reason of things.

The simple lesson in this passage is that rulers cannot legislate the structure of creation. True enough, it might be objected, but rather beside the point. If rulers cannot alter truths about triangles, they can certainly control the teaching of those truths. For Thomas to presume pedagogical autonomy is simply to ignore what happens when regimes systematically suppress or adulterate philosophy.

---

[21] *Super De causis* 1.
[22] *Super De Trin.* 5.1 *arg.* 10 and *ad* 10.
[23] *Super De Trin.* 3.1 corp, *De verit.* 14.10 corp, *Contra gent.* 1.4, *Summa theol.* 1.1.1 and 2–2.2.4.

Thomas's presumption of pedagogical autonomy is not ignorance or naïveté, but a sign of the abstractness that issues about the history of philosophy have for him. Thomas is perfectly familiar with the civic regulation of teaching and, indeed, with cases where certain teachings have been brutally repressed. He prays a liturgy that commemorates many martyrs, after all, and he belongs to an Order that championed the suppression of heresy. Thomas's best thoughts about teaching within the city are thoughts about teachings on faith within a Christian regime. Questions about the practice of philosophy must be abstract for Thomas because he takes "philosophy" as a name for the unfulfilled condition of wisdom under paganism. A Christian may not remain a philosopher, I repeat, and so a Christian can only conceive living philosophically as a prelude to the life of grace. If we want Thomas's best thoughts about esotericism, we must turn to his views on theological motives for it.

Christian Motives for Esoteric Writing

In the opening passage from Boethius's *On the Trinity*, there was an implicit allusion to Matthew 7.6: "Do not give a holy thing to dogs, nor put your pearls before pigs; that they might not trample them under their feet and, having turned about, break you into pieces." Thomas makes the Boethian allusion explicit. This is not the earliest mention of the verse in Thomas's corpus.[24] Earlier uses can be found in his *Scriptum* on the *Sentences* of Peter Lombard. Nor is the Boethian commentary the verse's last appearance. The verse reappears as Thomas writes. Moreover, it is hardly the only Gospel passage that puts the issue of esoteric teaching, but it is one that attracted attention in works of theological synthesis well known to Thomas.[25] The *Summa* "of Alexander," for example, devotes a whole section to the injunction from Matthew.[26] So it is not surprising that Thomas recalls the verse often, from the *Scriptum* on the *Sentences* to the great *Summa*.

The Matthean injunction is cited explicitly in the *Scriptum* four times. Thomas gives it two readings, each authorized by patristic authorities and by his immediate predecessors. The first reading applies to theological teaching. While discussing the "translative" application of names to God, Thomas

---

[24] For the dating, see Weisheipl, *Friar Thomas*, pp. 381–382, and Torrell, *Initiation*, 503.

[25] For an introduction to the patristic debates on these passages, see Marguerite Harl, "Origène et les interprétations patristiques grecques de l'«obscurité» biblique," *Vigiliae Christianae* 36 (1982): 334–371.

[26] "Alexander of Hales," *Summa theologica* 3.2.4.2.4.3 (CSB 4:936–939).

rehearses an argument that any teaching strives to make truth manifest. Metaphors and other symbolic locutions serve to conceal truth. They ought then not to be used in theology. Thomas replies that the truth should be made manifest in proportion to the recipient's capacity for receiving it. Some are hurt rather than helped by truth, either because they fight it impiously or because they cannot grasp it. So the truth of divine things should be hidden, as Matthew says.[27] The same sense is given to the injunction in arguing that the unbaptized should not be catechized because sacred doctrine may not be delivered to the unclean.[28] Thomas explains that the Scriptural text refers to those of the "unclean" who oppose faith, not to those who want to come to the faith.[29]

The second reading of the injunction in the *Scriptum* applies it to Eucharistic communion. When the issue is whether a priest ought to give the body of Christ to a known sinner, Matthew is cited to argue the negative.[30] Thomas emphasizes that the injunction prohibits not the giving, but the willingness to give, and elaborates a distinction between what the priest wills of himself and what he does as if by coercion.[31] Matthew appears again to argue that Jesus did not give his own body to Judas at the Last Supper.[32] Thomas replies that although Judas was truly a "dog" he was not one openly. Jesus did not want to expose him in front of the other disciples.[33]

Thomas also distinguishes these two readings of the injunction, the doctrinal and the sacramental, in his contemporary or slightly later *Lectura* of the Gospel of Matthew.[34] Thomas situates the particular injunction within the Sermon on the Mount's treatment of "judgments (*iudicia*)." Christ has already taught that human judgments are restricted to externals and that they ought to be congruent, equitable, and orderly.[35] The Lord now teaches that human judgments ought to be discriminating. Thomas appends two interpretations of Matthew's images. The first, drawn from Augustine, takes "dogs" to be heretics and "swine" to be those who are unclean. "Thus to give holy things to dogs is to minister holy things to heretics. Again if some-

---

[27] *Scriptum Sent.* 1.34.3.1 *ad* 3.
[28] *Scriptum Sent.* 4.6.2.2. *arg.* 2.
[29] *Scriptum Sent.* 4.6.2.2.1 *ad* 1.
[30] *Scriptum Sent.* 4.9.1.5.1 *arg.* 2.
[31] *Scriptum Sent.* 4.9.1.5.1 *arg.* 2.
[32] *Scriptum Sent.* 4.11.3.2.1 *arg.* 1.
[33] *Scriptum Sent.* 4.11.3.2.1 *ad* 1.
[34] On the best arguments, the *Lectura* would also have been delivered in Paris during Thomas's first regency, that is, between 1256 and 1259. For the dating, Weisheipl, *Friar Thomas*, 371–372, who relies on H.-V. Shooner, "La date de la '*Lect. Matt.*' de s. Thomas,' *Bulletin thomiste* 10 (1957–1959):153–157; compare Torrell, *Initiation*, p. 495.
[35] *Lect. Matt.* 7.1. The references in the rest of this paragraph are also to this passage.

thing spiritual is said, and this is treated with contempt, it is given to swine." The second reading takes "holy things" as the church's sacraments, the "pearls" as mysteries of truth. The sacraments are not to be taught to the unfaithful, and the spiritual senses are not to be given to the faithful who lead bad lives. Thomas pauses to imagine an objection, as he often does in the *Lectura*. Christ said many good things to the unfaithful and they trampled upon his words. Thomas replies, very explicitly in his own voice, "I say that he did this on account of the good who were with the bad, who profited from [Christ's words]."

In these contemporary texts from the *Scriptum* and the *Lectura* on Matthew, Thomas approves two motives for esotericism in theological teaching. The first is that teaching without regard for the condition of the learners will harm some of them. It will harm them not least by making it more difficult for them to hear the offer of salvation at any future time. The second motive is that unreserved teaching may betray or beget a lack of reverence in the teacher. If this is the case, then the teacher too is being harmed. Both motives justify a discernment of audience and the use of means of concealment.

The motives are more fully developed when Thomas comes to treat the Matthean injunction in the *Golden Chain*, his continuous gloss on the Gospels composed from patristic excerpts. For Matthew 7:6, the *Chain* consists almost entirely and almost equally of passages from Augustine's *On the Lord's Sermon on the Mount* and from the *Unfinished Work on Matthew* (*Opus imperfectum*), widely received in the medieval West as a work by John Chrysostom.[36] There is too much here to be summarized, but two excerpts can capture the reasons for esotericism in teaching. The first is from the *Opus imperfectum*:

> Again the mysteries of truth, that is pearls, are not to be given except to those who desire truth and who live according to human reason. For if you give them to pigs, that is to those burdened by the enjoyment of a filthy life, they do not understand their worth, but count them as like the other worldly fables. And so they crush them by their fleshly acts.[37]

---

[36] See the *Catena aurea: in Matt.* 7.3. Augustine occupies about 87 lines of printed text, "Chrysostom" about 77. The only other authorities used are Rabanus Maurus (4 lines) and the interlinear *Glossa* (2 lines). The *Opus imperfectum* is now attributed to a Latin-speaking Arian of the fifth century. On the text's authorship and its tangled medieval transmission, see J. van Banning, *Opus imperfectum in Matthaeum: Praefatio*, Corpus Christianorum Series Latina 87B (Turnhout: Brepols, 1988), pp. v–vii and ix–xiii.

[37] *Catena aurea: in Matt.* 7.3.

The deepest truths in Christianity are not to be spoken except to those who enact desire to hear them by living rationally. The rest, living against reason, cannot distinguish truth from glittering fiction, and they cancel the force of truth in their daily habits. This passage mixes the two motives distinguished above, but offers a more precise description of the condition of suitable learners: "those who desire truth and who live according to human reason." Human reason means here, not philosophy, but human rationality, which ought to be the highest internal power. Those who have seriously disordered souls are disqualified from hearing for the same reasons that Aristotle disqualified the followers of passion and the incontinent in the *Nicomachean Ethics*.

The end of this section of the *Chain* offers a last quotation from Augustine. It distinguishes those who cannot understand from those who cannot hear. The distinction lies between someone who covers her ears violently and someone who has them somehow plugged up. Nothing is to be taught openly to one who cannot understand, since such a person will "either infect it with hate, as a dog, or neglect it by contempt, as a pig." Someone who is prevented from hearing by uncleanness ought to be cleansed in order that she might begin to hear. The Lord was willing to speak before mixed crowds for the sake of those who could understand or who could be brought to understand. A competent Christian teacher may respond to earnest inquirers who might despair to think that their questions could not be answered.

The Augustinian passage balances the one from the *Opus imperfectum*. "Chrysostom" specifies the condition of suitable hearers rather rigorously, while Augustine insists on healing disordered souls whenever possible so that they can begin to hear the truth. Augustine urges the dangers of reserve – in his example, the dangers to earnest inquirers whose questions are met with silence. Between these two poles, Thomas stands much closer to Augustine, as the reader can see in his final uses of the text from Matthew.

Thomas applies the Matthean injunction to a number of cases in the *Summa*. It appears first and generally – as one would expect – in defense of the principle that Scripture should use metaphors. To the argument that theology is ordered to making truth manifest, Thomas replies that the "hiddenness of figures" is useful both for the "exercise of the studious" and against the "derision of the unfaithful."[38] Exercise helps the faithful, and derision rebuffs the unfaithful. The same argument from derision is made with the same Scriptural support in a freestanding disputed question (*quaes-*

---

[38] *Summa theol.* 1.1.9 *ad* 2.

tio de quolibet) roughly contemporary with the middle of the *Summa*.[39] The *Summa* itself then applies the injunction where we have not seen it before. Enumerating conditions that demand public confession of faith, Thomas judges that confession is not praiseworthy when it produces unrest in the unfaithful without any benefit.[40] Again, in answer to the question whether someone can deceive in time of war, Thomas argues that human beings are not always held to make clear what they propose or understand. "Even in holy teaching (*doctrina*) many things are to be hidden, especially from the unfaithful, so that they may not deride [them]."[41]

There are other cases in the dialectic of the *Summa* where the Matthean injunction supports an objection. May someone put off doing spiritual goods because of scandal? One argument says that it is permissible, on analogy to sacred doctrine and Matthew 7:6. Thomas replies with a distinction between the truth of teaching and the act of teaching – or any other act of mercy – to avoid scandalizing the petty-minded, so long as one is not obligated to teach by some special office. Where there is the obligation of office, the act of public confession becomes necessary to salvation.[42] A similar dialectic arises in applying the Matthean injunction to the case of Eucharistic communion. Should a priest deny the body of Christ to a sinner who asks for it? One argument holds that he should, because to admit a sinner to communion is an egregious case of giving something holy to dogs. Thomas replies that Christians are not to give holy things "to dogs, that is to manifest sinners. But hidden things cannot be punished publicly, but are rather reserved to the divine judgment."[43]

In these last four cases – three of which come from the heart of the *Summa*, from its persuasive and particular moral teaching, Thomas emphasizes prudential discernments. A Christian has to judge whether public confession will benefit the faith enough to justify the risk of public unrest. A theologian must decide how much to say before unbelievers, given the possibility of derision. A priest must determine which communicants are "manifest sinners." Perhaps most pointedly, Thomas requires that someone who holds a teaching office must put his own obligation against dangers of scandal.

---

[39]   *Qq. de quolibet* 6.1, paraphrasing Augustine's *De doctrina christiana*. Thomas here also adds a reference to Pseudo-Dionysius. For difficulties of dating, see Weisheipl, *Friar Thomas*, p. 367; Torrell, *Initiation*, p. 492.

[40]   *Summa theol.* 2–2.3.2 *ad* 3.

[41]   *Summa theol.* 2–2.4–3 *corp.*

[42]   *Summa theol.* 2–2.43.7 *arg.* 2 (with the Scriptural citation), *ad* 2, and especially *ad* 4, with the backwards reference to 2–2.32.2.

[43]   *Summa theol.* 3.80.6 *ad* 1.

Thomas's ever more nuanced rereading of a single Scriptural injunction recalls several larger lessons. The first is that Thomas never inaugurates a comprehensive theological project without insisting on the need for caution in teaching. Whether he is expounding Peter Lombard's *Sentences*, commenting on the Boethian corpus, exhorting to Christian wisdom in two stages, or inaugurating the *Summa* itself, Thomas commends the need for reserve and provides a defense of concealment.[44] In these discussions, as distinct from the discussions about philosophy, Thomas advocates not only a discernment of audiences, but obscure terminology, poetic forms, and multiple meaning. Indeed, he insists that Scripture has a unique textual multiplicity, far beyond the resources of a human author. The first task of the theologian is always to expound Scripture, to inhabit its multiple meanings. Clearly the theologian must then always be deciding how many of those meanings are to be clarified and before whom. Yet the reader should also note that here – perhaps especially here – Thomas does not permit the lie as a means of concealment. His esoteric devices are chiefly devices of postponement.

It might well be objected that the esoteric character of Scriptural language was a required topic in any academic discussion of theology by the time Thomas wrote. He could hardly have dispensed with it, any more than he could overlook the question, whether or how far theology was like a "science." The objection forgets that Thomas uses the reasoning behind theological esotericism not just in relation to Scripture. It is also the principle for the main structural division of *Against the Gentiles*. Truths that reason can touch are suitably argued before non-believers. Truths that reason cannot touch, much less comprehend, ought not to be debated before non-believers. Probable arguments for the truths beyond reason are only offered "for the exercise and consolation of the faithful."[45] If they were presented as arguments to unbelievers, the result would be to confirm them in their error, since they would conclude that faith rests on such flimsy foundations.

The esoteric writing of divine truths, in Scripture and in the discourses arising from Scripture, is no mere topic for Thomas. It is a conviction. More: it is a powerful impulse for the construction of new forms for the teaching of Christian wisdom. Whatever hesitations Thomas felt over the motives for philosophical esotericism, he feels none over the motives of their theological inheritors.

---

[44]   *Scriptum Sent. prol.* 1.5, *Super De Trin.* 2.4, *Contra gent.* 1.9, *Lect. Sent. prol.* 4.1 *arg.* 2–3 and *ad* 2–3, *Summa theol.* 1.1.10.

[45]   *Contra gent.* 1.9 (no. 54).

Thomas's Teaching

If Thomas takes theological motives for esotericism seriously, that only strengthens the original charge against him. He may have assented to the motives, but he appears to have failed entirely in executing them. After all, most of the evidence for Thomas's views on the philosophical distinction of audiences comes from his expositions of Aristotle – works famous for unlocking obscurities in the Aristotelian texts. Again, and whatever Thomas says, *Against the Gentiles* circulated as one work, with all four Books bound together for anyone to read. Finally, and most tellingly, the great *Summa*, which begins by reaffirming the need to speak cryptically, proclaims in its prologue that it will simplify things precisely for the sake of beginners.[46] Thomas appears to be convicted on his own standards of gross pedagogical irresponsibility.

Stated so bluntly, the charge can provoke two opposite responses. The first is that Thomas does not really mean what he says about esoteric teaching. The second is that he forgets it under the impulse to care for his readers by explaining everything clearly. The first response is improbable. If Thomas parrots philosophical and theological motives for esotericism without following them, then he mocks ancient Christian precepts. Mockery on that scale is plausible only if one believes that Thomas is a radically ironic writer – say, a philosopher pretending to be a theologian. The second response is uncharitable. It assumes that Thomas is a sloppy or distracted author, unable to remember, literally from one paragraph to the next, what he has in mind.

A more promising explanation is that Thomas entrusts his writings to a series of institutions that are supposed to protect them. He can write less cautiously because he writes inside nested walls that promise to keep out the wrong readers: the wall of the church, of course, but also of the Dominican order or the Parisian university's faculty of theology. Limited circulation of medieval theological texts was guaranteed not only by the means for their production, but by various kinds of institutions. Contemporary readers tend to forget these safeguards because Thomas's texts are produced and studied now under the prying gaze of a decidedly public scholarship. Under modern conditions of circulation, Thomas's readership is limited more by disinterest than by prudence. We would appreciate Thomas's circum-

---

[46] At least, this is the meaning of the prologue on most readings. In fact, the brief exposition there of 1 Corinthians 3.1 suggests that the *Summa* will be very careful to distinguish between what can be digested by beginners and what cannot.

spection in writing better, so the explanation suggests, if we would think about his texts under medieval conditions for reading. The explanation is suggestive, but not conclusive. I began this book by arguing that Thomas's trust in those institutions was misplaced. They badly misunderstood the pedagogical projects in his compositional structures. How could they be counted on to recognize or respect his rhetoric of teacherly caution? If Thomas entrusted his writing to the institutions he inhabited, he badly miscalculated how to protect secrets, not so much under the unforeseeable conditions of modernity, but precisely under the institutional conditions that he knew best.

Let me suggest instead that Thomas negotiates his notions of prudent teaching dialectically, page by page, in relation to authority. He relies on dialectic as a process in readers' souls and also as a judgment on how secrets are carried in Christian genealogies of authority. After all, the possibility of secret teaching haunts any transmission of textual authorities. Given the ancient precepts, how can Thomas know whether this inherited passage, this Scriptural verse or creedal formula, means anything like what it seems to mean on the surface? Once unleashed, the suspicion of a secret meaning may attach to any inherited text, no matter how plain it appears. What prevents the precept of esoteric writing from destroying the possibility that a coherent teaching will be passed down through writings? Thomas resists a destructive spiral of suspicion by subordinating it to two kinds of continuity. He trusts, first, in the continuity of the *sensus fidelium*, of living apostolic faith within the Christian church. The faith lives on until the end of historical time. At no point in time can it be exhaustively captured by writing. Thomas mirrors that trust, second, by writing a dialectic in which the secrets of faith are never assumed to be exhausted. His exegesis of authority becomes an affirmation of the possibility of secrets yet to be understood. Thomas writes disputation not just because his present puts new questions to the inherited texts, but because the inherited texts pose questions about their meanings to any (medieval or modern) reader. A reader glimpses Thomas's practice of esoteric writing in the pedagogical sequence of any article or any large compositional structure.

The sequence of the *Summa* exhibits this esotericism in several ways. Its persuasion aims at an end beyond the present life – and so it presumes its own incompletion for any present reading. The *Summa* is explicitly for beginners, and so it repeatedly offers the beginning of an education. It is a skeleton of typical authorities and arguments that must be filled in by classroom use. Finally, it is an experiment in both medieval and modern senses. It is an experience of learning by reading, but it is also a test or trial of the reader's capacity for formation. In these ways and others besides, the *Summa* teaches cautiously, selectively, by teaching without closure.[47]

In the first chapter, I raised questions about Thomas's success at resisting the various sorts of police who will inevitably be attracted by powerful moral pedagogy. I have just argued that his resistance to them is chiefly structural – and so necessarily vulnerable to excerpting, rearranging, rewriting into other genres. No text can prevent itself from being dismembered – nor would it want to. Dismemberment is the condition of reading in sequence. The question is not whether a text can protect itself from being taken to pieces, but whether its pieces are successful in reconstituting themselves within the best readers. The pieces of Thomas's *Summa* reconstitute themselves not so much by making a "more accurate" picture of Thomas as by influencing the practice of theology. What survives of the *Summa*'s structure, when it is read seriously, is a challenge to the theological writing of those who read it.

---

[47] I here read Thomas's famous clarity against its obvious implications and the standard interpretations. See, for example, Denys Turner, *Faith, Reason, and the Existence of God* (Cambridge: Cambridge University Press, 2004), p. 102: "Thomas is famous for his lucidity; as it were, the materiality of his theological signifiers disappears entirely into what is signified by them, and there is, in Thomas, an almost ruthless literary self-abnegation, a refusal of eloquence: the language is made to absent itself in any other role than that of signifying." Is it really necessary to argue, in our cultural moment, that minimalism can be a complex and fully eloquent choice in style?

Conclusion

Writing Theology after Thomas –
and His Readers

Since the nineteenth century, several dozen movements of intellectual renewal have claimed Thomas Aquinas. None has responded fully to the challenge laid down by his writing.

The styles or genres for retrieving Thomas have typically been borrowed without much thought from those near at hand: neo-Scholastic manuals, historical surveys, doctrinal paraphrases, philosophical systems, philological commentaries, or the essay in one or another version (from *belles lettres* to patches of symbolized logic). Thomisms are not alone among Christian theological or philosophical movements in overlooking the quandaries of form. Still the lack of formal invention is more culpable among self-proclaimed Thomists than among readers of many other authors or traditions. For Thomas, theological form is a central preoccupation. What kind of Thomism can ignore it? Given the history of Thomisms, medieval and modern, the question might rather be: how must Thomism as a disposition to intellectual inheritance be reconceived in order not to ignore theological form once again?

During certain decades of the last century, being a Thomist in Catholic circles meant adhering to an approved orthodoxy and the mechanisms for its enforcement. Thomism implied resistance to calls for theological renewal and innovation. So, for example, during the 1940s eminent Thomists launched attacks on the *"nouvelle théologie"* (which would wield such influence on Vatican II).[1] More recently, on this side of the council, many of those opposed to its "liberal" documents or implementations have trumpeted

---

[1] See the narrative by Aidan Nichols in "Thomism and the Nouvelle Théologie," *The Thomist* 64 (2000):1–19. Nicholas seems to assume that Labourdette and those who agreed with him held exclusive title in the term "Thomism."

calls for a return to (neo-)Thomistic orthodoxy, a "Fourth Scholasticism" (successor to those of the Middle Ages, the Counter-Reformation, and the nineteenth century).[2] Fortress neo-Thomism becomes the metonym for fortress Catholicism. Even those who are not particularly aggressive about Thomistic orthodoxy can participate in defensive provincialism. When a narrow band of technical disagreements becomes the only context for reading Thomas "professionally," Thomistic expertise is the enemy of the purposes in Thomas's writing.

Thomism has often exerted itself quite explicitly to superintend or restrict readers of Thomas. Those attacks in the 1940s were not only aimed at a preference for Greek patristic sources over medieval Latin ones. They had in their sights revisionist interpretations of Thomas.[3] A decade earlier, in the 1930s, Thomist rigorists (indeed, some of the same Thomist rigorists) had censured Marie-Dominique Chenu, whose attentive reading of Thomas brought to fruition a whole line of historically-instructed exegesis. The case of Chenu is worth some reflection, since it illustrates how severe the reactions of neo-Thomism can be when confronted by Thomas's own practice of theological writing. The case must also be told because it has shadowed this book from the beginning.

Chenu insisted – rightly, I think – that his methods for reading Thomas were the methods of his Dominican predecessor, Ambroise Gardeil, whose major works were published beginning in 1905.[4] So when Chenu began to teach Dominicans how to read Thomas in the late 1920s, he was giving them habits of reading conceived before the turn of the nineteenth century, in the first decades after *Aeterni patris*. When Chenu recorded these techniques of reading in 1950 as an *Introduction to the Study of St Thomas Aquinas*, he was showing the results of more than six decades of work.[5] Still Chenu became the target when this "historical turn" was condemned by neo-Thomists attached to Vatican offices. A privately circulated work setting

---

[2]   See the narrative in Nichols, *Discovering Aquinas*, p. 142.

[3]   See, for example, Marie-Michel Labourdette, "La théologie et ses sources," *Revue thomiste* 46/2 (1946): 353–371, p. 354, n. 2, which mentions Henri Bouillard, *Conversion et grace chez S. Thomas d'Aquin* (Paris: Éds. Montaigne, 1944) and Henri de Lubac, *Surnaturel: Études historiques* (1st edn., Paris: Éds. Montaigne, 1946). For a fuller picture of the reaction to de Lubac's rereading, see Kerr, *After Aquinas*, 134–148.

[4]   See the essays reprinted in Chenu, *La parole de Dieu*, 1: *La foi dans l'intelligence* (Paris: Éds. du Cerf, 1964), 243–282. There is some discussion of Gardeil in Gerald A. McCool, *The Neo-Thomists* (Milwaukee: Marquette University Press, 1994), in a chapter on the French Dominicans.

[5]   Marie-Dominique Chenu, *Introduction à l'étude de Saint Thomas d'Aquin* (Montreal: Institut d'études médiévales, and Paris: J. Vrin, 1950).

forth Chenu's "historical" method was delated to Rome. The Holy Office demanded that Chenu recant ten theses tainted by "subjectivism" or "historical relativism." In 1942, his private monograph was added to the *Index of Forbidden Books*, and Chenu was removed as regent of studies at Le Saulchoir and sent off to Paris to keep him away from Dominican students.[6] It is not only philosophy in the city that must fear silencing.

What was so provocative about Chenu's "historical" method of reading Thomas? The *Introduction* is a serene book that rarely registers preceding controversies. It is also subversive. It makes plain, as Alain de Libera says, how different the conditions of medieval intellectual life were from the modern, undermining any strong assertion of the unbroken unity of Scholasticism.[7] More subversively still it seeks to reactivate the teaching power in the structure of Thomas's writing.[8] Instead of trying to synthesize Thomas into a system, or reduce his multiplicity to a single narrative of development, Chenu analyzes rhetorical elements one by one. If he gives a chapter to biography and institutional setting, he gives four to Thomas's genres, terminologies, authorities, and argumentative styles. He then devotes seven chapters, fully half the book, to meticulous readings of Thomas's individual works as individual works.

Chenu urges his reader to respond as a reader to Thomas. The reader's response is to be energetic and open, not foreclosed by notions of authoritative mimicry, not constrained by the pretense of copying. In case the novice reader has missed that point, Chenu proposes exercises in which he raises questions or lays out a line of inquiry without predicting how it will end. Chenu's style of reading invites a response to the dialectical enactments in Thomas's texts by discouraging the fantasy of reproducing a Thomistic system divorced from the texts. Chenu writes that he wanted to lead his readers into an unfamiliar building: the "majestic – and disconcerting – edifice of Saint Thomas's writings."[9] Note the words "disconcerting" and "writings."

---

[6]   The documents and some narratives about them are contained in Giuseppe Alberigo, Marie-Dominique Chenu, Étienne Fouilloux, Jean-Pierre Jossua, and Jean Ladrière, *Une école de theologie: le Saulchoir* (Paris: Éds. du Cerf, 1985). Chenu's book was originally "published" in 1937, the expanded version of a talk he had given at the school's celebration of the Feast of St Thomas.

[7]   Alain de Libera, *Penser au Moyen Âge* (Paris: Éds. du Seuil, 1991), p. 44.

[8]   In his title and his intentions, Chenu also plays against Alexandre Kojève's *Introduction à la lecture de Hegel: Leçons sur La Phénoménologie de l'esprit, professées de 1933 à l'École des hautes-études*, ed. Raymond Queneau (Paris: Gallimard, 1947). His relation to Kojève resembles that of so many other French thinkers during the same decades.

[9]   Chenu, *Introduction*, p. 5: "Il s'agissait d'introduire, de 'faire entrer' dans l'édifice majestueux et déconcertant de l'œuvre de saint Thomas."

Aeterni patris hoped for a neo-Thomism that was anything but disconcerting. It needed a system that could condense philosophic truths across centuries into a secure foundation, a sure defense. The encyclical's hope was redoubled when Thomism allied itself so closely to the official campaign against "Modernism," that mythical construct meant to synthesize the threats of modern thinking. (It is the mirror image of the "Thomistic synthesis.") Chenu's method of reading was condemned as a kind of Modernism; so too were revisionist interpretations of Thomas proposed by the founders of the *nouvelle théologie*. Of course, the "relativism" discovered in their readings was no more than the "relativism" of Thomas's own writing-practice. His structural experiments, his thoroughly dialectical pedagogies, his orchestration of multiple languages have much more in common with the *nouvelle théologie* than with the neo-Thomism of Garrigou-Lagrange or Labourdette. Official neo-Thomism could not even consider Thomas's main theological accomplishment, his invention of pedagogical forms. How could it possibly acknowledge a challenge to improvise new ones?

My point is not about "bad scholarly writing," though it is abundant in Thomistic scholarship. Some allies of official neo-Thomism were accomplished writers. Maritain is a refined stylist – not to say, polemicist – and a fastidious reader of contemporary literature. Yet Maritain's forms for retelling Thomas are variations on established genres of constructive exegesis. Many anti-official writings are also not formally innovative. De Lubac writes out his revision of Thomas on grace fluently and passionately, but his form is that of doctrinal retrieval or reconstruction. The same could be said, with adjustments, about Étienne Gilson and Henri de Lubac or Joseph Maréchal and Pedro Descoqs. There are exceptions, of course. Karl Rahner's *Spirit in the World* undoes the genre of Thomistic commentary ironically, from within (as his later writings sabotage the essay and the systematic treatise).[10] Bernard Lonergan's articles on the notion of the mental "word" in Aquinas challenge the persistent reader to intellectual conversion through close reading.[11] Chenu gently mocks the standard introduction to Thomas, which summarizes principal doctrines without regard for where

---

[10] Karl Rahner, *Geist in Welt: Zur Metaphysik der endlichen Erkenntnis bei Thomas von Aquin* (Innsbruck: F. Rauch, 1939). The second edition was translated by William Dych as *Spirit in the World* (New York: Herder and Herder, 1968).

[11] The articles, originally published during the 1940s in *Theological Studies*, were anthologized by David B. Burrell as *Verbum: Word and Idea in Aquinas* (Notre Dame: University of Notre Dame Press, 1967), then re-edited (and translated) by Frederick E. Crowe and Robert M. Doran as *Word and Idea in Aquinas* (Toronto: University of Toronto Press, 1997).

or how they appear in the texts.[12] Still the inventions are few and the unthought borrowings many. Response to Thomas during the last century was not the site of striking formal experiment – unless one counts novellas like James Joyce's *Portrait of the Artist as a Young Man* or Pierre Klossowski's *La vocation suspendue.*

It would take a long time to tell a story about the genres of twentieth-century Thomism. The story would pass along shelves of books I have hardly mentioned. For example, Thomas Aquinas is not owned by Roman Catholics, nor is his reception controlled only by the dynamics of that church's protracted agony over the modern. Throughout the twentieth century there were famous non-Catholic Thomists. During its last quarter, some of the most interesting versions of Thomas appeared outside the confines of the Catholic problematic. In "analytic" philosophy, Thomas has been read apart from earlier traditions of Catholic interpretation – and sometimes with an explicit disavowal of them. In various programs of Anglican or Protestant theology, the figure of Thomas has served to recall, that is, to propose, another way forward. But I do not see that claiming Thomas outside Catholicism has always meant responding to his challenge over theological form – or escaping the police. "Analytic Thomism" gets written in the terminologies, logics, and genres of analytic philosophy. The Thomas of "radical Orthodoxy" speaks in the hybrid tones, alternately lyrical and caustic, of (post-) post-modern contestation. Both proceed under the surveillance of complex regimes of intellectual respectability. Analytic Thomism, for example, does not have to answer to ecclesiastical superiors, but does have to convince doubting colleagues by outdoing them in rigor, in approved "moves" around stipulated topics.

So what?, an impatient reader might well ask. Isn't it peculiar to expect that a project of repetition like neo-Thomism would lead to improvisations of style or genre? Or that the reception of Thomas in academic departments could escape their standards of epistemic conduct? My argument has been that Thomas's texts are successively more thorough improvisations of forms

---

[12] Even introductions that start off with the best intentions end up ignoring the structures for theology. Nicholas Healy insists on the importance of following Thomas's dialectic, but he then reverses the order of *Summa theol.* 2 and 3 in explaining what Thomas has to teach to Christian living. See Nicholas M. Healy, *Thomas Aquinas: Theologian of the Christian Life* (Aldershot and Burlington: Ashgate, 2003), pp. 40–41 and 50–51 for dialectic, but then notice the transposition of the treatment of Christ (87–103) before that of the theological virtues (119–129) and law (136–145), only to be interrupted by the sacraments (48–153), which are followed in last place by cardinal virtues (153–157). This scrambles the actually dialectical development of the *Summa.* A similar reordering of topics can be found in Davies, *Aquinas,* especially in the placement of chapters 18 and 19.

for epistemic conduct. I want to be surprised when astute readers of them fail to think first and last about form – including their chosen form for responding to Thomas. The peculiar thing for me is that we are no longer surprised.

When I reviewed the history of Thomism in the double narrative of the first chapter, I complained that Thomas had been casually rewritten without regard for his forms. My complaint now goes a step further. The failure of so many Thomisms is not that they rewrite Thomas, but that they fail to notice that his rhetorical forms demand reflective and inventive rewriting. Text-reception comes in varieties. The strongest kinds of reception do not pretend to be replications or imitations. The most appropriate response to a demanding text may not be submission. It may not even be agreement. A strong text may ask for disagreement and counter-proposal. The strongest texts, the ones that create their own genres, may require of their best readers an equivalent creation. I place Thomas's writing with the strongest, but I still want to distinguish responses to his rhetorical forms from disregard for them. Some misreading is so complete that it cannot be counted reception. This is true for a number of neo-Thomisms. Their projects prevent *a priori* any reception of Thomas. Before his texts can be received, they have already been consumed as mere authorizing occasions. The form of the new project has so completely screened the forms in Thomas that his texts cannot appear through it.

"Posterity" is a word I use to connect rhetorical form with its reception. All along I have used the rhetorical notion of form to describe a work's address. Address is an effect of structure, not of authorial psychology. (Indeed, the figure of the "author" is projected backward by rhetorical form as much as the ideal of a reader is projected forward.) Any serious reading of a persuasive structure must ask itself how it stands to the responses antici-pated by that persuasion. Otherwise it denies at once its continuity with the embodied project of the text being read. A credible reading begins by putting its form into play before the work's attempted persuasion. To put itself into play is not the same thing as agreeing in advance to be finally persuaded. Indeed, to fall within the intended posterity of a work is not necessarily to end by accepting the text or repeating its doctrines. The text's form may not anticipate either agreement or repeatable doctrines. If it does, it may be that there are possibilities latent within the rhetorical form that allow continuous dissents from its explicit anticipations. Or it may be that the form of the work anticipates unforeseen extensions and fruitful misinterpretations.

Many self-proclaimed Thomisms never consider how they stand to the persuasive form of Thomas's major works. I infer that they cannot be counted part of Thomas's rhetorical posterity. I then contrast these Thomisms with others in which motives of appreciation or adherence are turned through reading into something better. There is no pure repetition, especially across historical or cultural distances, but the desire for repetition (like the passion of fandom) can underwrite serious reception. Lonergan retells his own turn from Molinism to Thomas.[13] It feels like an epiphany to discover that Thomas's texts enact questions opposed to authoritative traditions about him. But that discovery needs to be completed by another: the quest for Thomas as original already mistakes the rhetorical function of his texts. The *Summa* was not written to be repeated. Its structure encourages neither doctrinal idolatry nor philological obsession. If I mean to respond to the *Summa* exactly and only as Thomas wrote it, my professed motive has been undoing itself all along. I have not asked clearly enough *how* he wrote it. I have not brought the form of my reading up against the form of his writing.

Receiving Thomas can evidently never be the same activity as Thomas composing. The space between composition and reception should displace fantasies of mimesis with a challenge to fuller response. The most self-aware reception takes up this provocation deliberately as a gift from the text. Thomas responds to his inheritance by inventing new forms. He wants to persuade his readers that the forms further the ends he learned from his authorities even as they exceed them. Our reception of Thomas ought to attempt the same. We receive Thomas most deliberately when we respond to the formal challenge posed by his inventions. The challenge is not a general imperative: "Be creative and do what you will." To claim that following Thomas today requires only engaging the latest science or proclaiming oneself a dissenter is a biographical fallacy. It is another way of reducing Thomas to a floating marker of authorization. His texts issue much more particular formal challenges to those who would inherit them.

What are the particular challenges posed by Thomas's texts? Let me name three. Each should be familiar from earlier chapters. Put together they can begin to specify the rhetorical posterity of Thomas's texts.

First, Thomas experiments with pedagogical structures for receiving authorities. He means to receive them alive rather than dead. The authorities are not objects of antiquarian interest. They do not function as bits of evidence in polemical proof.[14] They form no system. They are not bronze

---

[13] See, for example, Lonergan, *Method in Theology* (London: Darton, Longman and Todd, 1972), p. 163, n. 6.

[14] So the citations in Thomas should be distinguished from the controversial function of the modern footnote as described by Anthony Grafton, *The Footnote: A Curious History*

idols. On the contrary, Thomas hopes to invent structures that carry forward the activity of the authorities – their doctrines and topics, certainly, but also their pedagogies, inquiries, and linguistic improvisations. A commonplace Thomistic formula is pertinent just here: a science or body of knowledge is a habit of starting-points or principles. Theology is a disposition to produce discourses from its principles. Thomas's theological writings are instruments for inheriting and fostering the habit of theological discourse. Creating structures for handing down theology is like creating regimes for teaching virtue. To judge that a line of writers carries on a tradition of theology is like judging that successive generations in a family or a city exhibit the "same" virtue. The rhetorical forms for inheriting authorities are no different in kind from the rhetorical forms in authoritative texts. Inheritance cannot exempt itself on a plea that it is meta-discourse. If the inheritance is essentially a habit of artfully productive principles, then the form of inheritance has got to be a form for exercising the habit.

Here is a second particular challenge: Thomas invents rhetorical forms to keep inherited theology whole. On his account of the pilgrim state of the human mind within history, theology cannot possibly be whole as an accomplished system of propositions. Theology is the work of faith, and faith is restlessness on the way to beatitude. Thomas writes through forms that keep theology whole in the only way it can be: as pedagogy, as a curriculum of ascent. A theological curriculum ought to exercise all the faculties required for the highest human end. It conceives terminologies, topics, and arguments in relation to arts or disciplines that are indispensable to that end. Thomas's theological structures do not pretend to be encyclopedic. They do not reach to include every possible science. On the contrary, they must be pedagogically selective.

The third challenge is to protect inherited "secrets" by dialectical process. The secrets are not fevered scandals or bleak denials of every surface meaning. They are acts of trust in the activity of passing on. Thomas believes that thoughtless disclosure can damage. Students will be damaged if they are led to think that there is nothing to be learned; teachers, that there is nothing to be taught. In neither case is a secret actually given away. It is rather presumed to have been betrayed. The presumption is damaging, but inaccurate. The secret has not been communicated, because it cannot be communicated to those who are not ready to learn it. A failed effort at communication damages, not by revealing a secret, but by making it

---

(Cambridge, Mass.: Harvard University Press, 1997). One could argue that the unreflective use of the footnote – like this one – already presumes a different relation to intellectual inheritance than the one enacted by Thomas.

seem that there is nothing to be revealed. Take this as a parable of neo-Thomism.

Putting these points together prescribes certain challenges for any Thomism worthy of the name. It cannot prescribe responses. If Thomism is neither fantastic mimesis nor the manufacture of a police badge to be pinned on the current uniform, its forms cannot be predicted. So far as *neo*-Thomisms are mimicry or empty authorization, adequate responses to Thomas's writings will lie outside them, beyond them. The responses will be unrecognizable to neo-Thomism and perhaps even as "Thomism" in any ordinary sense.

The rhetorical forms in Thomas's best works lead the reader to ask, what rhetorical forms of inheritance make a tradition possible? That question haunts the writing of Roman Catholic theology. Many writers pass by the question because they presume that the answer is obvious. Having a tradition means submitting to an institutional authority. The form of their writing is quotation. Other writers, suspicious of authority but obligated to it, calculate degrees of permissible deviation from official lines. Their writing is ironic quotation, copying with deliberate redirection. Others still adopt or resort to the prevailing academic forms, as if the forms for theology could be nothing other than the forms of any other respectable discipline.

Thomas invents rhetorical forms that challenge his readers to have tradition by practices of active inheritance. The challenge anticipates responses that will balance attention and innovation, that complete mimesis in self-possession. Many will find this an improbable claim, but then Catholic notions of theological inheritance have become thoroughly entangled with the legal and social persistence of institutional authority. Thomas claims authority through experimental forms of theological discourse. Those who want to claim his authority must respond, first and last, to the particular challenges of his forms. If their responses begin by ignoring his forms in hot pursuit of current authority, then they have evidently failed to meet his challenges.

This book is not an adequate response to the challenge that Thomas poses. Its form has been a *via remotionis*, a series of subtractions or negations. It hopes to place itself in Thomas's rhetorical posteriority by clearing a way for the beginners called to read him.

Index

Note: The majority of Aquinas's works are cited under 'Aquinas, St Thomas', but those discussed at length are listed separately. They are entered under their English title whenever one has been provided in the text.